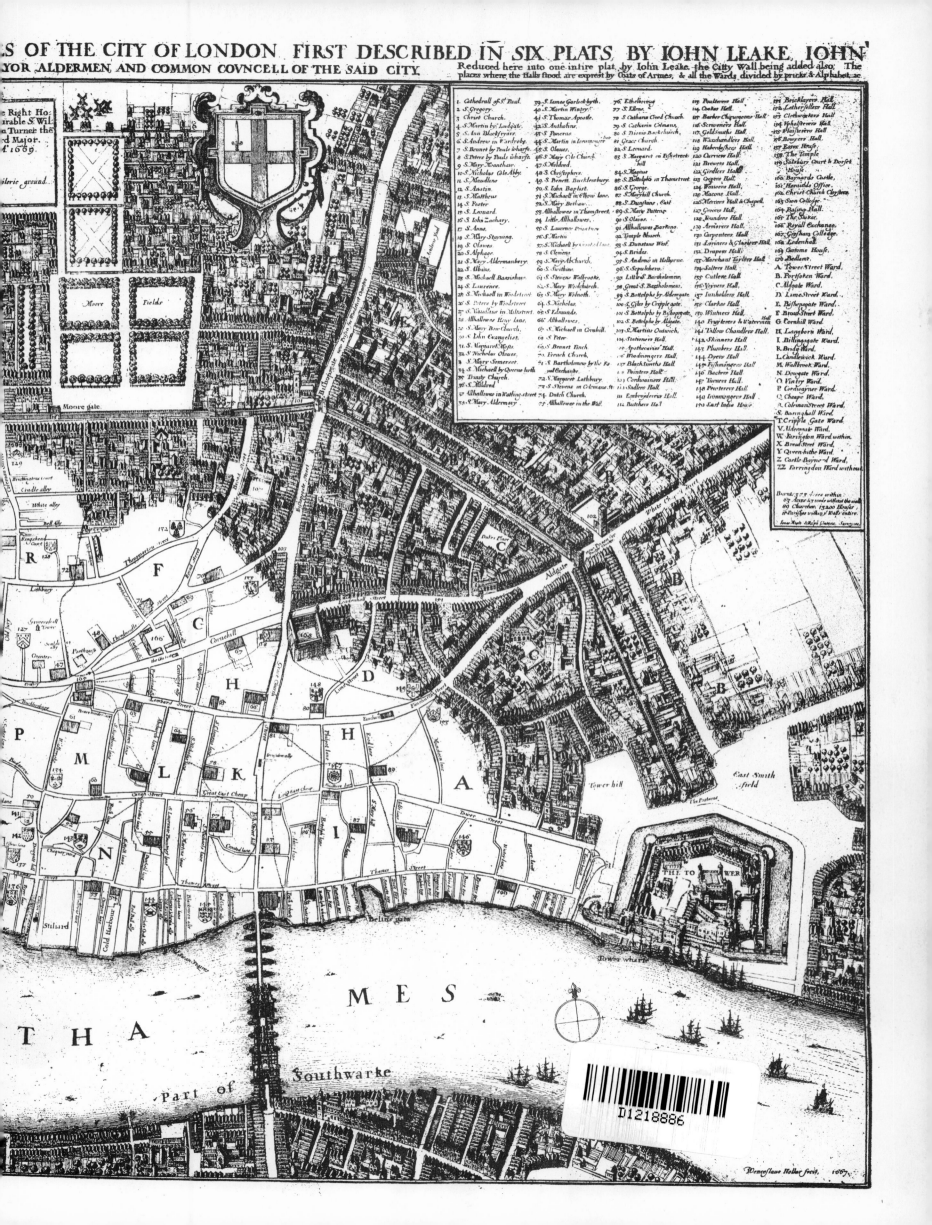

Ex Libris

THE COOPER UNION

purchased through the book fund
established by

J. PIERPONT MORGAN

Oversize
720.942
D314A

DA
682
.D4
1970

Defoe
A tour thro' London
about the year 1725

665

COOPER UNION LIBRARY
3 1206 00847 0607

ROOM USE ONLY ⬤

A TOUR THRO' LONDON

about the year

1725

Laudatur et *Alget*

Daniel Defoe
After the Engraving by M. Van der Gucht
prefixed to the Author's "De Jure Divino", 1706.

/A TOUR THRO' LONDON

about the year

1725/

Being Letter V and parts of Letter VI of

'A TOUR THRO' THE WHOLE ISLAND *of* GREAT BRITAIN'

Containing a Description of the City of LONDON,
as taking in the City of WESTMINSTER, Borough
of SOUTHWARK and Parts of Middlesex

by

DANIEL DEFOE

Reprinted from the Text of the Original Edition [1724-1726]

EDITED & ANNOTATED
by
SIR MAYSON M. BEETON, K.B.E., B.A.
and
E. BERESFORD CHANCELLOR, M.A., F.S.A.

ILLUSTRATED
with MAPS, specially drawn to delineate the LONDON of DEFOE'S
time and his *CIRCUIT* thereof, and reproductions of DRAWINGS,
MAPS, and PRINTS mostly contemporary with the period of his life
[1659-1731]

BENJAMIN BLOM, INC. *PUBLISHERS*
NEW YORK AND LONDON
1969

720.942
D314A

Oversize
DA
682
.D4
1970
c.1

First Published 1929
Reissued 1970 by
Benjamin Blom, Inc., Bronx, New York 10452

Library of Congress Catalog Card Number 68-56542

Printed in the United States of America

364665

OCT 1 9 1976   Cooper Union Library

A

TOUR

Thro' the whole ISLAND of

GREAT BRITAIN,

Divided into

Circuits *or* Journies.

GIVING

A Particular and Diverting ACCOUNT of Whatever is CURIOUS and worth OBSERVATION, *Viz.*

I. A DESCRIPTION of the Principal Cities and Towns, their Situation, Magnitude, Government, and Commerce.

II. The Customs, Manners, Speech, as also the Exercises, Diversions, and Employment of the People.

III. The Produce and Improvement of the Lands, the Trade, and Manufactures.

IV. The Sea Ports and Fortifications, the Course of Rivers, and the Inland Navigation.

V. The Publick Edifices, Seats, and Palaces of the NOBILITY and GENTRY.

With Useful OBSERVATIONS *upon the Whole.*

Particularly fitted for the Reading of such as desire to Travel over the ISLAND.

By a GENTLEMAN.

LONDON:

Printed, and Sold by G. STRAHAN, in *Cornhill.*
W. MEARS, at the *Lamb* without *Temple-Bar.*
R. FRANCKLIN, under *Tom*'s Coffee-house, *Covent-Garden.*
S. CHAPMAN, at the *Angel* in *Pall-Mall.*
R. STAGG, in *Westminster-Hall*, and
J. GRAVES, in St. *James's-Street.* MDCCXXIV.

(Facsimile of the Title page of the original issue of Defoe's ' Tour.')

CONTENTS

LIST OF PLATES

LIST OF PLATES

LIST OF PLATES

LIST OF PLATES

Plates

PREFATORY NOTE

IN *reprinting Defoe's original text of that portion of his 'Tour thro' Great Britain' which concerns London, our special object has been to reconstruct and present, as far as possible, to the eye of the reader of to-day, a living picture of London as our author saw it, supplementing for this purpose the text with annotations, maps, and reproductions of old drawings and engravings, mostly contemporary with the period of his life (1659-1731).*

Many volumes have been written about the London of the eighteenth century, but they have dealt mainly with the last three quarters of that period. For these ample raw material is available in a mass of contemporary records both descriptive and pictorial. The first quarter is comparatively lacking in this respect. Hence the special value of this first-hand record of London topography of about the year 1725, written by one who of all his contemporaries was perhaps best qualified to do justice to his subject, and who knew how to invest with a human touch even the dry annals of topography; hence also the justification for tearing this fragment from its context and issuing it in its present shape and form.

Defoe's 'Tour thro' the whole Island of Great Britain' was issued originally in three separate octavo volumes at short intervals during the years 1724-5-6. The title-page of the first volume, published in 1724, which is reproduced in facsimile on a previous page, indicates clearly in its long explanatory sub-title the general scope and purpose of the work. The various 'Circuits or Journies' into which it is divided, thirteen in all, each dealing with a more or less contiguous group of Counties, appear in the then fashionable form of Letters as being written 'By a Gentleman.'

We are here concerned with one of these Letters only (with a few extracts appended from another), printed in the second volume published in 1725, viz. 'Letter V. Containing a Description of the City of London, as taking in the City of Westminster, Borough of Southwark and the Buildings circumjacent.' This Letter, or Chapter, stands apart from the rest as a self-contained literary and topographical unit and, as such, we have reproduced it, detached from its context of the provincial Circuits, under the designation of 'A Tour thro' London about the year 1725,' adapting the title which Defoe used for his work as a whole. In producing this volume the Editors look on themselves merely as showmen exhibiting a supremely interesting, and till quite recently almost unknown, account of the London of the first quarter of the eighteenth century, here and there pausing to explain or illustrate with the help of annotations, maps and reproductions of old prints some reference in the text which might otherwise be obscure. Our readers will note that this text covers a wider field than a mere 'Description' of the London in being about the year 1725. They will find Defoe constantly recalling and contrasting in the course of his narrative the London of his early years, the London of Charles II and his immediate successors, with what he saw before his eyes, as he noted down in retrospective survey the great expansion and transformation which had been wrought within the sixty-five years of his own lifetime. To us, in the light of London's vast growth in the two subsequent centuries, the scale and the statistics of this expansion, with which Defoe, amid reiterated ejaculations of awed wonder, so frequently stimulates his readers, may seem relatively insignificant, for he speaks in acres and thousands where we speak in square miles and millions. But we must not forget that it was during the half century which elapsed between the Great Fire and the date of his 'Tour'—the half century which synchronises with the life work of Sir Christopher Wren—that, alike in the City and West End, the main outlines were drawn and the framework laid out on which until quite recent days the development of London's central areas continued to expand.

In Defoe's youth this expansion and transformation began with the era of vast building activity made necessary by the ravages of the Great Fire, and continued throughout his life; but he could remember the London that had vanished, and in his text he sets forth such changes in its appearance and size as struck him in his old age, just as, to-day, someone topographically-minded among the older of us might try to reconstruct a picture of Victorian London by noting the alterations brought about by successive phases of demolition and rebuilding. As such he would have to trace out the streets and structures which preceded the formation of, say, Shaftesbury Avenue and Victoria Street, Aldwych and Kingsway, to take out-standing examples of new street alignment and reconstructed areas, just as does Defoe when he describes the City area, as it was before the Fire, and tells us of the open fields and country lanes of the ' Out-parts ' which during his lifetime had become covered with the rising tide of bricks and mortar.

But save to those who have made a special study of the maps and records of ' Old London,' Defoe's text might easily present pitfalls and difficulties. His references to the public buildings, monuments, markets, prisons, churches, etc., of his day, would have been intelligible enough, doubtless, to his contemporaries, but are often cryptic to readers of two centuries later. In order, therefore, to make his text clearer to the reader, annotations have been added wherein ' we have endeavoured to avoid Prolixity and to omit no Remarkables, so far as our designed Brevity would admit,' as Delaune expresses it in the quaint language of his little pocket London guide-book. These additions are printed in smaller type than is Defoe's own account of London, so that anyone may have the choice either of reading our author's ipsissima verba straight through, regardless entirely of the annotations, or of perusing only those dealing with some subject or locality in which he may be specially interested. In working on Defoe's text other contemporary accounts of London have been drawn upon, including Strype's revised edition of Stow's Survey of London, for instance, and those smaller works of which the facsimile title-pages are printed in one of the Appendices. These are referred to in our notes for brevity's sake under the names of their authors or editors, and in quoting from these and other authorities of a later date it has not been thought advisable in a book of this character to overload its pages with a plethora of footnotes giving chapter and verse for every reference.

But when all is said, it is to contemporary plans and prints that we must chiefly look for a clear and graphic reconstruction of the boundaries and streets and an accurate presentation of the more important sites and build-ings referred to by Defoe. In the selection of our illustrations it has not been found possible to confine ourselves to sources wholly contemporaneous with the period of Defoe's life, but, except in a few cases for which there is a special reason, they represent scenes or subjects approximately, if not exactly, as they existed in his day. It must be remembered that there were no illustrations to the original edition of Defoe's ' Tour.' The great school of pictorial topography which, as the century advanced, was to be exemplified in the works of Canaletto, Scott, Sandby and their successors, had not then come into existence. The quality of such illus-trations as might have been available to our author, had he decided to add them, is sufficiently indicated in the few contemporaneous topographical publications of his day. They represent for the most part the crude beginnings, or rather revival, of an art which had had curiously enough at an earlier period the unique and splendid interpretation of Hollar. There are far fewer examples, moreover, of topographical illustrations dating from Defoe's time, quite irrespective of the question of quality, than might be imagined; and the present collection of such, often lacking both in artistic and technical merit, but always singularly typical of the period and invaluable as graphic records of a vanished London, has been brought together only after careful search and selection from a variety of public and private sources. Two small maps were indeed issued with the original edition of the Tour, one of England and one of Scotland, but they were drawn on too small a scale to be of much practical value to such as may have ' desired to travel over the whole Island '—the par-ticular class of readers to whom Defoe dedicates his work. To have illustrated all the thirteen sections of the Tour would have been obviously impossible if only on the score of the cost, and Defoe tacitly leaves his travellers to consult the excellent road maps published by Ogilby and his successors then available. But our author himself, when he comes to his chapter on London with its careful, and in some cases even minute, topographical details, seems to express a half apology to his readers for not adding a map when he exclaims : ' I have given as accurate a description as I could without drawing a Plan or Map of the Places.' However difficult it may have been for his contemporaries to follow in the footsteps of his perambulations without some illustrative aid to his written word it is doubly so for the modern reader, and the two large folding maps appended hereto have therefore been specially drawn with great care in order to delineate as accurately as possible both the Circuit of London as a whole and also the chief buildings in the City proper as set forth in the text. Two smaller single page ones have also been specially prepared, one to illustrate the plan and precincts of the proposed new Royal Palace at Whitehall and the other Defoe's description of the towns and villages in Middlesex adjacent to London. In these four maps there are indicated only those localities, streets and buildings which are specifically mentioned by Defoe, with the addition of a few familiar land-marks, and they have all been drawn and framed in decorative settings reminiscent of the embellishments which are so characteristic a feature of the cartography of this period.

As regards the contemporary Maps and Plans which have been reproduced here our task was simpler, and those which have been chosen may be said to speak for themselves. That on the back end-papers of this volume reproduces Hollar's plan of the ruined City of 1667 immediately after the Great Fire, while that on the front end-papers represents the London of (approximately) 1720, being a reproduction of that issued with Strype's revised edition of Stow's ' Survey of London ' referred to above. They were both, doubtless, well known to Defoe, and delineate, respectively, the London of his boyhood and of his old age. The third large folding map at the end of this volume is a copy, carefully redrawn from the worn and in places almost undecipherable original of the Plan of the Parish of St. George's, Hanover Square, dated 1725. This Plan was specially prepared in connection with the important ceremony of marking the straggling boundaries of this then newly created Parish, and its date coincides exactly with that of the publication of the Tour. It affords, therefore, a most important contribution towards our knowledge of the accurate topography of this interesting section of the West End in the early eighteenth century. One other small plan, contemporary with Defoe's early days, has been reproduced, that of the Whitehall Palace of Charles the Second's time, which serves to assist in the interpretation of Knyff's Bird's-eye View of the Palace of a later date, printed on the same page.

One last word with regard to the portrait of Defoe which forms our frontispiece. This has been selected as being in all probability the most lifelike and authentic of the five existing portraits of our author, which are enumerated by Mr. Wright in his Life. *Of these only two may be taken as being important, viz. the one engraved by Van der Gucht from a portrait by Taverner (the whereabouts of the original of which is unknown, if it actually survives), prefixed to a collection of Defoe's writings published in 1703, and that issued with his ' Jure Divino ' in 1706, without the artist's name attached, but also engraved by Van der Gucht. It is the latter which is here reproduced, as it seems likely that Defoe himself preferred it to the earlier one. Otherwise, it may be reasonably assumed, he would have been content to use the former again as the frontispiece to what he properly regarded as one of his major works. This theory is perhaps supported by Defoe's reference to this portrait in a letter to a friend, dated May 24th, 1706, in which with a conventional modesty he remarks: ' There is also a picture of your humble servant, prepared at the request of some of my friends, who are pleased to value it more than it deserves.' The significance of the words from Juvenal, ' Laudatur et Alget,' which Defoe caused to be inscribed under this portrait, will not be lost upon the reader who will remember that just before this date our author had undergone the bitter experience of the pillory, bitter notwithstanding its relative triumph, followed by a long imprisonment in Newgate, and the words are therefore something in the nature of a* cri de cœur *wrung from a man who had endured much for conscience' sake.*

With regard to the paper, type and binding of this volume, these have been specially chosen to harmonise with the style and fashion of our author's period and to give, as far as possible, further verisimilitude to the story of the ' Tour,' a point which we feel would not have been unacceptable to the great master of veri-similitude himself. Defoe, on the title-page of his original volume, described his work as designed to be ' particularly fitted for the Reading of such as desire to travel over the Whole Island of Great Britain.' Our concern here is with London only, and our task as Editors of this small section of the whole has been to make it more ' particularly fitted ' for such readers of to-day as may desire to travel over the London of Defoe's day with Defoe himself as their guide and companion ; and we would end with the words with which our author begins his own preface—' If this Work is not both Pleasant and Profitable to the Reader, the Editors most freely and openly declare the Fault must be in their Performance, as it cannot be any Deficiency in the Subject.'

M. M. B.
E. B. C.

September 1929

NOTE OF ACKNOWLEDGMENT

IN the course of their investigations the editors have received much kindly and valuable assistance. For this their thanks are due to the Librarians of various London Public Libraries and the authorities in the Print Room of the British Museum, as well as to H. L. Eason, Esq., Registrar of Guy's Hospital; Mervyn Macartney, Esq., F.S.A., Surveyor to St. Paul's Cathedral; Edmund Rudolf, Esq., Secretary of the Royal Exchange Assurance; G. C. Hast, Esq., of the Sun Fire Office; Denis Hyde, Esq., for the loan of the interesting picture of old Peterborough House; T. Owen Thirtle, Esq., A.R.I.B.A., who has with great care and accuracy drawn the maps and plans included in this volume; G. Gordon Godfrey, Esq., who has so appropriately added to these their decorative embellishments; Leonard Killby, Esq., M.A., for assistance kindly rendered in the revision of the proof sheets; and lastly to W. Hanneford-Smith, Esq., Hon.A.R.I.B.A., of Messrs. Batsfords', the publishers of the work, who has taken immense trouble in the matter of the illustrations and general format of the work, and to whose technical skill and advice the editors are deeply indebted.

A LIST OF SOME OF THE CHIEF AUTHORITIES ON THE LIFE AND WORKS OF DANIEL DEFOE CONSULTED IN THE PREPARATION OF THIS VOLUME

1. Memoirs of the Life and Times of Daniel Defoe, by *Walter Wilson*, 1830.

2. The Life of Daniel Defoe, by *William Hazlitt*, 1840.

3. Daniel Defoe, by *John Forster* (*Edinburgh Review*, 1845).

4. The Life and Times of Daniel Defoe, by *William Chadwick*, 1859.

5. Daniel Defoe: His Life and Recently Discovered Writings, by *William Lee*, 1869.

6. Daniel Defoe, by *Professor William Minto* ('English Men of Letters Series,' 1879).

7. The Life of Daniel Defoe, by *Thomas Wright*, 1894.

8. Defoe. 'Representative Selections,' edited by *John Masefield*, 1913.

'London is like a Laurel Leaf
May She be radiant still and
flourish like the Tree.' *Hatton 1708.*

INTRODUCTION

DANIEL DEFOE, like John Stow, the 'Father of London Topography,' before him, was a Londoner born and bred. His father, one James Foe (Daniel did not adopt the 'De' till late on in his life), was a butcher in St. Giles, Cripplegate, of whom little is known beyond that he was a prominent Nonconformist, who gave his son an excellent education at the Dissenters' School at Newington, intending him to become a minister. There has been some dispute as to the date of Daniel's birth, but this is now generally agreed to have occurred in the year 1659. He died in 1731, so that his life covers the period which extends from the days of Richard Cromwell through the reign of Charles II, James II, William and Mary and George I, down to the early years of George II. The whole of that life was spent either in London itself or in its immediate vicinity apart from short spells of residence in retirement at Bristol and Bury St. Edmunds, a visit to Spain and Portugal as a trader, and not infrequent journeys throughout England and Scotland as a Government agent.

It is with Defoe as Londoner and London Topographer that we are specially concerned in these pages, and it would be out of place to enlarge generally on the details of his long and active life. He has been lucky in having had many able biographers, who have dealt with all the phases and events of his strenuous career as Trader, Author, Editor, Pamphleteer, Secret Service Agent and Confidential Adviser of Ministers of State and the Crown.

Wilson and Lee and Chadwick and Wright have all produced long and detailed biographies of Defoe. Hazlitt, Forster, Professor Minto and Mr. John Masefield have given us important essays and studies on his writings, all of which, with their often divergent views on his career and character, are available to those who may wish to make a closer study of his life, whether as Man of Letters or Man of Affairs. Our readers will note from the list on the opposite page that the first of these Biographies appeared just a century ago.

DEFOE AS A LONDONER

Let us take a very brief glance at some of the incidents in Defoe's career in order to indicate more especially the localities in London with which he was from time to time connected. Thus in 1685, after his marriage with Mary Tuffley, which had taken place two years earlier, we find him beginning business as a hosier in Freeman's Court, near the Royal Exchange, and carrying on this trade for the space of ten years. In 1687 he was admitted to the freedom of the Butcher's Company and later he appears engaged in brick and tile making, with works on the Thames near Tilbury, where he himself at this time lived. He leapt into fame as a pamphleteer with the publication of *The True-Born Englishman* in 1701, and the next year emerges as the author of what by a vote of the House of Commons was described as ' a scandalous and seditious pamphlet.' This was his famous Satire on the bigots of the High Church Party entitled *The Shortest Way with the Dissenters*, and the warrant for his arrest in consequence of its publication describes him as ' a middle-sized spare man, about forty years old, of a brown complexion, and a dark brown coloured hair, but wears a wig; a hooked nose, a sharp chin, gray eyes, and a large mole near his mouth.' He was, in due course, apprehended, and on July 28th, 1703, stood in the pillory at the Conduit in Cheapside, and on the following days in those by the Royal Exchange and Temple Bar. It is significant that instead of being pelted while in the pillory by the populace, he was greeted with sympathy, and as he himself describes it, ' by loud shouts and acclamations when I was taken down.' He was then imprisoned for more than a year in Newgate, where he commenced the publication of his *Review,* a periodical which it seems probable gave Steele the idea for the *Tatler.* Writing of himself some years later, Defoe describes how he 'writ his Reviews and stated the affairs of the Nation for many years; and in the infancy of things men were pleased with his trifling labours well enough: after him the *Tatlers, Spectators,* etc., of Sir Dick amused us for a while and several bright things were said which pleased and entertained us.'

His next London residence was in Stoke Newington, and when John Forster was writing his biographical sketch of him (1845) he was able to state that his house was still standing; it was pulled down just thirty years later. It occupied a site in Church Street on the south side, rather to the east of Lordship's Lane, with gardens, extending to some four acres, bounded on the west by Cut-throat Lane. It would seem that Defoe was living in Stoke Newington in 1709, but that it was not till 1724 that he 'had newly built there a very handsome house as a retirement from London.' This is a statement by one Baker, who was afterwards to become his son-in-law, quoted by Lee in his *Life of Defoe,* in which work will be found a view and plan of the house and its gardens. The house is there shown to have been of considerable size with stabling at the side, facing Church Street, its grounds running back to Pawnbrokers Lane, being bounded on the west by a narrow way called Hussey's Lane. He is said to have written *Robinson Crusoe* at Stoke Newington, but it could not have been in this house, as that work appeared in 1719. It may be that his former residence stood on the site later to be covered by his more pretentious dwelling. A thoroughfare was subsequently run through the grounds of the house, and was named Defoe Street. His death did not occur here, however, but in a house in Rope Makers' Alley, Moorfields, opposite where the London Institution stands. Rope Makers' Alley is now Ropemaker Street, and connects Finsbury Pavement with what was once Greek Street but is to-day Milton Street. Defoe is buried in Bunhill Fields Cemetery, in a spot which he himself chose as being close to the grave of his sister, who had died some years previously.

DEFOE'S 'TOUR THRO' GREAT BRITAIN'

Daniel Defoe suffers, as a Man of Letters, from the overwhelming popularity of one immortal book. His name is familiar to the whole world as the author of *Robinson Crusoe,* but as regards the rest of his works, the average reader is probably content to remember that he wrote other stories of adventure, less fitted for tender years, such as *Colonel Jack* and *Moll Flanders,* with thieves and pirates as his heroes and loose women as his heroines, and was the author of the *Journal of the Plague* and the *Memoirs of a Cavalier.* But, generally speaking, except by the student, the great mass of his writings, apart from his fiction, is now almost entirely forgotten, many of them buried with the political and religious controversies of his time which gave them birth. Entirely forgotten, it might perhaps be said, until its recent reissue by Mr. G. D. H. Cole just two centuries after its first appearance, was the book, with a section of which we are here concerned, *A Tour thro' the whole Island of Great Britain.* And yet the book is in many ways a remarkable one, for it was, if we except Macky's much shorter work, the first systematic attempt to perambulate the United Kingdom and (to quote the author's preface) to present ' The Situation of Things, not as they have been, but as they are in each County and chief town; The Improvements in the Soil, the Product of the Earth, the Labour of the Poor, Improvement in Manufactures, in Merchandises, in Navigation, in all respects the present Time, not the Time Past.' It is, too, specially noteworthy as one of the products of Defoe's advancing years (he was over 65 when it was first issued), that period of amazing literary industry on his part which saw *Robinson Crusoe* given to the world in his sixtieth year to be followed before his death twelve years later by more than fifty other separate works, many of them long and important contributions to the literature of his country.

The fifth ' Letter ' of the *Tour* contains ' *A Description of the City of London, as taking in the City of Westminster, Borough of Southwark, and the Buildings circumjacent,*' while part of Letter VI deals with the suburbs of London situated in Middlesex. Several editions of the work were subsequently issued in the course of the eighteenth century, each revised and altered to bring it up to date. The continual addition of new matter would obviously have made the volumes too bulky for their purpose, which tended to become more and more that of the modern guide-book and much of the original text was therefore eliminated by successive editors, although, even so, the work had finally to be enlarged to four volumes. From the guide-book point of view this was both necessary and commendable. Whether you are reading the 1727 edition or the third, of 1742, or those which followed (there were eight altogether during the eighteenth century), you are supplied with adequate up-to-date information corresponding with the growth and development of the country. But all these successive revised editions naturally resulted in the essential character of Defoe's original text becoming well-nigh obliterated beneath the mass of alterations and additions. For instance, in 1778, an eighth edition of the work appeared bearing the statement that it was ' originally begun by the celebrated Daniel Defoe, continued by the later Mr. Richardson, and brought down to the present time by a Gentleman of Eminence in the literary world.' Concerning this edition, Lee, the devoted admirer and biographer of Defoe, to whose years of research we owe the discovery of so much that was previously unknown in regard to his life and writings, comments with force and justice: ' It is stripped of the finest passages illustrating the manners of the people; it has lost the charm of the simple narrative, and is, in fact, no longer the work of Defoe '; and he adds, ' The original edition, as Defoe left it, can never be out of date and is of increasing interest and value as a perpetual memorial of much that has no longer a visible existence. Respect for the character of the author and the integrity of his work demands that every edition subsequent to his death in 1731 be repudiated on his behalf.'

This injunction has been obeyed, it is needless to say, in this reprint of a portion of the *Tour* which reproduces textually and typographically the original edition, save that for the sake of greater clarity the paragraphs have been sub-divided, sometimes with cross-headings, sometimes with numerals, as seemed best suited for the purpose. This Circuit and Description of London differs very materially in character, just, of course, as does the subject, from the rest of the volume and contains far more topographical detail than the other twelve which deal with the provinces. As Mr. Cole points out in his scholarly Introduction to the reprint of the First Edition alluded to above, Defoe's *Tour* is important ' primarily as a guide to social and economic conditions. It is, indeed, an invaluable picture of the state of Great Britain between the Revolution of 1688 and what we are wont to call the Industrial Revolution.' In this respect his chapters on the provinces at once recall to the reader's mind and invite comparison with Arthur Young's *Tours* at the end of the eighteenth century, and William Cobbett's *Rural Rides* in the early years of the nineteenth. This comparison does not suggest itself to the same degree in the perusal of the few pages which Defoe devotes to London. He here confines himself more to a description of its actual physical growth than to any detailed analysis of its trade and commerce, or the social and industrial life of its inhabitants. The City is ' the centre of its Commerce and Wealth '; Westminster and Whitehall, the ' Court-end ' as he calls it, the ' centre of its Gallantry and Splendour '; while the ' Out-parts ' house its ' Numbers and Mechanicks.' Beyond this broad distinction between the East and West Ends and the Suburbs Defoe has comparatively little to tell us of the economic and industrial life of the London of his day, or of the various trades and occupations which were so largely localised at that time, each in its different district. But one feature is common to all the chapters in the *Tour*—the rejection of purely antiquarian matter. With antiquities and ' Time Past ' Defoe is not concerned; ' Time Present ' is his theme—and he seldom misses an opportunity of tilting at those who, like Leland, Stow, Camden, Strype and the rest, had been content to fill their ponderous tomes mainly with chronicles of the past. He strikes this note forcibly in his reference to the ' Two large Volumes in Folio ' (obviously Strype's revised and enlarged edition of Stow, recently published in 1720) in the opening lines of his London chapter.

Another marked feature which differentiates the London section from the rest of the *Tour* is the certainty of touch which instinctively tells the reader that its author is here describing at first hand the features, as well as the growth during his life-time, of a city with whose highways and byways he was intimately conversant. Defoe was not above borrowing information from others, and, indeed was, as all the world knows, a past-master in the art of inventing and giving verisimilitude to his inventions, and it is fairly certain that he must have ' conveyed ' largely, for at least certain parts of his *Tour*, in spite of his boast of ' having travelled for the purpose of this book in three or four several Tours over the whole Island, continually observing and carefully informing myself of everything worth observing in all the Towns and Counties through which I passed,' and also of having made already ' seventeen large circuits or separate journies in England, and three general Tours.'

In the case of London and its suburbs Defoe doubtless had need to make some special expeditions to fill in the gaps of his general knowledge. His description of ' tugging up ' to Hampstead and its Heath ' on the very summit,' for instance, would appear to record the impressions of a special excursion to an unfamiliar district. But generally speaking he had all the places before him in his mind's eye and all the facts at his fingers' ends. For Defoe it was an easy task to put pen to paper and present them to his readers in his own realistic and ' conversational ' style. The City was ' not difficult to be described,' as he phrases it in the opening sentence of his Letter, but ' to be concise and short ' and bring it 'within the narrow Compass of a Letter' was the 'Task difficult.' This peculiar 'conversational ' characteristic of our author's style has been noted by Mr. Masefield in his Appreciation of Defoe in his introduction to *Representative Selections* from his writings. As he says, ' Defoe wrote almost every day, with great fluency, for nearly fifty years, producing in that time about a hundred and fifty known works, many of them extremely long books; and many others, though ostensibly mere tracts and pamphlets, as long as an ordinary novel. Writing, to such a man, is not so much an art as a natural personal faculty, like conversation. We see no conscious striving for particular beauties of style.' ' Like conversation ' and ' no striving for beauties of style '—this may be said to sum up the qualities which distinguish Defoe's pen-picture of the London of his day from the bald and colourless descriptions of the average topographical works of the period (and—sad to say—many other periods), and constitute its peculiar interest and charm.

THE ' DESCRIPTION OF LONDON '

Let us very briefly epitomise the story of our author's Tour through—and round—the London of two centuries ago. He starts on his ' Circuit ' from Peterborough House on Mill Bank, and, so to speak, takes his reader by the arm, pointing out as he goes ' whatever is Curious and worth Observation ' in the long thirty-six miles tramp, expatiating on its ' prodigious ' and ' monstrous ' growth and development since his boyhood days, while deploring the 'Disaster of London as to the Beauty of its Figure ' in that it had been allowed to sprawl out its buildings anyhow and anywhere ' at the mercy of any Builder or Undertaker of Buildings.' With meticulous care and precision he takes his ' Line of Measurement ' as he goes, mile by mile, furlong by furlong, and rod by rod, to show his reader-companion just how far and where this lava-flow of bricks and mortar has impinged on the green fields of yesterday and is joining up the City with the adjacent villages. Note the exactitude with which, as he reaches the N.E. districts of the suburbs, most familiar to him as lying near his own home at Stoke Newington, he zig-zags in and out by this and that ale-house or brew-house or burying ground or garden wall or even 'the Cow-keeper's yard,' in order neither to minimise nor exaggerate ' the measure of this mighty, I cannot say uniform, Body,' whose continuous expansion since the Great Fire of his childhood's days had so deeply impressed his imagination. ' I have really not stretched my calculations to make it seem bigger than it is,' he ends up triumphantly. So he continues on to the eastern limit of his ' Circuit ' at Blackwall, crosses the river to Deptford and passes by Rotherhithe, the Borough, and the swampy open spaces of St. George's Fields back to his starting point. Having completed the circuit he then takes his fellow ' Itinerant ' on a sight-seeing tour of London, ' as divided into three, viz., the City, the Court and the Outparts,' dilating on the splendour of the new St. Paul's, the ' venerable antiquity ' of Westminster Abbey, the ' really mean ' Palace of St. James, the ' several beautiful conduits,' the ' not very valuable statues,' or discoursing on the ' new contrivance of the Penny Post,' this ' prodigious Paper Commerce called stock-jobbing,' the hospitals, churches, markets and prisons and so on; sometimes critical of defects, with perhaps a constructive suggestion for the remedy, but far more often exuberantly enthusiastic, he enlarges on all that had been achieved by his fellow citizens in the task of reconstruction since the Fire; the inauguration of new institutions, such as the Bank of England, the insurance offices, Guy's Hospital and the Charterhouse; and finally the amazing growth and development of the new Port of London with its long line of wharves, warehouses, and shipyards stretching down the Thames, and its fleet of ' 2,000 sail of all sorts ' in the Pool. With all this achieved almost within his own generation and before his own eyes mainly by the energy and enterprise of that great middle class to which Defoe himself belonged, of whose liberties and ideals he had been the life-long spokesman and champion, and which was now at last growing to be the real controlling power in the State, what wonder that he exclaims of London in an outburst of patriotic pride ' No City in the World can equal it—Nothing in the World can come up to it! '

DEFOE AS A REFORMER

And yet beneath the surface of this great material achievement there was much that was ugly and repulsive, much that was calling urgently for reform in the morals and manners of its inhabitants, more perhaps than at any other period of London's existence. A ' Society for the Reformation of Manners,' influentially supported both by Court and City, was indeed carrying on an active campaign against the grosser forms of licence and corruption then prevalent among all classes. To those who remember Defoe's zeal in such matters it will be a matter for surprise that scarcely a reference or even hint is made by him to this aspect of the London of his day. What suggestions for improvements he has to make are confined strictly to its structural and topographical deficiencies, the lack of an adequate Palace for its King and Parliament, the congestion at Charing Cross, the need for a new Bridge at Westminster and so on. There are two good reasons which manifestly explain his silence. Having strictly limited himself to a ' Description of London within the Compass of a Letter,' he would not extend or interfere with his topographical narrative by introducing matter which, although germane to his subject, would have been there inappropriately intruded; and secondly he had already evolved in his brain and contemplated the publication of another work dealing solely with the social problems of the London of his day, and submitting concrete suggestions for improvement and reform. This volume in due course appeared. The complete edition of the *Tour of Great Britain* was issued in June 1727, and within a year (to be precise, in March, 1728) Defoe published a book called *Augusta Triumphans or the Way to Make London the most flourishing City in the Universe.* The suggestions which he put forward for attaining this end threw an interesting sidelight on the manners and customs of the day, and were as follows:

(i) By Establishing a *University* where Gentlemen may have Academical Education under the Eyes of their Friends.
(ii) By an Hospital for *Foundlings.*
(iii) By forming an Academy of Sciences at *Christ's Hospital.*
(iv) By suppressing pretended *Mad Houses*, where many of the fair Sex are unjustly confined, while their husbands keep Mistresses, etc., and many Widows are locked up for the sake of their Jointure.
(v) To save our Youth from *Destruction*, by cleaning the Streets of impudent *Strumpets*, suppressing *Gaming Tables* and *Sundry Debauches.*
(vi) To save our Lower Class of People from utter *Ruin*, and render them useful, by preventing the immoderate use of Geneva.
With a frank Exposition of many other Common abuses, and incontestable Rules for Amendment. Concluding with an effectual Method to prevent *Street Robberies* and a Letter to Col. Robinson on account of the Orphans Tax.

DEFOE AS JOURNALIST

This is only one of the many glimpses of the social aspects of the London of his day which Defoe has given us. In that mass of ephemeral journalism which he poured out unceasingly in the intervals of producing his longer and better-known works, will be found passages in abundance which serve as a sort of prose commentary on what Gay tells us in the verses of his *Trivia.* Defoe was more familiar than was Gay with the City, and in the doings of Exchange Alley we find a supplement to the picture of the social life of the 'Court End' of the town, of its clubs and coffee-houses with which the poet was more concerned, and which Steele and Addison have painted for us in the familiar pages of the *Tatler* and *Spectator.*

They serve also to supplement the pictures preserved for us in the prints of the period where we generally see a foreground of figures and vehicles and so on, which the artist has inserted to give life to his delineations and proportion to his structures—and a picturesque *ensemble* these generally make. The hackney coach and the sedan-chair have for us both a pictorial and a historic interest. But we are apt to forget the annoyances and discomforts to which those who hired them were so frequently subjected. Gay tells us of the physical discomforts and difficulties of locomotion in the crowded cobbled streets, while Defoe reminds us that, where the 'licensed driver' is concerned, human nature was as perverse then as now. He writes of the 'insolence of Coachmen in demanding unreasonable sums for their fare,' their 'sauciness in giving ill language to Gentlemen,' and their 'refusing to go to particular places at their pleasure,' conduct which was sufficiently widespread as to occasion the introduction of a Bill in Parliament for its correction, Again, we read, with excitement, of the doings of those highwaymen and footpads who were being idealised by Gay in his *Beggar's Opera* as heroes of romance in the same year that saw the publication of Defoe's *Tour*. But in *Mist's Journal*, and *Applebee's Journal*, our author records instances of such depredations as must have effectually destroyed any illusions which may have been previously held by the victims of these gentlemen of the road. They are here found 'taking £400 from two ladies at Richmond,' and making a general dead-set at travellers leaving or arriving at London near the various turnpikes, especially in the area about Islington and Newington Green. To the tales of the exploits of those bands of ruffians known as 'Mohocks' and 'Nickers' and 'Scourers' and so forth, perambulating the streets and inflicting indecencies and injuries on all sorts of inoffensive pedestrians, which have been recorded by Addison, Swift and Gay, Defoe adds instances of outrages by other 'hooligans' of the day, such as the Spittlefields weavers, the London Catchpoles and even the Marshalsea officers, indicating that then the citizen had almost as much to fear from the guardians as from the breakers of the law. The state of the Debtors' prisons, the question of the advantage and propriety of what were wont to be called 'Sanctuaries,' 'The Mint,' Whitefriars and the rest, are also to be found discussed by one whose eyes were everywhere and to whom, indeed, nothing that was human was indifferent.

From these 'Press-Cuttings,' so to speak, one obtains a cumulative vision of the social London of two centuries ago, which supplements the author's topographical account of the city. For instance, here is a notice of a new and greatly improved fire-engine, from *Applebee's Journal* for July 20th, 1723: 'On Tuesday last, Mr. Newsham, in New Street, Cloth Fair, London, play'd his new-invented Engine at the Royal Exchange, before several Gentlemen then present. It play'd several Yards above the Dial, with a constant stream, above a hundred gallons each minute; which must be allow'd by all ingenious Men that saw it, to exceed all sorts of Engines whatsoever.'

Again, we get a glimpse of the official ceremony with which Bartholomew Fair was wont to be inaugurated, from the same source, dated August 20th, 1724:

' On Saturday last (22nd) in the Afternoon, the Lord Mayor came with great State and Solemnity to Smithfield, and proclaimed Bartholomew Fair. His Lordship's Coach stopp'd at the Lodge Door of Newgate, where Mr. Reuse, the chief Turnkey appeared, in the absence of Mr. Pitt, the Keeper (who is indisposed) and treated his Lordship, the Sheriffs and Aldermen with a Lemonade, after a very handsome and pleasing Manner; which Custom is observed to all the Mayors, at the Proclaiming of Bartholomew Fair.'

All is fish that comes to Defoe's net, and from the notice (1718) of an uproar in the Lincoln's Inn Theatre, caused by three gentlemen wanting to go behind the scenes, ' there being an order of the House made to the contrary,' to one telling us that two new bells had been put up in St. Bride's steeple, thus making a peal of twelve bells, ' being more than any other steeple in England '; from details (1724) of Jack Sheppard's famous escape from Newgate, his reapprehension, and his execution on November 1st of that year, to a long ' et cetera ' of topical gossip in which we learn much about the South Sea Bubble, we obtain all kinds of data which, scrappy as they may be, are yet of the utmost value and interest, and enable us to build up a microcosm of the London of two centuries ago.

There is one contribution in particular to *Applebee's Journal* which has a special bearing on Defoe's *Description of London*, being approximately of the same date, and is therefore reprinted as one of the Appendices to this volume. He writes, in the form of a letter, concerning the deserted state of Westminster owing to one of the frequent absences of the King and the Court in Hanover. These frequent absences caused much hostile comment and heartburning among the English subjects of the German king. Defoe, as a staunch supporter of the House of Hanover, tactfully treats the subject in a humorous way, and the letter, although a long one, is worth studying as an example of his conversational journalistic style and exceptional powers of realistic composition.

DEFOE'S CONTEMPORARIES

A word should be said concerning some of Defoe's more notable contemporaries because the period during which he lived was particularly rich in eminent men in all walks of life whose names are household words in our history. A ' small world ' indeed was the London of his time, and society was far less complex than it is to-day. Even in his later years it was still small enough for the ' man in the street ' to be familiar with the identity and personality of the ' Great Men ' of the day who were often to be pointed out in the streets, as were Dryden and Addison, as they wended their way to their favourite haunts in the coffee-houses of Covent Garden.

Going back to his early years, in the reign of Charles II, Defoe might thus have met Samuel Butler and John Hobbes and Andrew Marvell, and as a boy may have seen a blind man being led by a daughter for an airing from a house in Artillery Walk, Bunhill Fields, not far from the elder Foe's shop, who would have proved on enquiry to be one John Milton. Other poets and dramatists of a past day, who were still hanging on to life, were Davenant and Denham and Waller; and Shirley, the last of the older playwrights, who was living in St. Giles's at the time of his death in 1666, linked Defoe's childhood to the latter years of Shakespeare's greatness.

Contemporaries of Defoe's earlier manhood were Dryden, who died in Gerrard Street in 1700, and had long been an oracle at Wills's; Pepys who was in Buckingham Street in 1684, but subsequently (1700) removed to Clapham under his doctor's advice, and his great contemporary diarist Evelyn, who was accustomed to come to London from Sayes Court, Deptford, or from further Wootton, to attend meetings of the Royal Society in Crane Court, or consult with his friends, Dr. Wren or Mr. Flamsteed, taking lodgings sometimes in Whitehall (1686), sometimes in Soho Square (1690), or in Villiers Street, Strand (1683); or later still in Dover Street (1699). In 1694 John Locke was staying in Lincoln's Inn Fields ' over against the Plough Tavern ' off Carey Street, and Sir William Temple recalled an older generation, coming up to London from his ' little corner ' at Sheen, or from more remote Moor Park. But a greater than these was Isaac Newton who lived first in Jermyn Street, then in Haydon Square, Minories, and from 1710 to the year of his death (which, however, actually occurred at Kensington) in 1727 in the little house in St. Martin's Street, Leicester Square, which not even this famous association was able to preserve from demolition. Many of the not very long-lived Restoration dramatists survived into Defoe's manhood, Rochester and Dorset and Buckingham and Farquhar for instance. More nearly his contemporaries were Congreve, who died in 1729, and Wycherley and Vanbrugh, and these linked an earlier period with that great ' Augustan Age ' of which Defoe was one of the outstanding luminaries, the age of Swift and Addison and Steele, of Gay and Pope and Arbuthnot, the era when the *Tatler* and the *Spectator* were powers in the literary world, and when the *Dunciad* and *Gulliver's Travels* and Defoe's own masterpiece helped to create a golden age of letters.

Then, too, Vanbrugh was erecting his vast and massive palaces, and Grinling Gibbon was filling Wren's new churches with the fruits and flowers of his exquisite art; Flamsteed and Halley were discovering new worlds among the stars; Handel was introducing his Italian operas, and Bentley was systematising classic criticism. Hogarth at the age of twenty-eight, in 1724, while still an art student at Sir James Thornhill's new School of Painting, had published in his *Masquerades and Operas* the first slight sample of his genius as painter-satirist, which a few years later was to culminate in that series of plates which depict with such accuracy of social and topographical detail the London of the period immediately succeeding that of Defoe.

The background of the stage on which these great men of their day played their parts may perhaps be briefly sketched in without trespassing too far into the domain of history proper. During the five reigns in which Defoe lived, he witnessed many amazing events: the Great Plague and the Great Fire of London; the Rye House Plot; Monmouth's Rebellion (in which he took part as one of the ' rebels ') and the subsequent Bloody Assize; the Trial of the Seven Bishops; the Flight of James II and the Accession of William and Mary; the Massacre of Glencoe; the Act of Union with Scotland; the wars of Marlborough; the rise and bursting of the South Sea Bubble; the attempt of the Old Pretender to recapture the throne of his father; the abolition of the Censorship of the Press. He saw two revolutions: one that gave the throne of the Stuarts to a comparative stranger; and another by which, in the phraseology of the time, a branch of the family was called to take the position of the original trunk; and as once more the atmosphere of his surroundings changed, when the 'asthmatic little Dutchman ' came to sit where the gay Charles and the priest-ridden James had sat before him, so it was again when George I came not too willingly from Hanover to replace the last of the Stuart dynasty.

Defoe's life covers, indeed, seventy years of a sequence of more remarkable happenings and the effective careers of more notable men in all spheres of activity than does perhaps any other similar period in our history, and the period is specially significant as one which links up two distinct eras in our history. Just as in his early manhood the outward appearance of the capital itself changed to his wondering eyes, so did the social and moral life of its inhabitants, in strong reaction from the rigours of the Puritan régime, take on an altered and, to one born, bred and educated as a Dissenter, a strange and disagreeable complexion. Equally hateful to his instincts and convictions was the political re-action identified with the High Church Party's support of the revived Doctrine of the Divine Right of Kings and the Duty of Passive Obedience by their subjects. To the defeat of these forces of Re-action in all their varied manifestations Defoe devoted the chief energies of his life; he took a leading part as pamphleteer and journalist in common with his great contemporaries, Swift, Bolingbroke, Addison, Prior and Steele in all the religious and political controversies which mark the long-drawn-out struggle between the Whigs and Tories of the time and lived to see, with the accession of George I and the establishment of a Parliamentary system of Government under Walpole, the victory of those democratic principles which the influence of his powerful and prolific pen had done so much to secure. ' From my first entering into the knowledge of public matters,' he wrote, in eloquent appeal to the verdict of History against the indictments of his political adversaries, ' I was, and have ever been to this day, a sincere lover of the constitution of my country; zealous for Liberty and the Protestant interest; but a constant follower of moderate principles, a vigorous opposer of hot measures in all'—words which sum up the chief articles of his political creed and embody the basic theme of all his political writings. By Defoe himself, the services which he thus rendered to his country in helping to guide the national destinies along the paths of political freedom and religious toleration were doubtless regarded as the essential achievement of his life, far transcending the authorship of those works of realistic fiction for one of which he is now chiefly remembered; one which, moreover, by the irony of fate, has come to be regarded as the peculiar property of the ' boys and girls of England,' by whom the obelisk to his memory was set up just a hundred and forty years after his death to mark the spot where he had been laid to rest in the burial ground of Bunhill Fields.

PLATE II

VIEW OF LONDON FROM GREENWICH SHEWING DEPTFORD AND THE ISLE OF DOGS

From a contemporary Gouache Drawing.

By courtesy of Messrs. Walkers Galleries Ltd.

A TOUR IN CIRCUITS THROUGH ENGLAND, &c.

LETTER V.

Containing a Defcription of the City of LONDON, *as taking in the City of* WESTMINSTER, *Borough of* SOUTHWARK, *and the Buildings circumjacent.*

S I R,

AS I am now near the Center of this Work, fo I am to defcribe the great Center of *England*, the City of *London*, and Parts adjacent. This great Work is infinitely difficult in its Particulars, though not in itfelf; not that the City is fo difficult to be defcribed, but to do it in the narrow Compafs of a Letter, which we fee fo fully takes up Two large Volumes in Folio, and which, yet, if I may venture to give an Opinion of it, is done but by Halves neither.

However, be the Tafk difficult, as it is, yet it muft be done; to be concife and fhort, is abfolutely neceffary; to be plain and fignificant, as neceffary; I fhall obferve both, as near as I can.

The 'Center of this work' refers to the complete *Tour of Great Britain*, of which the portion concerning London, here reprinted, occupies approximately the centre. The 'Two large Volumes in Folio' are obviously Strype's edition of Stow, which had appeared in 1720, ' corrected, improved and very much enlarged,' but, for Defoe's taste, was far too full of purely antiquarian matter.

LONDON—' NOW IN THE MODERN ACCEPTATION '

London, as a City only, and as its Walls and Liberties line it out, might, indeed, be viewed in a fmall Compafs; but, when I fpeak of *London*, now in the Modern Acceptation, you expect I fhall take in all that vaft Mafs of Buildings, reaching from *Black-Wall* in the *Eaft*, to *Tot-Hill Fields* in the *Weft*; and extended in an unequal Breadth, from the Bridge, or River, in the *South*, to *Iflington North;* and from *Peterburgh Houfe* on the Bank Side in *Weftminfter*, to *Cavendifh Square*, and all the new Buildings by, and beyond, *Hannover*

NOTE.—The ornamental heading above and the tail-piece on the final page are enlarged reproductions in facsimile of those which appear on the opening pages of Defoe's *Tour* and are characteristic of the ' Printer's ornament ' of the period.

Square, by which the City of *London*, for fo it is ftill to be called, is extended to *Hide Park Corner* in the *Brentford Road*, and almoft to *Maribone* in the *Acton Road*, and how much farther it may fpread, who knows? New Squares, and new Streets rifing up every Day to fuch a Prodigy of Buildings, that nothing in the World does, or ever did, equal it, except old *Rome* in *Trajan's* Time, when the Walls were Fifty Miles in Compafs, and the Number of Inhabitants Six Millions Eight hundred thoufand Souls.

In connection with Defoe's allusion to the 'Walls and Liberties' it should be remembered that the old City Wall, with its seven land gates and its one Bridgegate, still remained *in situ* in his day. The Gates were not removed till the 'sixties of the eighteenth century. The Wall itself disappeared gradually. It is shown as still in existence in Rocque's plan of 1746, but in that of Horwood, 1799, is totally ignored, although small fragments still remained as they do to-day.

BLACKWALL was then, as now, and as it had been from early Tudor times, what Strype calls 'a notable harbour for ships.' 'Here,' he writes, 'is a well-known wet dock, called Blackwell Dock, belonging to Sir Henry Johnson, very convenient for building and receiving ships'; and during the eighteenth century, when ships were built of wood, many men-of-war were constructed here. Even down to the close of the nineteenth century, when iron and steel had replaced wood in ship construction, the shipbuilding and repairing industry, the pride of the Thames for so many centuries, continued to be carried on, but gradually disappeared owing, apparently, to the more favourable labour conditions on the Tyne and Clyde and elsewhere.

Concerning the name of Blackwall two explanations have been advanced; thus Norden in his *Speculum Britanniæ* states that 'the place taketh name of the blackness and darkness of the water bankes, or wall at that place,' but Strype is more particular, thus: it is, he says, ' so called, because it is a *wall* of the Thames and distinguished by the additional term Black, from the black shrubs that grew on it, as on Blackheath which is opposite to it on the other side of the river (or perhaps from the blackness of the place and situation).'

In earlier days the name had been indifferently spelt Blakwale, Blakewale and even Bralkwale, Sir Walter Raleigh writing it in the last two ways in a single letter addressed to Secretary Cecil. Pepys, on the other hand, spells it as it is to-day, when referring to the visits he paid there to see the docks, one of which, the West Dock, had been then (1661) but recently constructed. Four years later, on the occasion of another visit, the Diarist gives some interesting data: ' Sept. 22, 1665. At Blackwall. Here is observable what Johnson tells us, that, in digging the late Docke (i.e. the West Dock) he did 12 feet under ground find perfect trees over-covered with earth. Nut-trees with the branches and the very nuts upon them; some of whose nuts he showed us, their shells black with age; and their kernell, upon opening, decayed, but their shell perfectly hard as ever. And a yew-tree, upon which the very ivy was taken up whole about it, which, upon cutting with an addes [adze], we found it to be rather harder than the living tree usually is.'

TOTHILL FIELDS have long disappeared as such, although, as our reproduction of Capon's watercolour sketch shows, little building development took place before the nineteenth century, and Vincent Square is now the only remnant of any magnitude of the old open spaces of this district. Tothill Street, Westminster, preserves their name. In Defoe's time they extended from the ' Road to the Horseferry' next to the river, near where stood the Neat Houses, which he mentions, and which, originally inhabited by graziers, were in his day occupied by gardeners who supplied the London markets with vegetables. There was a place of entertainment called The Neat House close to the Thames, to which Pepys was wont occasionally to resort, and it was probably here that Nell Gwynn's mother fell into the river and was drowned.

What Defoe calls ' The Bank Side in Westminster' corresponds to what is known now as Mill Bank. Strype, in 1720, calls it so and defines it as ' a very long place which beginneth by Lindsey House, or rather by the Old Palace Yard, and runneth up into PETERBOROUGH HOUSE, which is the farthest house.' This house, he adds ' hath a large court-yard before it, and a fine garden behind it; but its situation is but bleak in the winter, and not over healthful, as being so near the low meadows on the south and west parts.' It was then leased and occupied by Mordaunt, first Earl of Peterborough, and his family continued to occupy it till it was taken over and rebuilt as ' Grosvenor House on Millbank' by the Grosvenors, and used by them as their Town residence till early in the nineteenth century. Strype's description of the courtyard and garden is confirmed by the accompanying illustration.

PLATE III

TOTHILL FIELDS TOWARDS THE END OF THE XVIIIth CENTURY

(showing the Pest Houses, or "Five Chimneys," on the left, Battersea Windmills and Church in the centre, and Chelsea Hospital on the right)

From a Water Colour by William Capon

Appended to this water colour is the following note in William Capon's handwriting:

" William Capon del. 1794—Pinx. September 1818 "

" View of Tothill or Tuttle Fields looking South West, as they appeared in the Summer of 1794. Taken from the bed-room windows of the last house except one, (where I then resided) in Marsham St. in Westminster. . . . The tent pitched in the field is for the use of the Westminster Scholars, when they play at cricket. The Horse Ferry Road, seen in front, is now built on. At that time only one house was built at the Western end and was not visible from the situation from whence this draught was made. I have seen persons skait [sic] on the green fields shewn near the rails in front and water came up with the tide of the river as here shewn."

The swampy nature of a large part of that indeterminate area lying in the triangle between Westminster, Chelsea and Pimlico and known as Tothill Fields, is clearly indicated, with its pasture grounds and market gardens intersected by streams and ditches, in our reproduction of the contemporary Plan of the Parish of St. George's, Hanover Square. As Capon's sketch and the notes which he appends to it show, much of this district then remained subject to chronic inundation from the Thames at exceptionally high tides, and was consequently undeveloped as a building site till long after Defoe's day. This neighbourhood was in fact still occasionally flooded throughout the 19th century, and it is only since the tragic loss of life, consequent on the inundation of the Millbank area in 1928, that steps have been taken by the construction of an adequate embankment, to render it free from further troubles of this kind.

PLATE IV

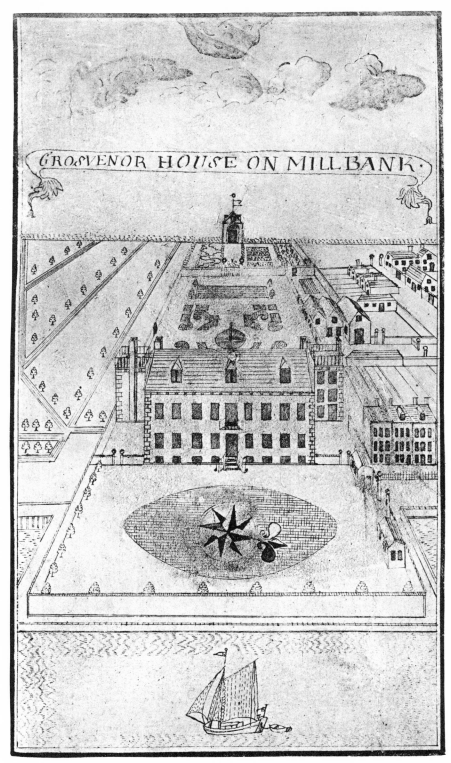

GROSVENOR HOUSE ON MILLBANK.

PETERBOROUGH (LATER GROSVENOR) HOUSE
From William Mackay's Plan of the Grosvenor Estate, dated 1723

CAVENDISH SQUARE was first laid out in 1718, but building operations were suspended for a time owing to the bursting of the South Sea Bubble. There is extant ' The Elevation of a New House intended for his Grace the Duke of Chandos, in Marybone Fields,' dated 1720. This was the famous house which was to have occupied the whole north side of Cavendish, or as it was for a time called Oxford, Square, but of which only the servants' wings were completed, to-day represented by the two corner houses.

When Defoe speaks of ' all the new buildings by, and beyond, Hannover Square,' he is referring to the development of the property round Grosvenor Square now known generically as the Grosvenor Estate. Grosvenor Square itself was actually begun during the early years of the eighteenth century, but its completion did not take place till 1725, in which year Sir Richard Grosvenor, ' the great builder,' as he was called, summoned his actual and intending tenants to a ' splendid entertainment ' at which the new streets of this district were solemnly christened.

The plan of the Parish of St. George's, Hanover Square, dated 1725, reproduced at the end of this volume, shows us all this area beginning to be covered with streets and houses much as it is to-day, and reaching, as Defoe points out, to Hyde Park Gate (now Corner) on one side and Marylebone ' in the Acton Road ' (Oxford Street) on the other.

LONDON—'AS TO THE BEAUTY OF ITS FIGURE'

It is the Difafter of *London*, as to the Beauty of its Figure, that it is thus ftretched out in Buildings, juft at the Pleafure of every Builder, or Undertaker of Buildings, and as the Convenience of the People directs, whether for Trade, or otherwife; and this has fpread the Face of it in a moft ftraggling, confuf'd Manner, out of all Shape, uncompact, and unequal; neither long or broad, round or fquare; whereas the City of *Rome*, though a Monfter for its Greatnefs, yet was, in a manner, round, with very few Irregularities in its Shape.

At *London*, including the Buildings on both Sides the Water, one fees it, in fome Places, Three Miles broad, as from St. *George*'s in *Southwark*, to *Shoreditch* in *Middlefex*; or Two Miles, as from *Peterburgh Houfe* to *Montague Houfe**; and in fome Places, not half a Mile, as in *Wapping*; and much lefs, as in *Redriff*.

> Defoe's love of hyperbole is well illustrated in this reference to the ' Disaster of London.' He seems to be echoing the remarks previously made by Hatton on this subject of the formless longitudinal growth of London, which ' some authors,' he says, ' have compared with that of a Laurel Leaf, . . . some to a Carpenter's rule; but it resembles the Shape of a great Whale, *Westminster* being the under Jaw; *St. James Park* the Mouth; *Pall Mall etc* the upper Jaw; *Cock & Pye Fields*, or the meeting of the 7 Streets the Eye; the rest of the City & Southwark to *East-Smithfield* the Body; and thence to Limehouse the Tail.' This suggestion of a Laurel Leaf has been taken as the *motif* of the pen-and-ink decorative heading used in our introductory pages.

'WHITHER WILL THIS MONSTROUS CITY THEN EXTEND?'

We fee feveral Villages, formerly ftanding, as it were, in the Country, and at a great Diftance, now joyn'd to the Streets by continued Buildings, and more making hafte to meet in the like Manner; for Example,

1. *Deptford*, This Town was formerly reckoned, at leaft Two Miles off from *Redriff*, and that over the Marfhes too, a Place unlikely ever to be inhabited; and yet now, by the Encreafe of Buildings in that Town itfelf, and the many Streets erected at *Redriff*, and by the Docks and Building-Yards on the River Side, which ftand between both, the Town of *Deptford*, and the Streets of *Redriff*, or *Rotherhith* (as they write it) are effectually joyn'd, and the Buildings daily increafing; fo that *Deptford* is no more a feparated Town, but is become a Part of the great Mafs, and infinitely full of People alfo; Here they have, within the laft Two or Three Years, built a fine new Church, and were the Town of *Deptford* now feparated, and rated by itfelf, I believe it contains more People, and ftands upon more Ground, than the City of *Wells*.

* Now represented by the British Museum.

Although Defoe speaks of DEPTFORD and REDRIFF or ROTHERHITHE, as then, through increase of buildings, being ' effectually joyned ' to London itself, it is not to be supposed that the former of those places in his day was, as it now is, wholly incorporated in this portion of the city. Even in Rocque's plan of some twenty years later than the date of which our author is writing, we see that the buildings linking it up with Rotherhithe were practically confined to the river bank, while the road to Deptford from Rotherhithe is shown unfinished, ending in open ground which is now thickly covered with streets and houses.

ROTHERHITHE, as being closer to the centre of things, was naturally more identified with London's main body, but even it extended only a short way back from the Thames, although its elongated area along the banks housed a considerable population. Originally a hamlet attached to the royal manor of Bermondsey, its name appears in a charter dated A.D. 898, as ' Ætheredes. hyd.' Its once alternative name of Redriff appears to have been given it in the seventeenth century, and in the large majority of local trade tokens it is so spelt.

Its church, which Defoe here speaks of as having been built within the last two or three years, was completed in 1715, and was erected on the site of a much earlier and smaller one. The name of its architect has not been recorded; but it partakes of that semi-classical character which was then in vogue, being a red-brick building with stone facings and Corinthian columns. Its steeple was not added till 1738. The Petition of the Parishioners for a Government grant-in-aid for the rebuilding of their church had been refused, and the necessary funds had to be raised by local subscription. As an original and special inducement subscribers were offered the opportunity of acquiring, not only a sitting in the church, but the title to a vault when required, for their own use or that of their family!

DEPTFORD—the place of the Deep Ford over the little river Ravensbourne at its junction with the Thames—first rose into importance from 'a small and contemptible fishing town' owing to the establishment there by Henry VIII of the Royal Dockyard. Its growth in population in Defoe's time is indicated by its division into two Parishes (St. Nicholas and St. Paul) by Act of Parliament in 1730, shortly after the publication of his *Tour*.

2. The Town of *Iflington*, on the *North* Side of the City, is in like manner joyn'd to the Streets of *London*, excepting one fmall Field, and which is in itfelf fo fmall, that there is no Doubt, but in a very few Years, they will be intirely joyn'd, and the fame may be faid of *Mile-End*, on the *Eaft* End of the Town.

3. *Newington*, called *Newington-Butts*, in *Surrey*, reaches out her Hand *North*, and is fo near joining to *Southwark*, that it cannot now be properly called a Town by itfelf, but a Suburb to the Burrough, and if, *as they now tell us is undertaken*, St. *George's Fields* fhould be built into Squares and Streets, a very little Time will fhew us *Newington, Lambeth,* and the *Burrough*, all making but one *Southwark*.

4. That *Weftminfter* is in a fair Way to fhake Hands with *Chelsea*, as St. *Gyles's* is with *Marybone*; and *Great Ruffel Street* by *Montague Houfe*, with *Tottenham-Court*: all this is very evident, and yet all thefe put together, are ftill to be called *London*: Whither will this monftrous City then extend? and where muft a Circumvallation or Communication Line of it be placed?

When Defoe states that ISLINGTON is ' joined to the streets of London, excepting one small Field,' he must be taken as speaking in a large and general way. For buildings here and there along the two highways to what was then practically a separate village, each known, according to plans of the time, simply as the ' Islington Roads ' (one is now St. John's Road and the other Goswell Road), may in a way be said to have connected it with London. But even considerably later than Defoe's day there were large undeveloped fields separating Sadlers Wells from London proper, extending between the two highways and almost to the backs of the houses on the north side of Compton Street, as is indicated in the annexed ' View of London from near Islington.'

Incidentally it may be remarked that the development of this northern part of London's surrounding area, before a similar extension took place in the south, was helped by the discovery of springs of more or less medicinal character, in these regions, which resulted first in the evolution of tea-gardens and pleasure haunts and subsequently the building of houses in their immediate vicinity.

THE NORTH-WEST PROSPECT OF DEPTFORD SHOWING THE ROYAL STOREHOUSE

Drawn and engraved by S. & N. Buck. 1739.

PLATE VI

A View from Constitution Hill Anno 1755.

Showing Buckingham House and Westminster Abbey with scaffolding on the unfinished West Tower
From a print published by R. Godfrey

HYDE PARK CORNER AS IT WAS IN THE MIDDLE OF THE XVIII CENTURY
From a contemporary wash drawing
This drawing shows Allen's apple stall, for which the site was granted by George II to a soldier of that name
who fought under him at Dettingen; and the 'Hercules Pillars' Tavern

In like manner NEWINGTON BUTTS was then but slightly linked on to south London by the extension to that village of the Borough High Street. All that portion, which we now know as Newington, of which St. George's Circus may be said to be the centre, was then the large open space called St. George's Fields, an area not destined to be developed till the early years of the nineteenth century. Defoe's prognostications on the other hand in the next paragraph, that it was 'very evident' that Chelsea would soon be linked up with Westminster, and St. Giles's with Marylebone, and Great Russell Street with Tottenham Court, were to be speedily verified within a few years.

On the South side of the Thames the rate of development was in fact far slower than on the North, as Sir Walter Besant has shown very clearly in his *South London*. It is interesting to compare with Defoe's comparatively meagre references here to this area the following account which he gives of Southwark in his chapter in the Tour which deals with Surrey:

'I am now come to *Southwark*, a Suburb to, rather than a Part of *London*: But of which this may be said with Justice.

A Royal City were not London *by.*

'To give you a brief Description of *Southwark*, it might be called a long Street, of about Nine Miles in length, as it is now built on Eastward; reaching from *Vaux-Hall* to *London-Bridge*, and from the Bridge to *Deptford* and up to *Deptford*-Bridge, which parts it from *Greenwich*, all the way winding and turning as the River winds and turns, except only in that Part, which reaches from *Cuckold's-Point* to *Deptford*, which indeed winds more than the River does.

In the Center, which is opposite to the Bridge, it is thicken'd with Buildings, and may be reckon'd near a Mile broad; (Viz) from the Bridge to the End of *Kent-street* and *Blackman-street*, and about the *Mint;* but else the whole Building is but Narrow, nor indeed can it be otherwise; considering the length of it.

The Principal Beauty of the Burrough of *Southwark*, consists in the prodigious Number of its Inhabitants: Take it as it was Antiently bounded, it contain'd Nine Parishes; but as it is now extended, and, as I say, joins with Deptford, it contains Eleven large Parishes: According to the Weekly-Bills, for the Year 1722, the Nine Parishes only bury'd 4166, which is about one Sixth Part of the whole Body, call'd *London:* the Bill of Mortality for that Year, amounting in all to 25750.

The first Thing we meet with considerable, is at the *Spring-Garden*, just at the Corner, where the Road turns away to go from *Vaux-Hall* Turnpike, towards *Newington*, there are the Remains of the Old Lines* cast up in the Times of the Rebellion, to Fortify this Side of the Town; and at that Corner was a very large *Bastion*, or rather a Fort, and such indeed they call it; which Commanded all the Pass on that Side, and farther on, where the Openings near *St. George's-Fields* are, which they now call the *Ducking-Pond*, there was another; the Water they call the *Ducking-Pond*, is evidently to this Day the Moat of the Fort, and the Lines are so high, and so undemolish'd still, that a very little matter would Repair and perfect them again.

From hence they turn'd South East, and went to the Windmill, at the End of *Blackman-street*, where they cross'd the Road, and going to the End of *Kent-street*, we see another great *Bastion;* and then turning S.E. till they came to the End of *Barnaby-street*, or rather beyond, among the Tanners, and there you see another Fort, so plain, and so undemolish'd, the Grass grows now over the Works, that is as plain as it was, even when it was thrown down.'

'A MEASURE OF THIS MIGHTY BODY'

I have, as near as I could, cauſed a Meaſure to be taken of this mighty, I cannot ſay uniform, Body; and for the Satisfaction of the Curious, I have here given as accurate a Deſcription of it, as I can do in ſo narrow a Compaſs, as this of a Letter, or as I could do without drawing a Plan, or Map of the Places.

As I am forced, in many Places, to take in ſome unbuilt Ground, ſo I have, on the other Hand, been obliged to leave a great many whole Streets of Buildings out of my Line: So that I have really not ſtretched my Calculations, to make it ſeem bigger than it is; nor is there any Occaſion of it.

* The Forts and Entrenchments which were constructed round London for the defence of the Capital against the armies of Charles I in the Civil War form the subject of a pamphlet by William Lithgow, entitled 'The Present Surveigh of London,' 1643, and more recently of a detailed and elaborate study by Mr. Norman G. Brett-James, M.A., in the fourteenth volume of the London Topographical Society's Records, to which we would refer our readers.

A LINE *of Meafurement, drawn about all the continued Buildings of the City of London, and Parts adjacent, including* Weſtminſter *and* Southwark, *&c.**

The Line begins, FOR THE MIDDLESEX SIDE *of the Buildings*,

	Miles	Fur.	Rods
1. AT *Peterborough Houfe*, the fartheft Houfe *Weft* upon the River *Thames*, and runs *N.W.* by *W.* by the Marfhes to *Tutthill Fields*, and paffing by the *Neat Houfes*, and *Arnold's Brewhoufe*, ends at *Chelfea Road*, meafured -	1	6	16
2. Then, allowing an Interval from *Buckingham Houfe* crofs the Park, about one Furlong and half to the Corner of my Lord *Godolphin*'s Garden Wall, the Line goes *North* behind the Stable-Yard Buildings, and behind *Park-Place*, and on the Park Wall behind the Buildings; on the *Weft* Side of St. *James*'s *Street*, to the Corner in *Soho*, or *Pickadilly*, then croffing the Road and goes along the *North* Side of the Road *Weft* to *Hide Park Gate* -	1	2	11
3. Then the Line turns *N.E.* by *E.* and taking in the Buildings and Streets, called *May-Fair*, and holds on *Eaft* till the New Streets formed out of *Hide Houfe Garden*, caufe it to turn away *North*, a Point *Weft* reaching to *Tyburn-Road*, a little to the *Eaft* of the great Mother Conduit; then it goes *North*, and croffing the Road, takes in the *Weft* Side of *Cavendifh Square*, and the Streets adjoining, and leaving *Marybone*, goes away *Eaft*, 'till it reaches to *Hampftead-Road*, near a little Village called *Tottenham Court* - - -	2	5	20
4. From *Tottenham Court*, the Line comes in a little *South*, to meet the *Bloomfbury* Buildings, then turning *Eaft*, runs behind *Montague* and *Southampton* Houfes, to the *N.E.* Corner of *Southampton Houfe*, then croffing the Path, meets the Buildings called *Queen's Square*, then turning *North*, 'till it comes to the *N.W.* Corner of the Square, thence it goes away *Eaft* behind the Buildings on the *North* Side of *Ormond Street*, 'till it comes to *Lamb*'s *Conduit* - - - - - - - - -	1	1	13
5. Here the Line turns *South*, and indents to the Corner of *Bedford Row*, and leaving fome few Houfes, with the Cock-Pit, and Bowling Green, goes on the Back of *Gray*'s *Inn Wall*, to *Gray*'s *Inn Lane*, then turns on the Outfide of the Buildings, which are on the *Weft* Side of *Gray's Inn Lane*, going *North* to the Stones End, when turning *Eaft*, it paffes to the New River Bridge without *Liquor-pond Street*, fo taking in the *Cold Bath* and the *Bear Garden*; but leaving out Sir *John Old-Caftle*'s and the *Spaw*, goes on *Eaft* by the *Ducking-Pond* to the End of *New Bridewell*, and croffing the Fairfield, comes into the *Iflington* Road by the Diftiller's Houfe, formerly Juftice *Fuller*'s, - - - - - - - -	1	2	6
Carried over - - - - - - - -	8	1	26

* Our readers are here referred to the folding map where Defoe's 'Line of Measurement' has been carefully traced, street by street, and as far as possible house by house, as is explained in the Prefatory Note. The general appearance of the open fields in the Sadler's Wells district to which Defoe refers is also well indicated in the View from near Islington.

	Miles	Fur.	Rods
Brought over - - - - - - - - -	8	1	26

6. Here to take in all the Buildings which joyn *Iflington* to the Streets, the Line goes *North* on the *Eaft* Side of the Road to the *Turk's Head* Ale-houfe; then turning *North Weft*, paffes to the *New River Houfe*, but leaving it to the *Weft*, paffes by *Sadler's Well*, from thence to *Bufby's* Houfe, and keeping on the *Weft* Side of *Iflington*, 'till it comes oppofite to *Cambray Houfe-Lane*, turns into the Road, and paffes *South* almoft to the Lane which turns *Eaft* down to the lower Street, but then turns *Eaft* without the Houfes, and goes to the *Cow-keeper's* in the lower Street croffing the Road, and through the *Cow-keeper's* Yard into *Frog-lane*, then running *Weft* on the *South* Side of the Town, juft without the Buildings, joyns again to the Buildings on the *Weft* Side of *Wood's-Clofe*, paffing behind the *Sheep-market* Wall - - 2 4 39

7. From *Wood's-Clofe*, the Line goes due *Eaft* to *Mount Mill*, where, leaving feveral Buildings to the *North*, it paffes on, croffing all the Roads to *Brick-lane*, to the *North* Side of the great new Square in *Old-ftreet*, and taking in the *Pefthoufe* Wall, turns *South* at the *North Eaft* Corner of the faid Wall, to *Old-ftreet* Road; then going away *Eaft* till it meets the Buildings near *Hoxton Square*, it turns *North* to the *North Weft* Corner of the Wall of *Ask's* Hofpital, then floping *North Eaft*, it paffes by *Pimlico*, the *Cyder Houfe*, and the Two Walls to the *North* End of *Hoxton*, when it turns *Eaft*, and inclofing the Garden Walls, comes into the *Ware* Road, juft at the *King's Head* in the New Buildings by the *Land of Promife* - - - - 2 0 16

8. From the *King's Head*, the Line turns *South*, running to the Stones End in *Shoreditch*, then turning *Eaft*, it takes in a Burying Ground and fome Buildings in the *Hackney* Road, when floping *South Eaft* by *South*, it goes away by the *Virginia Houfe* to a great *Brewhoufe*, and then ftill more *Eaft* to the back of *Wheeler-ftreet*, and then *Eaft* by *South*, to *Brick-Lane*, croffing which, it goes away *Eaft* towards *Bethnal Green*; but then turning fhort *South*, it goes towards *White Chapel Mount*, but being intercepted by New Streets, it goes quite up to the *South* End of the *Dog-Row* at *Mile End* 1 6 19

9. From the *Dog-Row*, the Line croffes the Road, and takes in a little Hamlet of Houfes, called *Stepney*, tho' not properly fo, and coming back *Weft* to the Streets End at *White Chapel Mill*, goes away *South* by the *Hog-houfes* into *Church Lane*, and to *Rag Fair*, when turning again *Eaft*, it continues in a ftrait Line on the *North* Side of *Ratcliff High-way*, 'till it comes almoft to the farther *Glafs-houfes*, then turning *North*, it furrounds all *Stepney* and *Stepney* Caufway to *Mile End* Road, then turning *Eaft* again, and afterwards *South*, comes back to the New Streets on the *North* Side of *Lime-houfe*, and joyning the Marfh, comes down to the Water Side at the lower Shipwright Dock in *Lime-houfe Hole* - - - - 3 7 01

	18	4	21

N.B. *This Line leaves out all the* North *Side of* Mile End *Town, from the End of the* Dog-Row, *to the* Jews Burying Ground, *which is all built; alfo all the* North *Part of the* Dog-Row, *and all* Bethnal Green: *Alfo all* Poplar *and* Black-Wall, *which are, indeed, contiguous, a Trifle of Ground excepted, and very Populous.*

FOR THE SOUTHWARK SIDE *of the Buildings, the Line is as follows :*

HAVING ended the Circumference of the *Middlesex* Buildings at *Lime-house*, and the Street extending towards *Poplar*, the Hamlets of *Poplar* and *Blackwall*, tho' very near contiguous in Buildings, being excluded, I allow an Interval of Two Miles, from *Poplar*, crofs the Ifle of *Dogs*, and over the *Thames*, to the Lower Water Gate at *Deptford*, and tho' in meafuring the Circumference of all Cities, the River, where any fuch runs through any part of the Buildings, is always meafured; yet, that I may not be faid to ftretch the Extent of the Buildings which I include in this Account, I omit the River from *Lime-house* to *Deptford* (where, if included, it ought to begin) and begin my Line as above.

Miles Fur. Rods

1. From the faid Upper Water-Gate at *Deptford*, the Line goes *Eaft* to the Corner next the *Thames*, where the Shipwright's Yard now is, and where I find a continued Range of Buildings begins by the Side of a little Creek or River, which runs into the *Thames* there, and reaches quite up the faid River, to the Bridge in the great *Kentifh* Road, and over the Street there, taking in the *South* Side of the Street, to the *Weft* Corner of the Buildings in that Street, and then meafuring down on the *Weft* Side of the long Street, which runs to the *Thames* Side, 'till you come to the new Street which paffes from *Dept-ford* to *Rederiff*, then turning to the Left, paffing on the back Side of the King's Yard to Mr. *Evelin*'s Houfe, including the New Church of *Deptford*, and all the New Streets or Buildings made on the Fields Side, which are very many, this amounts in the whole, to - - - - - 3 1 16

2. From Mr. *Evelin*'s Garden Gate, the Line goes *North Weft*, taking in all the New Docks and Yards, the *Red-houfe* and feveral large Streets of Houfes, which have been lately built, and by which the faid Town of *Deptford* is effectually joined to the Buildings, reaching from *Cuckold*'s *Point, Eaftward*, and which are carried out, as if *Rederiff* ftretch'd forth its Arm to embrace *Deptford*; then for fome length, the faid Street of *Rederiff* continues narrow 'till you come to *Church-Street*, where feveral Streets are alfo lately built *South*, and others Parallel with the Street, till gradually, the Buildings thicken, and extend farther and farther to the *South* and *South* by *Eaft*, 'till they crofs over the *Eaft* End of *Horflydown* to *Ber-mondfey* Church, and thence *Eaft* to the Sign of the *World's End*, over againft the great Fort, being the Remains of the Fortifications drawn round thefe Parts of *Southwark* in the late Civil Wars. This Extent is, by Computation, Four Miles; but being meafured, as the Streets indented, the Circuit prov'd 5 6 12

3. From this Fort, to the Corner of *Long Lane*, and through *Long Lane* to the *Lock*, at the End of *Kent-ftreet*, is - - - - - - 1 7 02

4. From the Corner of *Kent-ftreet* to the Town of *Newington Butts*, draw-ing the Line behind all the Buildings as they ftand, and round the faid Village of *Newington*, to the *Haberdafhers* Alms Houfes, and thence by the Road to the Windmill, at the Corner of *Blackman-ftreet*, is - - - - 3 2 16

5. From the Windmill croffing St. *George*'s Fields, on the Back of the *Mint*, to the *Fighting Cocks*, thence to the *Reftoration* Gardens, and thence on the Outfide of all the Buildings to *Lambeth-Wells*, and on to *Faux-Hall Bridge*, over againft the other Fort of the old Fortifications, being juft the fame Length that thofe old Fortifications extended, tho' infinitely fuller of Buildings; this laft Circuit meafures - - - - - 3 5 12

17 6 18

THE 'CIRCUMFERENCE OF THE CONTINUED BUILDINGS'

Thus the Extent or Circumference of the continued Buildings of the Cities of *London* and *Weftminfter*, and Borough of *Southwark*, all which, in the common Acceptation, is called *London*, amounts to Thirty Six Miles, Two Furlongs, Thirty Nine Rods.

N.B. *The Town of* Greenwich, *which may, indeed, be faid to be contiguous to* Deptford, *might be alfo called a Part of this Meafurement; but I omit it, as I have the Towns of* Chelfea *and* Knights Bridge *on the other Side, tho' both may be faid to joyn the Town, and in a very few Years will certainly do fo.*

Were it poffible to reduce all thefe Buildings to a compact Situation, 'tis generally thought, that the whole Body fo put together, allowing the neceffary Ground, which they now employ for the feveral Trades in the Out-Parts, fuch as the Building Yards by the River, for *Shipwrights, Tanners* Yards, *Dyers, Whitfters,** &c. I fay, 'tis believed the whole would take up Twenty Eight Miles in Circumference, very compactly built.

THE PRESENT NUMBER OF INHABITANTS

The Gueffes that are made at the Number of Inhabitants, have been varioufly form'd; Sir *William Petty*, famous for his Political Arithmetick, fuppofed the City, at his laft Calculation, to contain a Million of People, and this he judges from the Number of Births and Burials; and by this Rule, as well by what is well known of the Increafe of the faid Births and Burials, as of the prodigious Increafe of Buildings, it may be very reafonable to conclude, the prefent Number of Inhabitants within the Circumference I have mentioned, to amount to, at leaft, Fifteen Hundred Thoufand, with this Addition, that it is ftill prodigioufly increafing.

Nor is it hard to account for this Increafe of People, as well as Buildings in *London*; but the Difcourfe feems too Political to belong to this Work, which, rather, relates to the Fact than the Reafon of it, and is properly to defcribe the Thing, not to fhew why it is fo, for which Reafon I omit entring into the Enquiry.

THE 'GOVERNMENT OF THIS VAST COLLECTED BODY OF PEOPLE'

The Government of this great Mafs of Building, and of fuch a vaft collected Body of People, though it confifts of various Parts, is, perhaps, the moft regular and well-ordered Government, that any City, of above Half its Magnitude, can boaft of.

The Government of the City of *London* in particular, and abftractedly confidered, is, by the Lord Mayor, Twenty Four Aldermen, Two Sheriffs, the Recorder and Common Council; but the Jurifdiction of thefe is confined to that Part only, which they call the City and its Liberties, which are marked out, except the *Borough*, by the Walls and the Bars, as they are called, and which the particular Maps of the City have exactly lin'd out, to which I refer.

Befides this, the Lord Mayor and Aldermen of *London* have a Right Prefidial, as above, in the Borough of *Southwark*, as Confervators of the Bridge, and the Bridge itfelf is their particular Jurifdiction.

Alfo the Lord Mayor, &c. is Confervator of the River *Thames*, from *Stanes* Bridge in *Surry* and *Middlefex*, to the River *Medway* in *Kent*, and, as fome infift, up the *Medway* to *Rochefter* Bridge.

The Government of the Out Parts, is by Juftices of the Peace, and by the Sheriffs of *London*, who are, likewife, Sheriffs of *Middlefex*; and the Government of *Weftminfter* is,

---

* *i.e.* 'Whiteners' or Bleachers.

by a High Bailiff, conftituted by the Dean and Chapter, to whom the Civil Adminiftration is fo far committed.

The remaining Part of *Southwark* Side, when the City Jurifdiction is confidered, is govern'd, alfo, by a Bench of Juftices, and their proper fubftituted Peace Officers; excepting out of this the Privileges of the *Marfhalfeas*, or of the *Marfhal's Court*, the Privilege of the *Marfhal* of the *King's Bench*, the *Mint*, and the like.

'I WRITE IN MANNER OF A LETTER AND IN THE PERSON OF AN ITINERANT'

To enter here, into a particular Defcription of the City of *London*, its Antiquities, Monuments, &c. would be only to make an Abridgment of *Stow* and his Continuators, and would make a Volume by itfelf; but while I write in manner of a Letter, and in the Perfon of an *Itinerant*, and give a curfory View of its prefent State, and to the Reader, who is fuppofed to be upon the Spot, or near it, and who has the Benefit of all the Writers, who have already entered upon the Defcription; it will, I believe, be allowed to be agreeable and fufficient to touch at thofe Things principally, which no other Authors have yet mentioned, concerning this great and monftrous Thing, called *London*.

'I MEAN NOT THE CITY ONLY' —

N.B. *By this may be plainly underftood, that I mean not the City only, for then I muft difcourfe of it in feveral Parts, and under feveral Denominations and Defcriptions, as,*

1. Of the City and Liberties of *London*.
2. Of the City and Liberties of *Weftminfter*.
3. Of the *Tower* and its Hamlets.
4. Of the Suburbs or Buildings annex'd to thefe, and called *Middlefex*.
5. Of the Borough of *Southwark*.
6. Of the Bifhop of *Winchefter*'s referv'd Privileg'd Part in *Southwark*, called the *Park* and *Marfhalfea*.
7. Of *Lambeth*.
8. Of *Deptford*, and the King's and Merchants Yards for Building.
9. Of the *Bridge-houfe* and its referv'd Limits, belonging to the City.
10. Of the Buildings on *Southwark* Side, not belonging to any of thefe.

—'BUT ALL CONTAINED IN THE CIRCUMVALLATION AS ABOVE'

But by *London*, as I fhall difcourfe of it, I mean, all the Buildings, Places, Hamlets, and Villages contain'd in the Line of Circumvallation, if it be proper to call it fo, by which I have computed the Length of its Circumference as above.

We ought, with refpect to this great Mafs of Buildings, to obferve, in every proper Place, what it is now, and what it was within the Circumference of a few Years paft; and particularly, when other Authors wrote, who have ventured upon the Defcription of it.

It is, in the firft place, to be obferved, as a particular and remarkable Crifis, fingular to thofe who write in this Age, and very much to our Advantage in Writing, that the great and more eminent Increafe of Buildings, in, and about the City of *London*, and the vaft Extent of Ground taken in, and now become Streets and Noble Squares of Houfes, by which the Mafs, or Body of the whole, is become fo infinitely great, has been generally made in our Time, not only within our Memory, but even within a few Years, and the Defcription of thefe Additions, cannot be improper to a Defcription of the whole, as follows.

PLATE VII

A SONG TO CELEBRATE THE RURAL CHARMS OF SADLER'S WELLS

From a print by G. Bickham, 1728

PLATE VIII

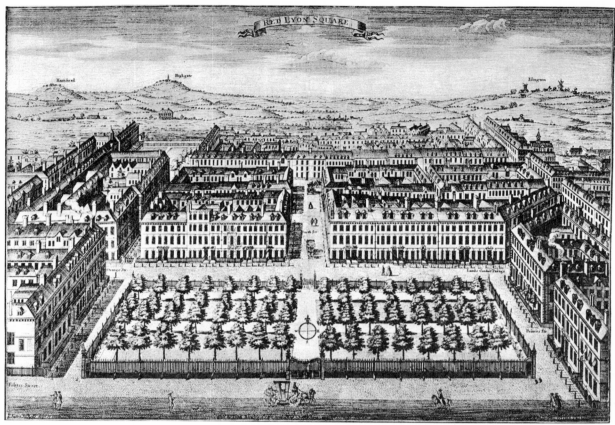

RED LION SQUARE
From a print by Sutton Nicholls, circa 1720

DEVONSHIRE SQUARE
From a print by Sutton Nicholls

A Brief Defcription of the New Buildings erected in and about the Cities of London and Weftminfter and Borough of Southwark, fince the Year 1666.

THIS Account of New Buildings is to be underftood,
1. Of Houfes re-built after the great Fires in *London* and *Southwark, &c.*
2. New Foundations, on Ground where never any Buildings were erected before.

Concerning the Great Fire of London, here referred to, practically all that is to be known is given in Mr. Walter Bell's exhauftive volume.

The ftory of the other fire, that which devaftated Southwark in 1676, is lefs familiar. While it was not comparable in fize, or the amount of the damage done, with that which had occurred in the heart of the city ten years earlier, the Southwark fire was of vaft extent as it deftroyed not only practically the whole of this area, but in its courfe burnt out many of thofe beautiful old galleried inns for which this part of London was famous.

Incendiarifm was at the time fufpected. Indeed, if we are to go by a paffage in the diary of the Rev. John Ward, it was proved, for his account of the circumftance runs thus: ' Grover and his Irifh ruffians burnt Southwark, and had 1,000 pounds for their pains. The 26th May, 1676, was the difmal fire of Southwark. The fire begunne att one Mr. Welfh, an oilman, near St. Margaret's Hill, betwixt the George and Talbot innes, as Bedloe in his narration relates.' Defoe, then a boy of feventeen, may well have feen the flames as the fire raged along the Surrey fhore; juft as, when a child, he may have had fome recollection of the earlier and greater difafter on his own fide of the river.

When our author fpeaks of ' New Foundations, on Ground where never any Buildings were erected before,' he is referring to the extenfion of London's fuburban area, the complaints againft which had been continuous fince Tudor times. A pamphlet, offering *An Apology of the Builder*, and giving reafons for the neceffity for new houfes, had been publifhed in 1682.

LONDON BEFORE THE GREAT FIRE

Take, then, the City and its adjacent Buildings to ftand, as defcribed by Mr. *Stow*, or by any other Author, who wrote before the Fire of *London*, and the Difference between what it was then, and what it is now, may be obferved thus:

It is true, that before the Fire of *London*, the Streets were narrow, and publick Edifices, as well as Private, were more crowded, and built clofer to one another; for foon after the Fire, the King, by his Proclamation, forbid all Perfons whatfoever, to go about to re-build for a certain Time, *viz*. till the Parliament (which was foon to fit) might regulate and direct the Manner of Building, and eftablifh Rules for the adjufting every Man's Property, and yet might take Order for a due inlarging of the Streets, and appointing the Manner of Building, as well for the Beauty as the Conveniency of the City, and for Safety, in Cafe of any future Accident; for though I fhall not inquire, whether the City was burnt by Accident, or by Treachery, yet nothing was more certain, than that as the City ftood before, it was ftrangely expofed to the Difafter which happen'd, and the Buildings look'd as if they had been form'd to make one general Bonefire, whenever any wicked Party of Incendiaries fhould think fit.

11

NARROW STREETS AND OVERHANGING ' PAPER WORK ' HOUSES

The Streets were not only narrow, and the Houfes all built of Timber, Lath and Plaifter, or, as they were very properly call'd *Paper Work*, and one of the fineft Range of Buildings in the *Temple*, are, to this Day, called the *Paper Buildings*, from that ufual Expreffion.

But the Manner of the Building in thofe Days, one Story projecting out beyond another, was fuch, that in fome narrow Streets, the Houfes almoft touch'd one another at the Top, and it has been known, that Men, in Cafe of Fire, have efcaped on the Tops of the Houfes, by leaping from one Side of a Street to another; this made it often, and almoft always happen, that if a Houfe was on Fire, the oppofite Houfe was in more danger to be fired by it, according as the Wind ftood, than the Houfes next adjoining on either Side.

How this has been regulated, how it was before, and how much better it now is, I leave to be judged, by comparing the Old unburnt Part of the City with the New.

NOW ARE WIDER STREETS BUT MANY MORE HOUSES

But tho' by the New Buildings after the Fire, much Ground was given up, and left unbuilt, to inlarge the Streets, yet 'tis to be obferved, that the Old Houfes ftood feverally upon more Ground, were much larger upon the Flat, and in many Places, Gardens and large Yards about them, all which, in the New Buildings, are, at leaft, contracted, and the Ground generally built up into other Houfes, fo that notwithftanding all the Ground given up for beautifying the Streets, yet there are many more Houfes built than ftood before upon the fame Ground; fo that taking the whole City together, there are more Inhabitants in the fame Compafs, than there was before. To explain this more fully, I fhall give fome particular Inftances, to which I refer, which there are living Witneffes able to confirm: For Example,

1. *Swithen*'s *Alleys* by the *Royal Exchange*, were all, before the Fire, taken up with One fingle Merchant's Houfe, and inhabited by one Mr. *Swithin*; whereas, upon the fame Ground where the Houfe ftood, ftands now about Twenty-two or Twenty-four Houfes, which belong to his Pofterity to this Day.

2. *Copt-Hall-Court* in *Throckmorton-ftreet*, was, before the Fire, alfo a fingle Houfe, inhabited by a *Dutch* Merchant; alfo three more Courts in the fame Streets, were fingle Houfes, Two on the fame Side of the Way, and One on the other.

Sweetings Alley was apparently named after a Dutch merchant of the 17th century named Henry Swieten whom Defoe refers to here as 'one Mr. Swithin.' The site of 'Swithens' or 'Sweetings' Alley is on the East of the Royal Exchange and is not to be confused—as it may have been by Defoe—with the neighbouring St. Swithin's Lane, named after the famous saint.

On the other hand, the name of Copt Hall was a familiar one in old London, Copthall Avenue to-day running through the site of the mansion specifically mentioned by Defoe. There was a Copped or Copt Hall, in Dowgate, on the site of the present Skinner's Hall, and another in St. Botolph without Aldersgate; while still another tenement was so called in St. Andrew by the Wardrobe. Copt Hall at Vauxhall and also in Southwark are also recorded. ' Copped ' implies pointed, and the inference is that houses bearing this name were distinguished by a sharp gable on their fronts; and as this feature was common in Elizabethan and Jacobean architecture, the frequency of the name throughout the country is accounted for.

The feveral Alleys behind St. *Chriftopher*'s Church, which are now vulgarly, but erroneoufly, call'd St. *Chriftopher*'s-*Churchyard*, were, before the Fire, One great Houfe, or, at leaft, a Houfe and Ware-houfes belonging to it, in which the famous Mr. *Kendrick* lived, whofe Monument now ftands in St. *Chriftopher*'s Church, and whofe Dwelling, alfo, took up almoft all the Ground, on which now a Street of Houfes is erected, called *Prince's-ftreet*, going through into Lothbury, no fuch Street being known before the Fire.

King's-Arms-Yard in *Coleman-ftreet*, now built into fine large Houfes, and inhabited by principal Merchants, was, before the Fire, a Stable-yard for Horfes and an *Inn*, at the Sign of the *King's Arms*.

The church of St. Christopher, or more properly ST. CHRISTOPHER LE STOCKS, stood in Threadneedle Street, and was demolished when the Bank of England buildings were enlarged in 1781. It took its additional title from the fact that it faced the old Stocks Market in which stood the famous statue of Charles II trampling on a Turk, erected at the cost of Sir Robert Vyner. The Stocks Market occupied the site of the present Mansion House, and was so called because stocks used to stand here in earlier days.

The church partly escaped the Great Fire. Wren repaired it in 1671, and it was again restored and beautified in 1697. The Mr. Kendrick referred to by Defoe was a London draper; he was Sheriff in 1645, and gave by will a cloth gown and a shilling a year to sixty poor men of the parish. But this was but a small part of his benefactions, a list of which, amounting to a total of £32,889 13s. 4d., occupies four columns in Hatton's *New View of London*, 1708.

The approximate position of the Kendrick mansion can be estimated by the fact that Prince's Street was formed on its site and that of its garden. The Prince's Street here referred to, however, was a very different one from the present thoroughfare bearing that name; instead of being a wide straight street, it zigzagged from Threadneedle Street to Lothbury, and Kendrick's house stood in the narrower, and more southerly, portion of it.

The KING'S ARMS YARD is clearly shown in Rocque's map, as being on the east side of Coleman Street, a little way north from Lothbury, so that although 'fine large houses' had been built in it, in Defoe's time, the yard itself, if not the tavern from which it took its name, remained, as indeed it does to-day. Coleman Street had been for centuries an important thoroughfare. It was so named, not as Stow suggests from a ground-landlord, but as Riley states from the charcoal-burners or colemen who in early days settled in this then extreme north portion of the city near the open moor. In Stuart times the street was a centre of Puritanism, and it was here that the 'Five Members,' sought for by Charles I, when they fled to the City, secreted themselves. It was in a conventicle held in Swan Alley, close by, that Venner of 'Venner's Insurrection' (1661) used to preach.

I might fill up my Account with many fuch Inftances, but 'tis enough to explain the Thing, *viz*. That fo many great Houfes were converted into Streets and Courts, Alleys and Buildings, that there are, by Eftimation, almoft 4000 Houfes now ftanding on the Ground which the Fire left defolate, more than ftood on the fame Ground before.

A glance at Ogilby and Morgan's Map of the City (1677) illustrates the great increase in the number of houses built even within the first decade after the Great Fire. Sir Walter Besant in his *London in the Time of the Stuarts* points out that ' new courts and alleys were formed, as the demand for land grew, by running narrow lanes between the backs of houses and swallowing up the gardens. In Ogilby's Map can be counted 479 courts, 472 alleys, and 172 yards, besides 128 inns, each of which, with its open courts for the standing of vehicles and its galleries, stood retired from the street on a spot which had once been the fair garden of a citizen's house.'

'PRODIGIOUS ENLARGEMENTS' ALSO OUTSIDE THE FIRE AREA

Another Increafe of Buildings in the City, is to be taken from the Inhabitants in the unburnt Parts following the fame Example, of pulling down great old Buildings, which took up large Tracks of Ground in fome of the well inhabited Places, and building on the fame Ground, not only feveral Houfes, but even whole Streets of Houfes, which are fince fully inhabited; for Example:

(*a*) WITHIN THE CITY

Crofby-Square within *Bifhhopfgate*, formerly the Houfe of Sir *James Langham* Merchant. *Devonfhhire-Square* and *Street*, with feveral back Streets and Paffages into *Petticoat-Lane* one Way, and *Hounfditch* another Way, all built on the Ground where the old Earl of *Devonfhire* had a Houfe and Garden and are all fully inhabited.

Bridgwater-Square, and feveral Streets adjoyning all fully inhabited, built on the Ground where the Earl of *Bridgwater* had a large Houfe and Garden in *Barbican*.

Billeter-Square, and feveral Paffages adjoyning, built upon the Grounds of one great Houfe, in which, before that, one Merchant only lived.

Of the four city squares here recorded by Defoe as having arisen on the sites of large mansions, CROSBY SQUARE was never anything but quite a small one, and even when Horwood produced his elaborate plan in 1799 contained only eight houses.

But the house belonging to Sir James Langham (it should be Sir John) was no other than the famous Crosby Place so intimately associated with Richard III, Sir Thomas More, and later the Spencer family. It was subsequently leased by Sir John Langham, who was Sheriff in 1642, and at his death his son, Sir Stephen Langham, continued to occupy the place. But during his tenancy a disastrous fire so seriously damaged the mansion that it was never afterwards occupied as a private dwelling. Luckily, however, the great hall was preserved, to be re-erected again in our own day, by a happy inspiration, on a portion of the site of Sir Thomas More's famous house at Chelsea, as part of the College of the International Federation of University Women.

DEVONSHIRE HOUSE, which gave its name to the square and street formed on its site, was the town house of the Earls of Devonshire from about the beginning of Charles I's reign. It had been earlier known as Fisher's Folly, having been originally erected by one Jasper Fisher, a Clerk in Chancery, and Stow describes it as being in his day both large and beautiful with ample pleasure grounds, bowling alleys, etc. It had a succession of notable owners before the Earls of Devonshire acquired it. When they gave it up, it was put to a variety of uses, its chapel being occupied for a time as a conventicle, and Pepys records being present at a funeral here. The mansion itself was let out for commercial and other purposes, the office for the Penny Post, inaugurated by Robert Murray and Dockwra in 1680, among them. Delaune, in his *Present State of London*, 1681, gives a long and interesting account of the inauguration and method of this new enterprise from which we reproduce extracts in the appendices to this volume to illustrate Defoe's later reference to this subject.

The print which we reproduce here from Bowles's *Several Prospects of Publick Buildings in London*, published in 1724, shows Devonshire Square, as it was ten years earlier, with trees planted close to the houses whose doors opened directly on to it, but long before that date all trace of Devonshire House itself had apparently disappeared.

BRIDGEWATER SQUARE is described by Strype about this time as being ' neatly enclosed with palisado pales, and set round with trees,' which he remarks ' renders the place very delightful.' The house itself faced Barbican, its grounds extending northwards. These grounds were afterwards developed into Bridgewater Gardens, and what remains of the old square has recently been acquired and dedicated to the public as an open space by the Corporation of the City. What the Earl of Bridgewater's house itself was like is not known, as there appears to be no extant view of it; while of its history all that can be stated with certainty is that it was destroyed by fire on April 11th, 1687, and that the two sons of the third Earl of Bridgewater perished in the flames, as recorded by Narcissus Luttrell, in his *Relation of State Affairs*.

Of BILLITER SQUARE a contemporary topographer writes that it is a ' very handsome, open, and airy place, graced with good new brick buildings, very well inhabited.' It was, indeed, in those days, when people of importance lived in these easterly haunts, quite a fashionable locality, and Defoe may have seen, perchance, when passing through it, a wizened little French gentleman, with a sardonic smile, coming out of one of its houses, that inhabited by a ' Mr. Cavalier,' who, on enquiry, would have turned out to be M. Arouet de Voltaire then a refugee in this country.

In Ogilby's map (1682) the site later occupied by the square is shown with a house of considerable size, marked ' Mr. Papillion's House,' which identifies at least the owner of the property at that time, and incidentally proves that the square was formed approximately about the same time as those we have been noticing here.

(b) ALONG THE STRAND

All thofe Palaces of the Nobility, formerly making a moft Beautiful Range of Buildings fronting the *Strand*, with their Gardens reaching to the *Thames*, where they had their particular Water-gates and Stairs, one of which remains ftill, viz. *Somerfet Houfe*, have had the fame Fate, fuch as *Effex, Norfolk, Salifbury, Worcefter, Exceter, Hungerford*, and

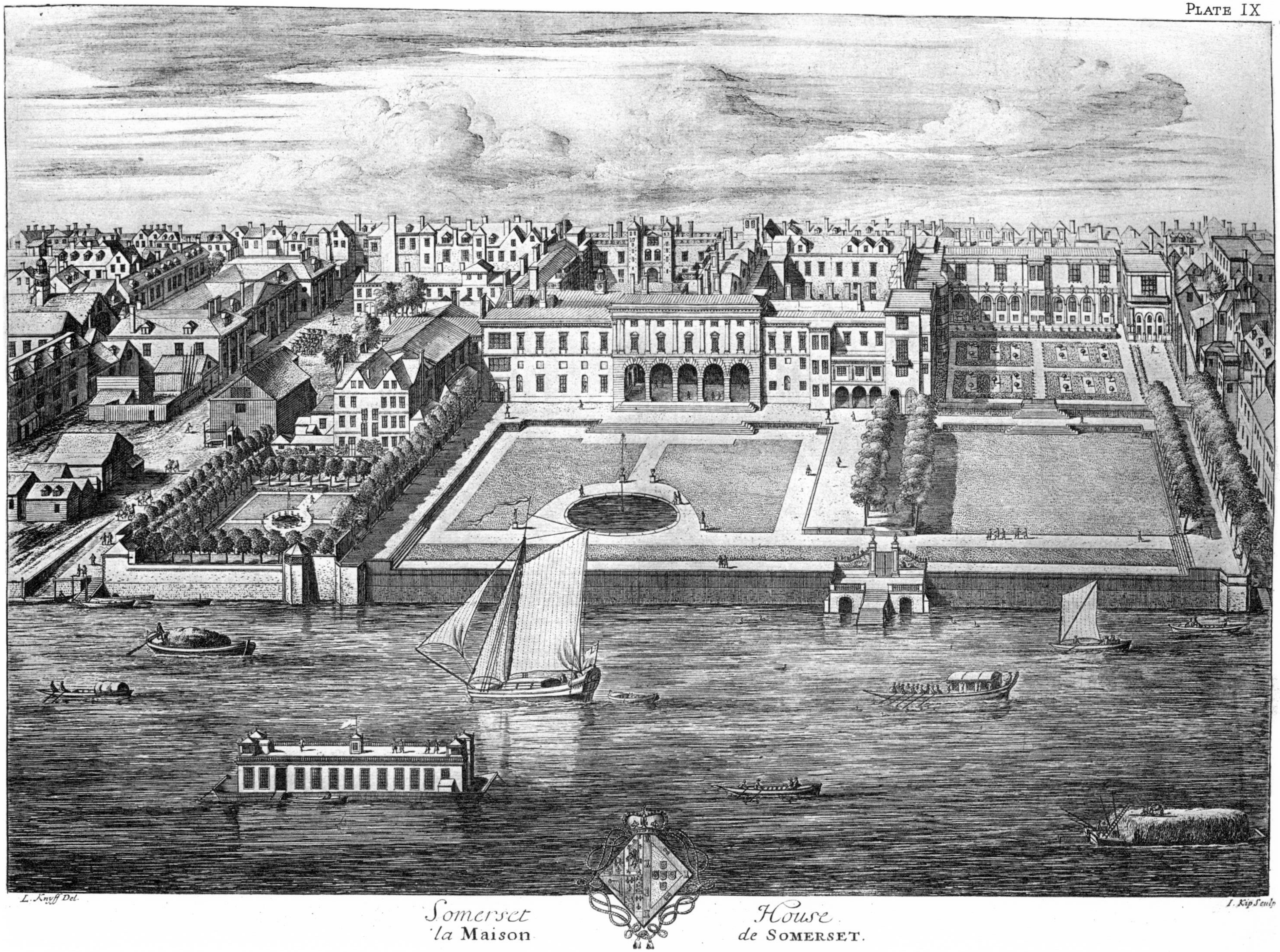

PLATE IX

L. Knyff. Del.

J. Kip Fecit.

Somerset   *House*
la Maison   *de* SOMERSET.

OLD SOMERSET HOUSE AS IT APPEARED IN 1724

From a contemporary print by J. Kip.

PLATE X

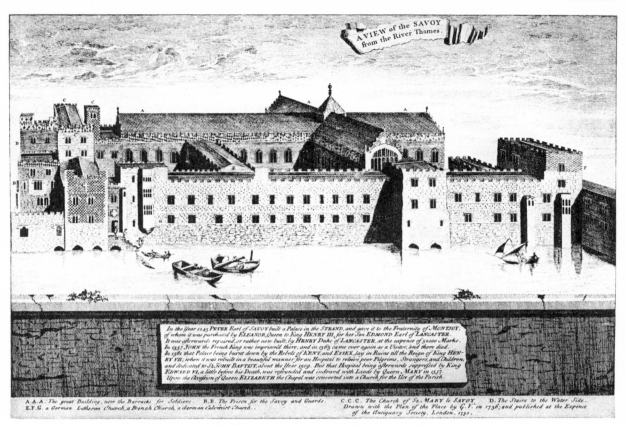

THE SAVOY PALACE OF THE TUDORS

As reconstructed from the old records by G. Vertue in 1736

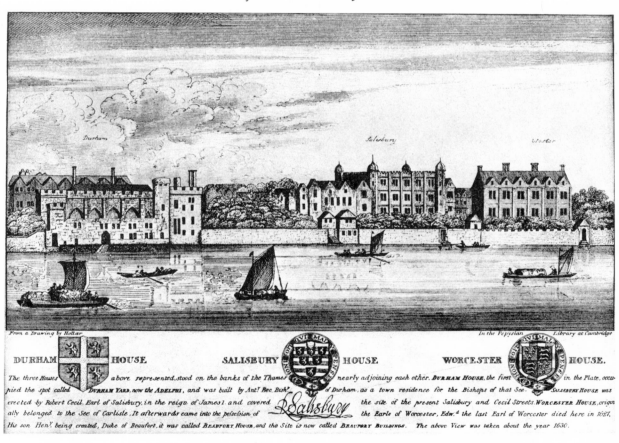

DURHAM, SALISBURY, AND WORCESTER HOUSES

After an original drawing by Hollar in the Pepysian Library

York Houfes; in the Place of which, are now fo many noble Streets and beautiful Houfes, erected, as are, in themfelves, equal to a large City, and extend from the *Temple* to *North-umberland Houfe*; *Somerfet-Houfe* and the *Savoy*, only intervening; and the latter of thefe may be faid to be, not a Houfe, but a little Town, being parted into innumerable Tenements and Apartments.

Of the 'Palaces of the Nobility fronting the Strand,' here enumerated by Defoe, of which we here reproduce the riverside fronts from Hollar's drawings, ESSEX HOUSE was, in his lifetime, purchased by Dr. Barbon, 'the great builder' who died in 1698, and was 'by him and other undertakers converted into buildings as now it is' (Strype). A portion of the old structure, however, remained untouched for a time, and in it the Cottonian library was kept from 1712 to 1730, before it was removed to Ashburnham House, Westminster, where so much of it was destroyed by fire on October 23rd, 1731. This relic of old Essex House remained till 1777 when it was demolished; but its water-gate, at the south end of Essex Street, is still in existence.

The NORFOLK HOUSE, mentioned above, is better known as Arundel House, where the Earl of Arundel had collected his famous marbles and had acted as a Mæcenas to the artists, Hollar among them, of the day. It was under the fourth Earl that the place was dismantled and eventually pulled down to make way for the houses and streets now perpetuating the family titles and names. The approximate date of the final dismemberment of the property can be arrived at by a private Act dated 1689 'for building into tenements the remaining part of Arundel Ground as now enclosed.'

SALISBURY HOUSE, on the site of Cecil Street and Salisbury Street, had before its destruction been divided into two, known respectively as 'Great Salisbury House' and 'Little Salisbury House'; the former remaining the residence of the Cecil family; the latter being let, and, in 1692, pulled down, the houses bordering Salisbury Street being erected on its site. A central portion connecting the two was converted into an Exchange—'The Middle Exchange' it was called. It, however, rightly or wrongly, obtained so unenviable a notoriety, and was commonly called by so unenviable a name, that, as Strype says, 'few or no people took shops there.' This apparently induced the then Earl of Salisbury to pull it and 'Great Salisbury House' down and convert the site into Cecil Street, with houses 'fit for persons of repute.' This occurred in 1695, so that Defoe could deplore from personal knowledge the loss of one of the finest of the Strand palaces, and its ample grounds.

WORCESTER HOUSE, as our author knew it, was the property of the Somersets, but had been let to Lord Clarendon who remained here till the Great Fire, when he went to Berkshire House, St. James's. After that it was used for a variety of public functions for which the great hall it contained was specially suitable. According to Pennant, the first Duke of Beaufort had it demolished, although some authorities state that it was burnt down in 1695. What seems more likely is that the Duke, having acquired a house in Chelsea in 1682, caused Worcester House to be pulled down, and a smaller one erected on its site, probably cutting up some of the property at the time for development, and that it was this smaller house that was destroyed by fire; after which various structures, Beaufort Buildings among them, were erected here.

EXETER HOUSE, though grouped by Defoe with those whose gardens extended to the river, was obviously that on the north side of the thoroughfare, the home of the elder branch of the Cecil family, where Exeter 'Change was afterwards to come, and later Exeter Street and Burleigh Street, and to-day the 'Strand Palace' Hotel. After the Restoration, Exeter House was occupied by the first Earl of Shaftesbury until 1676, when he moved into 'Thanet House' in the City, referred to elsewhere in these pages, and it was then pulled down. With the Earl of Shaftesbury at Exeter House lived John Locke, as 'family physician, tutor and private friend.'

HUNGERFORD HOUSE stood where Hungerford Market was to come in 1680, and where Charing Cross Station is to-day. This house had been destroyed by fire in April 1669 (Pepys records the event), and Sir Edward Hungerford, of Farleigh Castle in Somersetshire, demolished the ruined house, and erected the market as well as other buildings on its site, some ten years later. He was but following the example of other landlords in this neighbourhood, and particularly the Duke of Buckingham who, in 1672, sold the splendid and historic mansion he had inherited from his brilliant father, to a syndicate of 'undertakers,' as building speculators were then called, named Eldyn, Higgs and Hill, who pulled it down, and erected houses and streets (each of which bore a word of the Duke's title, a conditional clause, it is said, in the agreement) which to-day perpetuate rather the memory of the first Duke of magnificent memory than that of his profligate and inconstant son.

NORTHUMBERLAND HOUSE, mentioned incidentally here and more fully described on a later page, was happily to remain intact till 1874, when it too went the way of all bricks and mortar, and was replaced by the eponymous avenue and its great club and hotels. SOMERSET HOUSE was the beautiful old building which had long been a dower-house for the Queens Consort until George III bought Buckingham House for Queen Charlotte. It was destined to remain till 1776 when Chambers began the present vast and splendid structure, in many ways the finest building in London.

When Defoe speaks of THE SAVOY as 'a little Town of innumerable Tenements,' he but says in a few words what Strype, writing in 1720, amplifies with much interesting detail regarding the fate which had befallen this 'very ruinous building,' the one-time palace of John of Gaunt and the happy resort of Chaucer. 'The large hall is now divided into several apartments. A cooper hath a part of it for stowing of his hoops and for his work. Other parts of it serve for two Marshalseas for keeping prisoners, as Deserters, men pressed for military service, Dutch recruits, etc. . . . In this Savoy, how ruinous soever it is, are divers good houses. First the King's Printing Press for Proclamations, Acts of Parliament, Gazettes and such like public papers; next a Prison; thirdly a Parish Church and three or four of the churches and places for religious assemblies, viz. for the French, for Dutch, for High Germans and Lutherans; and lastly for the Protestant Dissenters. Here be also harbours for many refugees and poor people.' Strype's description of the decay into which the Savoy had fallen compares sadly with Vertue's print (here reproduced) of the splendid palace reconstructed by the Tudors.

(c) IN HOLBORN AND NEW CONVENT GARDEN

Many other great Houfes have, by the Example of thefe, been alfo built into Streets, as *Hatton-Houfe* in *Holborn*, and the Old Earl of *Bedford*'s great Garden, called *New Convent Garden*; but thofe I omit, becaufe built before the Year 1666; but I may add the Lord *Brook*'s House in *Holborn*; the Duke of *Bedford*'s laft remaining Houfe and Garden in the *Strand*, and many others.

Thefe are prodigious Enlargements to the City, even upon that which I call Inhabited Ground, and where infinite Numbers of People now live, more than lived upon the fame Spot of Ground before.

The memory of HATTON HOUSE is preserved in Hatton Garden, just as that of its predecessor, Ely Place, is in the adjoining street. Defoe here remarks that the houses built on the site of this once fine mansion had been erected before the Great Fire. As a matter of fact this property had become ruinous in Cromwell's time, and certain portions of it were removed in 1659 for street improvements. Evelyn, writing on June 7th of that year, tells how he visited the spot 'to see ye foundations now laying for a long streete and buildings in Hatton Garden designed for a little towne, lately an ample garden.' Even then portions of the old structure remained, and it was not till 1772 that an Act was passed for the purchase of the property by the Crown, with the resultant demolition of what still remained of the brickwork.

With regard to BEDFORD HOUSE which Sorbière in his *Voyage en Angleterre* mentions as 'Le Palais de Bethfordt,' although Covent Garden had been formed on a ' portion of its grounds,' it was occupied as a residence by the Russell family till 1704, when they went to their magnificent new abode in Bloomsbury Square. Strype describes it as ' a large but old-built house, having a good yard before it for the reception of coaches: with a spacious garden having a terrace walk adjoining to the brick wall next the garden.' This wall formed the boundary of the piazza of Covent Garden which had been contrived out of the ' pleasance ' of old Bedford House.

BROOKE HOUSE where Pepys went on one occasion (1668) to see the Commissioner of Accounts, ' the first time he was ever there,' was probably pulled down during the early years of the eighteenth century, as Hatton, writing in 1708, mentions Brooks (*sic*) Street which marks its site in Holborn as ' a pleasant uniform street.'

Defoe emphasises here the point that these great houses with their ample gardens, when cleared away, afforded space for numbers of new dwellings and accommodation for a much greater population than had previously existed on the same area.

PLATE XI

St. Giles   James St.

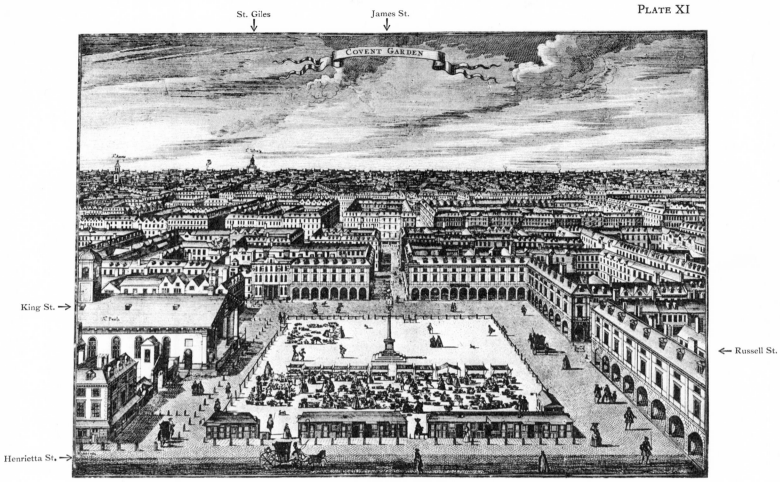

King St. →

← Russell St.

Henrietta St. →

COVENT GARDEN
From a print by Sutton Nicholls, 1720

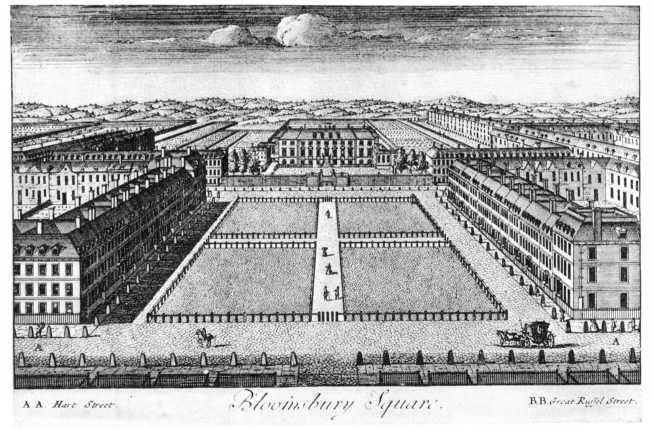

A.A. *Hart Street.*   *Bloomsbury Square.*   B.B *Great Ruffel Street.*

BLOOMSBURY SQUARE SHOWING SOUTHAMPTON (LATER BEDFORD) HOUSE
From a print by J. Harris, 1727

PLATE XII

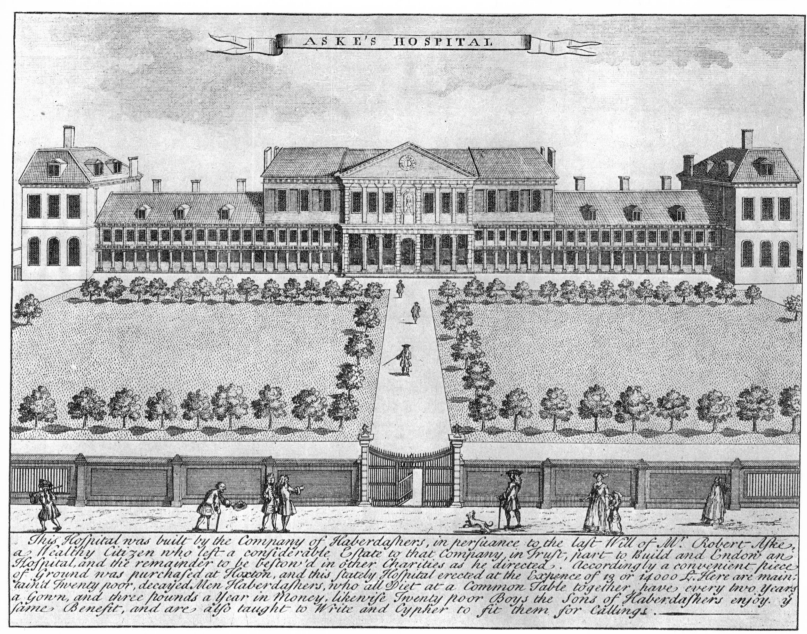

ASKE'S HOSPITAL

This Hospital was built by the Company of Haberdashers, in persuance to the last Will of M^r. Robert Aske, a Wealthy Citizen who left a considerable Estate to that Company, in Trust, part to Build and Endow an Hospital, and the remainder to be bestow'd in other Charities as he directed. Accordingly a convenient piece of Ground was purchased at Hoxton, and this stately Hospital erected at the Expence of 13 or 14000 £. Here are maintain'd Twenty poor, decayed Men Haberdashers, who all Diet at a Common Table together, have every two years a Gown, and three pounds a Year in Money. likewise Twenty poor Boys the Sons of Haberdashers enjoy ye same Benefit, and are also taught to Write and Cypher to fit them for Callings.

ASKE'S HOSPITAL AT HOXTON

From a print published by John Bowles, 1725

The even Greater Growth of the 'Out Parts'

But all this is a fmall Matter, compared to the New Foundations raifed within that Time, in thofe which we juftly call the *Out Parts*; and not to enter on a particular Defcription of the Buildings, I fhall only take Notice of the Places where fuch Enlargements are made; as

(1) THE DISTRICTS OF SPITTLE FIELDS, HOXTON AND BETHNAL GREEN

Within the Memory of the Writer hereof, all thofe numberlefs Ranges of Building, called *Spittle Fields*, reaching from *Spittle-yard*, at *Northern Fallgate*, and from *Artillery Lane* in *Bifhopfgate-ftreet*, with all the New Streets, beginning at *Hoxton*, and the back of *Shoreditch* Church, *North*, and reaching to *Brick-Lane*, and to the End of *Hare-ftreet*, on the Way to *Bethnal Green, Eaft*; then floping away quite to *White Chapel* Road, *South Eaft*, containing, as fome People fay, who pretend to know, by good Obfervation, above Three hundred and Twenty Acres of Ground, which are all now clofe built, and well inhabited with an infinite Number of People, I fay, all thefe have been built new from the Ground, fince the Year 1666.

> The area here indicated, as having been built over during the writer's lifetime, can be easily distinguished by a comparison of a 1720 plan of London with the earlier map issued by Ogilby in 1677. By this it will be seen that in the interval between these publications what was called ' The Old Artillery Ground,' an open space of large area off Bishopsgate Street (Artillery Lane and Street mark its site), had been entirely developed. It was in 1641 that the site of the existing Artillery Ground near Bunhill Fields was substituted for the old Bishopsgate one. It is described in old records as the 'third great field from Moorgate, next the six windmills,' and became famous as the drilling ground of the London Train Bands during the Civil War and later as the Headquarters of the Honourable Artillery Company. It had been originally an archery practice field for the citizens of London in the old days, before the musket superseded the earlier artillery of bow and arrow. Both the new and the old Artillery Grounds and five of the ' six windmills ' are depicted in Hollar's Map of 1667, reproduced as the back end-papers of this volume.
> Meanwhile the open spaces of the SPITTLE FIELDS themselves lying just to the east of the Artillery Ground had been cut up into a formal pattern of streets and houses, with Spittle Fields Market in their centre.

The Lanes were deep, dirty, and unfrequented, that Part now called *Spittlefields-Market*, was a Field of Grafs with Cows feeding on it, fince the Year 1670. The *Old Artillery Ground* (where the Parliament Lifted their firft Soldiers againft the King) took up all thofe long Streets, leading out of *Artillery Lane* to *Spittle-yard-back-Gate*, and fo on to the End of *Wheeler-ftreet*.

Brick-Lane, which is now a long well-pav'd Street, was a deep dirty Road, frequented chiefly by Carts fetching Bricks that Way into *White-Chapel* from *Brick-Kilns* in thofe Fields, and had its Name on that Account; in a Word, it is computed, that above Two Hundred Thoufand Inhabitants dwell now in that Part of *London*, where, within about Fifty Years paft, there was not a Houfe ftanding.

> The rustic character of the area around Spittle Fields here recorded by Defoe who, it must be remembered, passed many years of his youth in more or less proximity to it, with its grass fields and its cows feeding, and the carts fetching bricks from the neighbouring kilns, and, by the way, a windmill not far east of Brick Lane, on the south side of the Whitechapel Road, can best be realised by a study of Faithorne's fine plan of 1658, and the interesting though smaller scaled one of Porter, *circa* 1660; and it was naturally a matter of amazement to such a close observer as our author to find that within a period of half a century the population was to be numbered in tens of thousands in these parts where as a young man he had not seen a single habitation.

D

With regard to one or two places specially mentioned in the two foregoing paragraphs, it may be noted that the SHOREDITCH CHURCH to which he refers was the original fabric dedicated to St. Leonard, of which there are records as far back as 1218, and that it was not till 1736 that, being then in a ruinous condition, it was pulled down and the present structure, designed by the elder Dance, erected in its place.

The street Defoe calls NORTHERN FALLGATE is that, of course, which we know as Norton Folgate (Hatton calls it Norton Falgate), the second word being the old English for a four-barred gate; and the position of this barrier indicates that 'Northern' is after all the correct first word.

It was the coming of the French refugees to this district in 1685, as a result of the Revocation of the Edict of Nantes, that crowded it with workers to whom low rents were a necessity. The silk industry which they established here was to give Spitalfields a world-wide fame. There was once a 'cross,' not dissimilar, according to Stow, from that in St. Paul's Churchyard, where the Spital Sermons were preached. The original Spital or Hospital seems rather to have been an almshouse than what was wont to be termed a 'lazar house.' The present church was designed by Hawksmoor and was in process of erection during 1723-9, so that Defoe could have seen it in its completed state.

Hatton, who mentions Wheeler Street without comment, remarks that Brick Lane was 'the longest in London,' by which he no doubt means the longest thoroughfare designated a lane; of Hare Street he says that it is 'a considerable pleasant street between Brick Lane and the Fields.' It is still in existence.

(2) THE 'MORE EASTERN PART' AROUND WHITECHAPEL AND RATCLIFF-HIGHWAY, ETC.

On the more *Eaftern* Part, the fame Increafe goes on in Proportion, namely, all *Goodman's Fields*, the Name gives Evidence for it, and the many Streets between *White-Chapel* and *Rofemary Lane*, all built fince the Year 1678. *Well Clofe*, now called *Marine Square*, was fo remote from Houfes, that it ufed to be a very dangerous Place to go over after it was dark, and many People have been robbed and abufed in paffing it; a Well ftanding in the middle, juft where the *Danifh* Church is now built, there the Mifchief was generally done; beyond this, all the hither or *Weft* End of *Ratcliff-high-way*, from the Corner of *Gravel-Lane*, to the *Eaft* End of *Eaft Smithfield*, was a Road over the Fields; likewife thofe Buildings, now called *Virginia-ftreet*, and all the Streets on the Side of *Ratcliff-high-way* to *Gravel-Lane* above named.

Turning once again to Strype, whose meticulous topographical records are especially useful for these 'East End' districts, we find, 'Goodman's Fields are no longer fields and gardens, but buildings, consisting of many fair streets, as Maunsell Street, Pescod or Prescot Street, Leman Street, etc., and Tenters for Cloth-workers, and a large passage for carts and horses out of Whitechapel into Well-close; besides many other lanes;' and elsewhere, referring to the quantities of Roman remains found there, indicating that the site was once a Roman burial ground, he observes that these were discovered when building operations were taking place 'about 1678.'

The large extent of this open space is shown in Ogilby and Morgan's survey made after the Great Fire and before Ogilby's death in 1676. In this plan the site of WELLCLOSE SQUARE is shown as open ground with pathways crossing it diagonally. Defoe, who knew it in this condition and records the danger of crossing it after dark, was destined to see it entirely covered by streets and houses, with a church in its centre. This edifice was erected by Caius Gabriel Cibber, at the expense of King Christian V. of Denmark, in 1696, for the use of Danish merchants and seamen who affected this quarter of London on their visits here; hence its alternative name of Marine Square.

Hatton describes Wellclose Square, about 1708, as 'very near a geometrical square, whose area is about 2¾ acres,' and in Rocque's plan it is shown well planted with double avenues of trees surrounding what he calls 'Danes Church'; just as he shows Princes Square, a little to the east, with the Swedish Church in its centre.

The way from Gravel Lane to EAST SMITHFIELD, which has, of course, nothing to do with the better known West Smithfield, but was on the north-east of the Tower leading out of Little

Tower Hill, was in Defoe's earlier day pasture ground, and even in Rocque's map (1746) is shown only partially built over; Virginia Street ran due south through its western end, from Ratcliffe Highway towards Wapping. But to chart out the progressive increase of building in this 'more eastern part' of Defoe's description with any degree of accuracy is not possible. No plans or records exist which could tell us exactly what stage had been reached in any given year in the spinning of this intricate spider's-web of mean streets across the open fields and spaces of the East End.

(3) ON THE NORTH SIDE FROM SHOREDITCH AND HOXTON TOWARDS ISLINGTON

To come to the *North* Side of the Town, and beginning at *Shoreditch*, *Weft*, and *Hoxton-Square*, and *Charles's-Square* adjoyning, and the Streets intended for a Market-Place, thofe were all open Fields, from *Annifeed-clear* to *Hoxton* Town, till the Year 1689, or thereabouts; *Pitfield-ftreet* was a Bank, parting Two Pafture Grounds, and *Ask's* Hofpital was another open Field: Farther *Weft*, the like Addition of Buildings begins at the Foot way, by the *Peft-houfe*, and includes the *French* Hofpital, *Old ftreet* Two Squares, and feveral Streets, extending from *Brick-Lane* to *Mount-Mill*, and the Road to *Iflington*, and from that Road, ftill *Weft*, to *Wood's Clofe*, and to St. *John's*, and *Clerkenwell*, all which Streets and Squares are built fince the Year 1688 and 1689, and were before that, and fome for a long Time after, open Fields or Gardens, and never built on till after that Time.

HOXTON (formerly Hogsdon, and so referred to by Ben Jonson) was in 1658 open ground, and Faithorne places half a dozen windmills on the spot, just north of Upper Moor Fields, whose one-time presence was perpetuated later by Windmill Hill Row (now Worship Street). Ogilby, in 1676, shows all this part still open ground which, as we see from Defoe's statement above, was developed about 1689. ANNISEED CLEAR might seem cryptic, could we not identify it with Anna St. Clear (as Hatton writes it) or St. Agnes le Clare as given by Rocque, the eastern continuation of Old Street, from which Pitfield (or Petfield as Rocque spells it) debouched to the north by Charles Square. ASKE'S HOSPITAL was erected by the Haberdashers' Company in 1692, Robert Aske having left money in 1688 for that purpose; and it is interesting to know that Dr. Robert Hooke, the famous mathematician who designed Bethlehem Hospital, was its architect. The chapel attached to it was a somewhat later erection and was consecrated by Tillotson in 1695.

The PEST HOUSE referred to by Defoe stood rather to the north of Old Street, between the present King Street and Richmond Street, on the west of Bath Street, the northern continuation of Bunhill Row. MOUNT MILL, perpetuating in its name the site of one of the forts built round London in the time of the Civil War, as does Mount Street in the West End, was in open fields overlooking on the west WOODS CLOSE through which Goswell Street now runs. The name of Woods Close was later applied to a thoroughfare parallel with St. John's Street, connecting Compton Street with the Islington Road (now St. John Street), but before development Woods Close was a large field separating the highway from Goswell Street. The two squares mentioned by Defoe may have been Kings Square and Northampton Square, although there were several smaller ones formed in this neighbourhood whose shape and size were hardly equal to their designation.

(4) GOING WEST FROM GRAY'S INN, ' A PRODIGIOUS PILE OF BUILDINGS ' BETWEEN ORMOND STREET AND KING'S GATE IN HOLBORN

From hence we go on ftill *Weft*, and beginning at *Gray's-Inn*, and going on to thofe formerly called *Red Lyon* Fields, and *Lamb's Conduit* Fields, we fee there a prodigious Pile of Buildings; it begins at *Gray's-Inn Wall* towards *Red-Lyon ftreet*, from whence, in a ftrait Line, 'tis built quite to *Lamb's Conduit* Fields, *North*, including a great Range of Buildings yet unfinifh'd reaching to *Bedford Row* and the *Cockpit*, *Eaft*, and including *Red Lyon Square*, *Ormond ftreet*, and the great New Square at the *Weft* End of it, and all the Streets between that Square and *King's Gate* in *Holbourn*, where it goes out; this Pile of Buildings is very great, the Houfes fo magnificent and large, that abundance of Perfons of Quality, and fome of the Nobility are found among them, particularly in *Ormond ftreet*, is the D—— of *Powis*'s Houfe, built at the Expence of *France*, on Account of the former Houfe being burnt, while the Duke *D'Aumont*, the *French* Ambaffador Extraordinary lived in it; it is now a very Noble Structure, tho' not large, built of Free-Stone, and in the moft exact Manner, according to the Rules of Architecture, and is faid to be, next the *Banquetting Houfe*, the moft regular Building in this Part of *England*.

Here is alfo a very convenient Church, built by the Contribution of the Gentry Inhabitants of thefe Buildings, tho' not yet made Parochial, being called St. *George*'s Chapel.

As a general principle it may be accepted that before the great building activity of Defoe's time, all the ground north of Gray's Inn, east and west, was undeveloped. The New River Pond, as it was called, with the Ducking Pond to its south, was in open fields; further west Lamb's Conduit was in the same isolated position; and Red Lion Fields were just behind the houses on the north of Holborn, whose back windows looked over a wholly rural environment. Defoe himself sufficiently indicates the extent of building operations over this area in his day, without his remarks requiring much annotation, but there are one or two points that should be noticed. For instance, the date generally assigned to the formation of Red Lion Square is 1698; but we think it was considerably earlier, for Narcissus Luttrell, writing in his Diary for June 10th, 1684, speaks of some trouble arising between Dr. Barbon who had ' sometime since bought the Red Lyon Fields, to build on,' and ' the gentlemen of Gray's Inn,' and it seems probable that the dispute was quickly settled and building operations proceeded with. In any case fourteen years would have been a long time to wait before Barbon turned his purchase into a paying concern. Before the square came into existence Red Lyon Fields were used for public recreation; and on a part of them ' a large four-square house, with three galleries round, for the killing of wild bulls by men on horseback, after the manner as in Spain and Portugal, which was about this time to have been performed,' was erected. The discovery of the so-called Popish Plot (1695) seems to have interfered with this project which may possibly have had a patroness in Queen Catherine of Braganza.

The COCKPIT referred to by Defoe was in a turning off Theobalds Road opposite Bedford Mews (which ran between Bedford Row and Gray's Inn Gardens), Cockpit Court and Cockpit Yard perpetuating it by name. The ' GREAT NEW SQUARE ' was Queen's Square, which was formed about the beginning of the eighteenth century, and was first known as Devonshire Square, but was rechristened in compliment to Queen Anne in 1706. The chapel of St. George, referred to by Defoe in the succeeding paragraph, was at the south-west corner of the square and was built in 1706, by private subscription; it was intended as a chapel of ease for St. Andrew's, Holborn.

The 'D——' (as Defoe writes it) of Powis's house in Ormond Street stood back from the thoroughfare on the site now filled by Powis Place. While being rented by the Duc d'Aumont it was burned down on January 26th, 1713, Swift in a letter of the same date to Mrs. Dingley referring to the catastrophe. The new house was designed by Colin Campbell, and, wise by experience, an immense reservoir of water was formed on the roof as a protection against fire. Defoe writes 'D——' instead of Duke, the dukedom being only a nominal title conferred by James II. in exile on the Marquess of Powis, who adhered to his cause and was outlawed.

(5) FARTHER WEST ' NUMBERLESS STREETS QUITE INTO THE HAMSTEAD ROAD '

Farther *Weft*, in the fame Line, is *Southampton* great Square, called *Bloomsbury*, with *King-ftreet* on the *Eaft* Side of it, and all the numberlefs Streets *Weft* of the Square, to the Market Place, and through *Great-Ruffel-ftreet* by *Montague* Houfe, quite into the *Hamftead* Road, all which Buildings, except the old Building of *Southampton* Houfe and fome of the Square, has been form'd from the open Fields, fince the Time above-mentioned, and muft contain feveral Thoufands of Houfes; here is alfo a Market, and a very handfome Church new built.

Before building development took place in this more westerly quarter, SOUTHAMPTON (later Bedford) House and MONTAGU House (where the British Museum is now) stood well back in their courtyards from Great Russell Street, with their ample gardens behind abutting on open

PLATE XIII

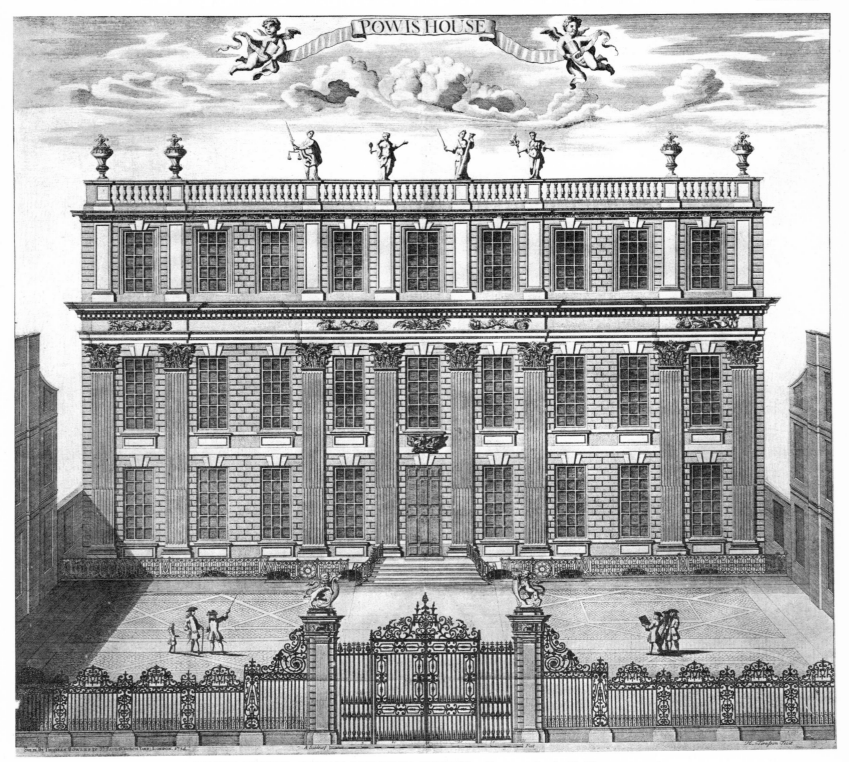

POWIS HOUSE, GREAT ORMOND STREET. *From a print by H. Terasson, 1714*

A phœnix has been introduced over the entrance to symbolize the re-building of the mansion after the fire. The Gallic cocks on the capitals denote that it was re-erected at the expense of the French Government. The back of the house overlooked the fields, and can be seen (No. 66) in the Prospect of London from Islington (Pl. XXIX).

PLATE XIV

MONTAGU HOUSE AS REBUILT IN 1687

Purchased by the Government in 1753 for the British Museum and replaced by the existing building a hundred years later

fields. Building activity had been begun, however, as early as 1655, when Evelyn, on the 9th February of that year, records dining with the Earl of Southampton in Bloomsbury, 'where he is building a noble square or Piazza; a little towne.' Southampton House itself, not improbably designed by John Webb, arose during the reign of Charles II in place of, but apparently somewhat to the north of, the earlier residence of that name. Here William, Lord Russell, was living when he was tried and executed in Lincoln's Inn Fields,* in 1683, and here his widow, Lady Rachel, died just forty years later, in what she called 'that desolate habitation of mine . . . a place of terror to me.' Defoe must have known, at least the exterior of the mansion, as well as did Strype who describes it as 'a large building with a spacious court before it for the reception of coaches, and a curious garden behind, which lieth open to the fields, enjoying a pleasant and wholesome air.' The square formed by Lord Southampton is shown in Ogilby and Morgan's plan, but is given no name; the houses on the east side, however, are called Seymour Row, and those on the left, Allington Row.

How great was the increase of houses in this area during the last quarter of the seventeenth century can be gauged by what Defoe here remarks, and how short a time it was before Montagu House began to lose the almost rural character it enjoyed for a few years, can be realised when it is remembered that the first mansion of that name had only itself been erected in 1675, from the designs of Robert Hooke 'after the French manner,' as Evelyn, who went to see it in the May of the following year, states. This was destroyed by fire in 1686 and rebuilt after the designs of Puget the French architect.

(6) THE GROWTH OF ST. GILES AND ST. MARTIN'S IN THE FIELDS, 'REALLY A KIND OF PRODIGY'

From hence, let us view the Two great Parifhes of St. *Giles*'s and St. *Martin's in the Fields*, the laft fo increafed, as to be above Thirty Years ago, formed into Three Parifhes, and the other about now to be divided alfo.

The Increafe of the Buildings here, is really a kind of Prodigy; all the Buildings *North* of *Long Acre*, up to the *Seven Dials*, all the Streets from *Leicefter Fields* and St. *Martin's-Lane*, both *North* and *Weft*, to the *Hay-Market* and *Soho*, and from the *Hay-Market* to St. *James's-ftreet* inclufive, and to the Park Wall; then all the Buildings on the *North* Side of the Street, called *Picadilly*, and the Road to *Knight's-Bridge*, and between that and the *South* Side of *Tyburn* Road, including *Soho-Square*, *Golden-Square*, and now *Hanover-Square*, and that new City on the *North* Side of *Tyburn* Road, called *Cavendifh-Square*, and all the Streets about it.

To appreciate what Defoe here says regarding 'a kind of Prodigy' of new buildings in the parishes of ST. GILES and ST. MARTIN'S IN THE FIELDS, one must consult Faithorne and Newcourt's plan of 1658. We shall there see that practically all the ground behind the houses on the north side of Long Acre was open, being known as St. Giles's Fields, and that beyond this to the west was what was called 'The Military Yard,' and then open fields, with a few houses straggling up a country road, approximately the Regent Street of to-day. There were a few detached houses near what is now Piccadilly Circus, including the well-known gaming house, Hicks's Hall, at the north-east corner of the Haymarket (then a broad open country road), and west of this were again open fields with Berkshire House, at the south-west corner of St. James's Street, the only neighbour to St. James's Palace. Where St. James's Square was to come, a decade later, was a large square plot of ground along the southern end of which stretched a double row of trees called Pall Mall, marking the spot where that game was played, before it was transferred to the neighbouring park. That park, then of somewhat more ample extent than it is to-day, divided the west-end from Westminster.

With regard to the new squares which Defoe had seen come into existence, SOHO SQUARE was laid out, in 1861, by one Gregory King, and it was in consequence known for a time alternatively as Soho and King's Square; Strype calls it the former, in 1720; Hatton in 1708 gives it both titles; while Maitland writing later (1739) says it was 'denominated King's Square, but vulgarly Soho Square.' The Duke of Monmouth's town residence occupied its south side. This house was, after

---

* According to Narcissus Luttrell, on the west side of the square, and not in the centre, as stated on the inscription affixed to the shelter in the garden.

the Duke's death, purchased by Lord Bateman whose name is preserved in Bateman's Buildings which stand on a portion of the site of the mansion. By the way, it may be remembered that Steele in *The Spectator* for March 2nd, 1711, makes Sir Roger de Coverley a lodger in the square. Now it is a curious fact that a certain Lady Coverly was actually living in it four years previously, and her name duly appears in the Rate Books.

GOLDEN SQUARE was a product of the building activity of *circa* 1688, being formed on a part of the Pest House Fields, a waste piece of land on which a Lazaretto, used during the Plague, had stood, having been built by that fine soldier and philanthropist, Lord Craven. During Defoe's time, Lord Bolingbroke was one of several noble residents in the square, the Earl of Peterborough being another, and here Swift was a frequent visitor.

HANOVER SQUARE as is implied by Defoe, and as the name indicates, was a later creation. Indeed it seems not to have been formed till roughly 1717. Defoe refers to this district in his contribution to *Applebee's Journal*, of Sept. 4th, 1725, which is reprinted in the Appendices.

CAVENDISH SQUARE, which was designed as the central feature in the development of Lord Harley's estate, referred to by Defoe as ' that new City,' was also commenced about the same year, although at first the houses arose but slowly, largely owing to the bursting of the South Sea Bubble. However, in time Harcourt House, the first in the square to be built, was completed for Lord Bingley, and it was not long before the whole ' quadrate ' was filled with those dignified structures which seem to be disappearing in these days as rapidly as they arose two centuries ago.

This laft Addition, is, by Calculation, more in Bulk than the Cities of *Briftol*, *Exeter* and *York*, if they were all put together; all which Places were, within the Time mentioned, meer Fields of Grafs, and employ'd only to feed Cattle as other Fields are.

The many little Additions that might be named befides thefe, tho' in themfelves confiderable, yet being too many to give Room to here, I omit.

This is enough to give a View of the Difference between the prefent and the paft Greatnefs of this mighty City, called *London*.

'THREE PROJECTS'—'LEFT TO THE WISDOM OF FUTURE AGES'

N.B. *Three Projects have been thought of, for the better regulating the Form of this mighty Building, which tho' not yet brought to Perfection, may, perhaps, in Time, be brought forwards, and if it fhould, would greatly add to the Beauty.*

1. Making another Bridge over the *Thames*.

2. Making an Act of Parliament, abrogating the Names as well as the Jurifdictions of all the petty privileged Places, and joyning or uniting the whole Body, *Southwark* and all, into One City, and calling it by one Name, *London*.

3. Forbidding the Extent of the Buildings in fome particular Places, where they too much run it out of Shape, and letting the more indented Parts fwell out on the *North* and *South* Side a little, to balance the Length, and bring the Form of the whole more near to that of a Circle, as particularly ftopping the running out of the Buildings at the *Eaft* and *Weft* Ends, as at *Ratcliff* and *Deptford*, *Eaft*, and at *Tyburn* and *Kenfington* Roads, *Weft*, and encouraging the Building out at *Moor-fields*, *Bunhil-fields*, the *Weft* Side of *Shoreditch*, and fuch Places, and the *North* Part of *Gray's-Inn*, and other adjacent Parts, where the Buildings are not equally filled out, as in other Places, and the like in St. *George's* Fields and behind Redriff on the other Side of the Water.

But thefe are Speculations only, and muft be left to the Wifdom of future Ages.

(i) The ' Three Projects ' which Defoe here specifies, even had they been ' generally thought of,' as he says, were such as might well have been evolved by his own brain, one always receptive of new ideas and always full of new Projects. With regard to the first of these suggestions—that for a new Bridge—this was inaugurated not long after, for the Act for Constructing Westminster Bridge was passed in 1736, the architect of the structure being a Swiss, naturalised in England,

PLATE XV

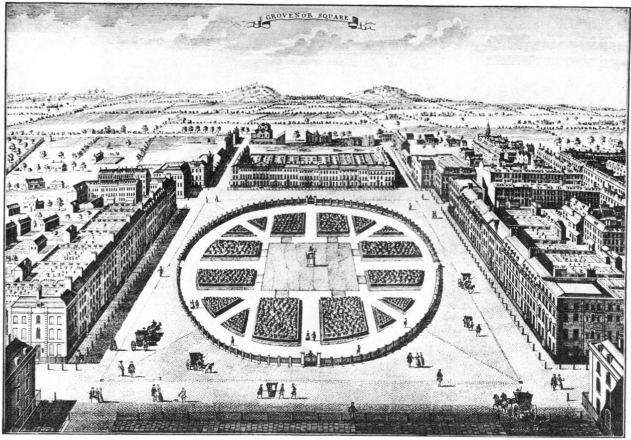

GROSVENOR SQUARE
From a print by Sutton Nicholls

HANOVER SQUARE
From a print by J. Overton, dated 1727

Plate XVI

THE MOUTH OF THE FLEET RIVER

From an original painting by S. Scott.

Charles Lebeyle. The first stone was laid in January, 1739, and the bridge opened for traffic in November, 1750. This bridge, familiar to us in a variety of pictures (some lovely Canalettos among them), was that on which Wordsworth wrote his famous sonnet. It remained till 1846, when it was closed and the present one begun in 1854, but owing to various delays the first half was not opened till 1860, the second two years later.

(ii) In this passage Defoe, departing from his usual rule of restricting his observations to the topographical aspect of his subject, adumbrates what has since come to pass—the unification of London under one supreme body known to us as the London County Council, with its satellite local Borough Councils. The City is still ruled by its Corporation; Westminster may still be regarded as a city in itself; and the name of the Borough still clings unofficially to Southwark; but all has now become merged in the generic title of London, as connoting one great entity which has extended its boundaries far beyond what even Defoe's imagination and prophetic instinct could have conceived possible.

What James I, in 1619, contemplated, and what Charles I, in 1636, attempted to carry out, did not actually materialise as a concrete fact till the year 1899, when the new County of London and its County Council came into existence and 'united the whole body' under one central administration. In this connection we would refer the reader to the interesting and instructive pamphlet issued by Norman G. Brett-James, Esq., F.S.A., entitled, 'A 17th Century L.C.C.' in which the attempts of the first two Stuart kings in this direction are traced, and the reasons for their failure analysed, with the resultant chaos in London's Local Government services during the XVIIIth and XIXth centuries.

(iii) In his third 'speculation' our author aims at a counsel of proportional perfection, which has to some extent been attained, unconsciously perhaps, by the natural working of the laws of supply and demand for housing accommodation within easy access of the centre, supplemented by improved methods of transport and recently by town planning schemes. For the city, which in his day may be said roughly to have been an ovoid oblong, has rounded off its shape and form, through, as he suggests, 'the more indented parts swelling out on the North and South side . . . to balance the Length, and bringing the Form of the whole more near to that of a Circle.' But, whereas to attain this end he advocates the 'stopping the running out' of building developments east and west, it has come about by no such restriction, but by an immense increase in these directions together with even greater amplifications on the north and south. It is only necessary to call to mind the present appearance of such then open spaces as those he mentions: Moor-fields, Bunhill Fields, Shoreditch, 'parts' north of Gray's Inn, St. George's Fields and Rotherhithe, as they are to-day, to realise how all these gaps have been filled up, save here and there where those open spaces, for which in size and number London is unique among Capitals, form the necessary lungs to London's mighty organism.

'NOW TO SPEAK OF THE INSIDE, THE BUILDINGS, THE INHABITANTS, Etc.'

I return now, to fome fhort Defcription of the Parts; hitherto I have been upon the Figure and Extent of the City and its Out-Parts; I come now to fpeak of the Infide, the Buildings, the Inhabitants, the Commerce, and the Manner of its Government, &c.

It fhould be obferved, that the City being now re-built, has occafioned the building of fome Publick Edifices, even in the Place which was inhabited, which yet were not before, and the re-building others in a new and more magnificent Manner than ever was done before.

THE MONUMENT

1. That beautiful Column, called the *Monument*, erected at the Charge of the City, to perpetuate the fatal Burning of the Whole, cannot be mentioned but with some due Refpect to the Building itfelf, as well as to the City; it is Two hundred and Two Feet High, and in its Kind, out does all the Obelisks and Pillars of the Ancients, at leaft that I have feen, having a moft ftupendous Stair-Cafe in the middle to mount up to the Balcony, which is about Thirty Feet fhort of the Top, and whence there are other Steps made even to look out at the Top of the whole Building; the Top is fafhioned like an Urn.

The MONUMENT, erected during the years 1671-7, from the second design prepared by Wren, according to the survey made by Hooke, Leybourn and others, cost £8,000, which sum, however, did not include what Caius Gabriel Cibber received for the bas-relief on the pediment; while Edward Pierce for carving the four dragons at the corners was paid, according to Walpole, two hundred guineas. As is generally known, the Great Fire was at the time supposed to be the work of religious zeal, and in 1681 two offensive inscriptions, indicating the Papists as its originators, were placed on the plinth of the column. When James II came to the throne they were obliterated, but on the accession of William III and Mary, were recut, and so remained till the good sense of the Common Council caused them to be finally expunged in 1831. Pope's well-known lines refer to this:

> 'Where London's column, pointing at the skies,
> Like a tall bully, lifts its head and lies.'

Delaune, also, in his *The Present State of London* (Edition of 1681), begins an Acrostic on the title of his book, which embodies the then very general belief in the guilt of the Papists:

> ' **T**—his is that City which the *Papal* crew
> **H**—ave by their damned devices overthrew
> **E**—rected on her old Foundations, New.'

During Defoe's time no one is recorded as having thrown himself from the top of the Monument, although quite a number of people did so subsequently, but in *Read's Weekly Journal* for September 26th, 1730, there is a notice of a wager in connection with it which reads thus: ' Last Thursday a nimble little drawer at the Baptist Head Tavern in the Old Bailey, ran up to the gallery on the top of the Monument and down again, for a considerable wager laid by some gentlemen frequenting the house. He had three minutes to do it in, but performed it in Two Minutes and a half and two seconds; which is looked upon as an extraordinary performance of the kind, and not one in a hundred of the fraternity can do. We understand that as he was running down, he often cried, " Coming, Coming, Sir! " '

THE FLEET DITCH

2. The *Canal* or River, called *Fleet-ditch*, was a Work of great Magnificence and Expence; but not anfwering the Defign, and being now very much neglected, and out of Repair, is not much fpoken of, yet it has Three fine Bridges over it, and a Fourth, not fo fine, yet ufeful as the reft, and the Tide flowing up to the laft; the *Canal* is very ufeful for bringing of Coals and Timber, and other heavy Goods; but the Warehoufes intended under the Streets, on either Side, to lay up fuch Goods in, are not made Ufe of, and the Wharfs in many Places are decay'd and fallen in, which make it all look Ruinous.

Few parts of London have become so altered in appearance as that which divides Fleet Street from Ludgate Hill, through the covering by a roadway of the Fleet River which, until 1765, ran as an open stream to the Thames. Previously to the Great Fire its banks were lined by sheds and stalls, and the refuse from these thrown into the water caused the stream to be choked and horribly insanitary. Official orders were constantly being given for the cleansing of the stream, but it was not till 1670 that Parliamentary powers were obtained to enlarge it so that vessels from the Thames might be able to come up and unload their cargo on its quays. The old earthen banks were faced with brick or stone, and wooden railings were fixed along the top. In fact, the stream was converted into a regular canal, with four bridges crossing it at Bridewell, Fleet Street, Fleet Lane and Holborn respectively. It was, however, a speculation that did not succeed, and from Gay's *Trivia* and other sources, we realise that the Fleet remained little better than an open sewer, even if its banks were kept more or less in order. This was its character in Defoe's time, and it was not till 1737 that, on the building of the Mansion House on the site of the Stocks Market, the upper portion of the Fleet Ditch between Ludgate and Snowhill was arched over and the Fleet Market built to take its place. The lower portion of the stream remained open till 1765 when, on the occasion of Blackfriar's Bridge being constructed, it was covered by the roadway now known as New Bridge Street. Farringdon Market which subsequently took the place of the Fleet Market was swept away in its turn, and Farringdon Avenue erected on its site in 1892.

PLATE XVII

THE ROYAL EXCHANGE AS REBUILT AFTER THE GREAT FIRE. With inset view of Gresham's original Building

PLATE XVIII

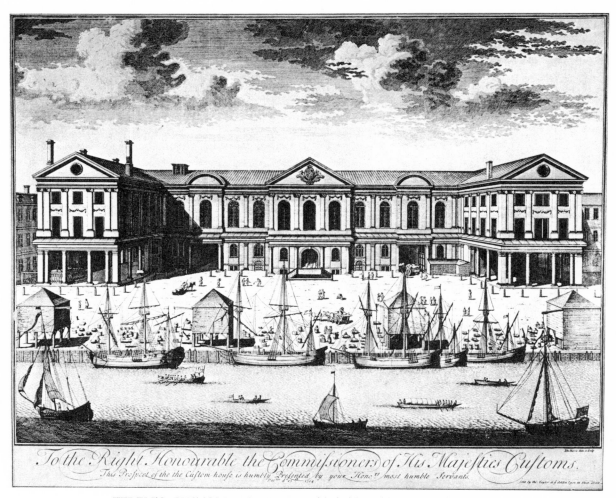

WREN'S CUSTOM HOUSE, BUILT AFTER THE GREAT FIRE
From a print by John Harris, 1714

RIPLEY'S CUSTOM HOUSE ERECTED AFTER THE DESTRUCTION OF WREN'S BY FIRE IN 1718
(This in its turn was destroyed by fire in 1814)
From a print by G. Toms

THE ROYAL EXCHANGE

The *Royal Exchange*, the greateſt and fineſt of the Kind in the World, is the next publick Work of the Citizens, the Beauty of which anſwers for itſelf, and needs no Deſcription here; 'tis obſervable, that tho' this *Exchange* coſt the Citizens an immenſe Sum of Money re-building, ſome Authors ſay, Eighty Thouſand Pounds, being finiſhed and embelliſhed in ſo exquiſite a Manner, yet it was ſo appropriated to the grand Affair of Buſineſs, that the Rent or Income of it for many Years, fully anſwered the Intereſt of the Money laid out in Building it: Whether it does ſo ſtill or not, I will not ſay, the Trade for Millenary Goods, Fine Laces, &c. which was ſo great above Stairs for many Years, being ſince ſcattered and removed, and the Shops, many of them, left empty; but thoſe Shops, of which there were Eight double Rows above, and the Shops and Offices round it below, with the Vaults under the whole, did at firſt, yield a very great Sum.

The Royal Exchange which Defoe here describes was the second building of the name. The original, or Gresham's Exchange, had been destroyed in the Great Fire so completely that Pepys going to see its ruins found nothing remaining but the statue of its founder. One of the earliest works undertaken after the catastrophe was the rebuilding of this important civic centre, and Edward Jarman, or Jerman, was commissioned to prepare plans for a new Exchange. His design followed in some special features that of the earlier structure, in that it formed a square, had a clockt ower, an inner courtyard, and, above, what was called a *pawn*, for the sale of haberdashery and so forth. Statues were also placed about it, and the majority of these were carved by Caius Gabriel Cibber; but a new statue of Gresham was the work of Pierce, and the one of Charles II of Grinling Gibbon. The first stone was laid by Charles II on October 23rd, the new building being opened on September 28th, 1669. It is said to have cost nearly £59,000. In its turn, it was destroyed by fire on January 10th, 1838. Before the completion of his work, Jarman had died, and his chief mason, one Cartwright, publicly declared that he was the 'master of the whole designe of the Exchange.' The print by Sutton Nicholls, dated 1712, which is reproduced here, shows the points of resemblance between the old and new structure.

BEDLAM

Among other publick Edifices, that of the Hoſpital of *Bethlehem*, or *Bedlam*, ſhould not be forgot, which is at the very Time of Writing this, appointed to be inlarged with Two new Wings, and will then be the moſt magnificent Thing of its Kind in the World.

The BETHLEHEM ROYAL HOSPITAL as known to us has been in Lambeth for so long (since 1812, indeed) that one is apt to forget that the original hospital occupied a site where Liverpool Street Station now stands, then a comparatively rural spot. It was founded there, in 1246, by Simon Fitz Mary, one of the City Sheriffs; but although the Fire did not affect it, changes in building and street alignment after that event determined the authorities to rebuild on a new site in Moorfields not far from the old one, and in consequence, Robert Hooke having prepared designs, the new structure* was begun in April 1675 and proceeded with so rapidly that it was completed in the July of the following year at a cost of £17,000. The French traveller, Misson, speaks of Bethlehem Hospital as being 'well situated and having in front several spacious and agreeable walks,' adding that 'all the mad folks in London are not in this hospital!' In Evelyn's Diary and the pages of *The Tatler*, and in *The London Spy*, will be found references to visits being paid here. For in those days the place and its inmates formed a kind of London show, and one of the rules reads that 'no person do give the lunatics strong drink, wine, tobacco, or spirits: Nor be permitted to sell any such thing in the hospital.' Curiosity and prurience were the reasons for many of these visits which are said to have resulted in an income of at least £400 a year. Evelyn, we need hardly say, went from other motives, and on April 18th, 1678, we find him recording that he visited 'new Bedlam Hospital, magnificently built and most sweetly placed in Morefields, since the dreadful fire in London.' Once more again is 'Bedlam' to be removed, and this time, even more 'sweetly placed,' outside London on the Surrey Hills. The present site has been purchased by Lord Rothermere for conversion into a public park, a splendid gift which adds one more 'lung' to London in a district sadly lacking in its open spaces.

* Illustrated in plate xlvii, facing page 76.

THE CUSTOM HOUSE

Likewife the *Cuftom-Houfe*, an accidental Fire having demolifhed Part of it, and given the Commiffioners Opportunity to take in more Ground, will, when it is finifhed, out-fhine all the *Cuftom-Houfes* in *Europe*.

Defoe could have seen at least three CUSTOM HOUSES in London: that which had been erected in Elizabeth's reign; that which Wren designed in 1671, in place of the earlier one destroyed in the Great Fire; and the third which Ripley built in 1718 when Wren's structure was burnt to the ground in that year. It is, of course, the last to which he here refers, destined also to be destroyed by fire in 1814. It possessed what was called a ' Long Room ' for the transaction of general business to which Macky makes an interesting reference in his *Journey Through England*. The views of the new and the old Custom Houses here given show the exteriors both of Wren's and Ripley's structures. Defoe's concluding remark indicates that when he was writing this portion of his *Tour* Ripley had not quite completed his building.

THE CHURCHES IN LONDON

The Churches in *London* are rather convenient than fine, not adorned with Pomp and Pageantry as in *Popifh* Countries; but, like the true Proteftant Plainnefs, they have made very little of Ornament either within them or without, nor, *excepting a few*, are they famous for handfome Steeples, a great many of them are very mean, and fome that feem adorned, are rather deform'd than beautified by the Heads that contrived, or by the Hands that built them.

Some, however, hold up their Heads with Grandeur and Magnificence, and are really Ornaments to the whole, I mean by thefe, fuch as *Bow*, St. *Brides*, the new Church in the *Strand*, *Rood-Lane* Church, or St. *Margaret Pattons*, St. *Antholins*, St. *Clement Danes*, and fome others, and fome of the Fifty Churches, now adding by the Bounty and Charity of the Government, are like to be very well adorned.

Three or Four *Gothick* Towers have been rebuilt at the proper Expences of the Fund appointed, and are not the worft in all the City, namely St. *Michael* at *Cornhill*, St. *Dunftan* in the *Eaft*, St. *Chriftophers*, St. *Mary Aldermary*, and at St. *Sepulchre*'s.

The half a dozen churches mentioned by Defoe above are specially referred to on account of the beauty of their steeples, and of these the first two are properly regarded as Wren's masterpieces in this direction. The original ST. MARY LE BOW was destroyed during the Great Fire, the present structure being put in hand a few years after that event, and completed in 1673. But the spire was not set up till some six or seven years later; just about the time that ST. BRIDE'S was finished and opened to the public. In this case, too, Wren added various embellishments at a later date (1699), but did not crown his achievement with his beautiful steeple till 1701-3. The Steeple of ST. MARGARET PATTENS in Eastcheap is notable because here lead has been so cleverly adapted by Wren to fulfilling what is generally the function of stone, and because it approximates more nearly to the Gothic style than does any other in the City. Of ST. ANTHOLINS' spire little can be said, because the original was destroyed by lightning, and its successor, together with the church it dominated, taken down in 1874. The original St. CLEMENT'S DANES suffered from the effects of time, not of fire, and being in a ruinous condition was demolished in 1680, when the present one was re-erected from Wren's designs; the spire being added in 1719. The ' New Church in the Strand,' as Defoe here styles it, and as for long what we know as St. MARY-LE-STRAND was generally called, was the first independent work of James Gibbs. It was erected approximately on the site of the famous Maypole, in 1714, and completed three years later. Pope has a much-quoted reference to it in *The Dunciad*:

> ' Amid that area wide they took their stand,
> Where the tall Maypole once o'erlooked the Strand,
> But now (so Anne and Piety ordain)
> A church collects the saints of Drury Lane.'

The 'gothic' churches here specified by Defoe were all the work of Wren working successfully in a style with which he was not generally sympathetic. ST. MICHAEL'S, rebuilt by him in 1672, was not wholly completed, especially as regards its spire (the tower was modelled, it is said, on that of Magdalen College, Oxford), till 1723. ST. DUNSTAN'S was one of the first churches to be rebuilt after the Fire, being taken in hand in 1667 and finished two years later. Wren was justifiably proud of its exquisite steeple, and one of his biographers describes it as 'the noblest monument of geometrical and constructive skill in existence, and unequalled for lightness and elegance.' As to its strength, an anecdote attests its designer's belief in this, for after a terrific hurricane had swept over the City, on being told that all the spires and steeples had been damaged, he is said to have replied: 'Not St. Dunstan's, I am quite sure.' The present body of the church is a rebuilt affair, having been undertaken in 1817. Another of the churches mentioned by Defoe has entirely disappeared, viz. St. CHRISTOPHER LE STOCKS, which was demolished in 1781 when the Bank of England buildings were enlarged.

ST. MARY ALDERMARY is another example of the great architect's restoration work, being superimposed on the original structure set up in 1518 by Sir Henry Keble, Lord Mayor. The upper portion of the tower was constructed in 1711. Wren was here obliged to work on the lines of the original design, and although he had the half-contemptuous feeling, characteristic of his generation, towards all Gothic architecture, which he labelled 'Saracenic,' he has succeeded wonderfully in carrying out his task, while leaving something of the stamp of his own individuality on it. ST. SEPULCHRE'S was another of the City churches which was but partially injured (although in its case severely) by the Great Fire. So impatient were the parishioners to get it restored that they would not wait for Wren's attention, and proceeded to repair it themselves. But they bungled it so much that it was a considerable time before he would give a certificate enabling them to obtain a grant for the work. During the eighteenth century the churchyard extended far into the street on the south, and was bounded by a high wall; but this wall was removed in 1761, and the formation of Holborn Viaduct further curtailed the cemetery. The connection of St. Sepulchre's with old Newgate, the presenting of a nosegay to those on their way to Tyburn, and the passing bell tolled from its tower, are all well-known incidents in the past history of the church.

THE CATHEDRAL OF ST. PAUL'S

But the Beauty of all the Churches in the City, and of all the Proteſtant Churches in the World, is the Cathedral of St. *Paul*'s; a Building exceeding Beautiful and Magnificent; tho' ſome Authors are pleaſed to expoſe their Ignorance, by pretending to find Fault with it: 'Tis eaſy to find Fault with the Works even of God himſelf, when we view them in the Groſs, without regard to the particular Beauties of every Part ſeparately confidered, and without ſearching into the Reaſon and Nature of the Particulars; but when theſe are maturely inquired into, viewed with a juſt Reverence, and confidered with Judgment, then we fly out in due Admirations of the Wiſdom of the Author from the Excellency of his Works.

The vaſt Extent of the Dome, that mighty Arch, on which ſo great a Weight is ſupported (meaning the upper Towers or Lanthorn of Stone Work Seventy Feet high) may well account for the Strength of the Pillars and Butments below; yet thoſe common Obſervers of the ſuperficial Parts of the Building, complain, that the Columns are too groſs, that the Work looks heavy, and the lower Figures near the Eye are too large, as if the *Dorick* and the *Attick* were not each of them as beautiful in their Place as the *Corinthian*.

'A COMPLEAT MASTER OF HIS BUSINESS'

The Wife Architect, like a compleat Maſter of his Buſineſs, had the Satisfaction, in his Lifetime, of hearing thoſe ignorant Reprovers of his Work confuted, by the Approbation of the beſt Maſters in *Europe*; and the Church of St. *Peter*'s in *Rome*, which is owned to be the moſt finished Piece in the World, only exceeds St. *Paul*'s in the Magnificence of its inſide Work; the Painting, the Altars, the Oratories, and the Variety of its Imagery; Things, which, in a Proteſtant Church, however ornamental, are not allowed of.

If all the Square Columns, the great Pillafters, and the Flat Pannel Work, as well within as without, which they now alledge are too heavy and look too grofs, were filled with Pictures, adorned with Carved Work and Gilding, and crowded with adorable Images of the Saints and Angels, the kneeling Crowd would not complain of the Grofsnefs of the Work; but 'tis the Proteftant Plainnefs, that divefting thofe Columns, &c. of their Ornaments, makes the Work, which in itfelf is not fo large and grofs as that of St. *Peter*'s, be called grofs and heavy; whereas, neither by the Rules of Order, or by the Neceffity of the Building, to be proportioned and fufficient to the Height and Weight of the Work, could they have been lefs, or any otherwife than they are.

SIR CHRISTOPHER WREN ANSWERS FOR THE SAFETY OF THE DOME

Nay, as it was, thofe Gentlemen who in Parliament oppofed Sir *Chriftopher Wren*'s Requeft, of having the Dome covered with Copper, and who moved to have had the Lanthorn on the Top made fhorter, and built of Wood; I fay, thofe Gentlemen pretending Skill in the Art, and offering to reproach the Judgment of the Architect, alledged, That the Copper and the Stone Lanthorn would be too heavy, and that the Pillars below would not fupport it.

To which Sir *Chriftopher* anfwered, That he had fuftained the Building with fuch fufficient Columns, and the Buttment was every where fo good, that he would anfwer for it with his Head, that it fhould bear the Copper Covering and the Stone Lanthorn, and Seven Thoufand Ton weight laid upon it more than was propofed, and that nothing below fhould give way, no not One half quarter of an Inch; but that, on the contrary, it fhould be all the firmer and ftronger for the Weight that fhould be laid on it; adding, That it was with this View that the Work was brought up from its Foundation, in fuch manner, as made common Obfervers rather think the Firft Range of the Buildings too grofs for its upper Part; and that, if they pleafed, he would undertake to raife a Spire of Stone upon the whole, a Hundred Foot higher than the Crofs now ftands.

When all thefe Things are confidered complexly, no Man that has the leaft Judgment in Building, that knows any Thing of the Rules of Proportion, and will judge impartially, can find any Fault in this Church; on the contrary, thofe excellent Lines of Mr. *Dryden*, which were too meanly applied in Allegory to the Praife of a paltry Play, may be, with much more Honour to the Author, and Juftice to this Work, be applied here to St. *Paul*'s Church.

> *Strong* Dorick *Pillars form the Bafe,*
> Corinthian *fills the upper Space;*
> *So all below is Strength, and all above is Grace.*

WHERE SIR CHRISTOPHER'S DESIGN WAS 'UNHAPPILY BAULKED'

Sir *Chriftopher*'s Defign was, indeed, very unhappily baulked in feveral Things at the beginning, as well in the Situation as in the Conclufion of this Work, which, becaufe very few may have heard of, I fhall mention in Publick, from the Mouth of its Author.

I. IN THE SITUATION

He would have had the Situation of the Church removed a little to the *North*, that it fhould have ftood juft on the Spot of Ground which is taken up by the Street called *Pater-nofter-Row*, and the Buildings on either Side; fo that the *North* Side of the Church fhould have ftood open to the Street now called *Newgate-ftreet*, and the *South* Side, to the Ground on which the Church now ftands.

By this Situation, the *Eaft* End of the Church, which is very beautiful, would have looked directly down the main Street of the City, *Cheapfide*; and for the *Weft* End, *Ludgate* having been removed a little *North*, the main Street called *Ludgate-ftreet* and *Ludgate-Hill*, would only have floped a little *W.S.W.* as they do now irregularly Two Ways, one within, and the other without the Gate, and all the Street beyond *Fleet-Bridge* would have received no Alteration at all.

> Those who are acquainted with the history of the rebuilding of ST. PAUL'S know under what disabilities Wren had to work: disabilities due to the ultra-conservatism of certain of the Commissioners, with Chichley and Pratt at their head, who kept insisting on the reconstruction of the old building rather than the building of a new one, added to the ' red-tape ' of officialdom and a perennial lack of funds. As Defoe states, the architect was over-ruled, too, with regard to the position in which he was anxious to place the new cathedral. It is obvious that had Wren had his way St. Paul's would have stood in a much more open situation than it does, with the result that its inherent impressiveness would have been far more arresting to the eye. Its east end would have faced Cheapside, and would thus have commanded a vista, and its west end would have looked almost immediately down Ludgate Hill instead of being partly hidden, as at present, by the alignment of that thoroughfare.
>
> Infinite troubles and petty annoyances beset Wren before his masterpiece was completed and the absurd accusation of trying to delay the construction was actually levelled against him, and, if it can be believed, his salary was withheld for a time in order to expedite his labours! One striking feature of his plans for the adornment of his Cathedral remained unfinished at his death in 1723, for from a passage in *Parentalia* we learn that the east end was ' intended only to serve till such time as Materials could have been procured for a magnificent Design of an Altar consisting of four Pillars wreathed of the richest Greek marbles supporting a Canopy hemispherical, with proper decorations of Architecture and Sculpture, for which the respective Drawings and a Model were prepared.'

By this Situation, the common Thorough-fare of the City would have been removed at a little farther Diftance from the Work, and we fhould not then have been obliged to walk juft under the very Wall as we do now, which makes the Work appear quite out of all Perfpective, and is the chief Reafon of the Objections I fpeak of; whereas, had it been viewed at a little Diftance, the Building would have been feen infinitely to more Advantage.

Had Sir *Chriftopher* been allowed this Situation, he would then, alfo, have had more Room for the Ornament of the *Weft* End, which, tho' it is a moft beautiful Work, as it now appears, would have been much more fo then, and he would have added a Circular Piazza to it, after the Model of that at *Rome*, but much more Magnificent, and an Obelisk of Marble in the Center of the Circle, exceeding any Thing that the World can now fhew of its kind, I mean of Modern Work.

But the Circumftance of Things hindered this Noble Defign, and the City being almoft rebuilt before he obtained an Order and Provifion for laying the Foundation; he was prefcribed to the narrow Spot where we fee it now ftands, in which the Building, however Magnificent in itfelf, ftands with infinite Difadvantage as to the Profpect of it; the Inconveniences of which was fo apparent when the Church was finifhed, that Leave was at length, tho' not without difficulty, obtained, to pull down one whole Row of Houfes on the *North* Side of the Body of the Church, to make Way for the Ballifter that furrounds the Cimetry or Church-yard, and, indeed, to admit the Light into the Church, as well as to preferve it from the Danger of Fire.

2. IN THE COVERING OF THE DOME

Another Baulk which, as I faid, Sir *Chriftopher* met with, was in the Conclufion of the Work, namely, the covering of the Dome, which Sir *Chriftopher* would have had been of Copper double Gilded with Gold; but he was over-ruled by *Party*, and the City thereby, deprived of the moft glorious Sight that the World ever faw, fince the Temple of *Solomon*.

Yet with all thefe Difadvantages, the Church is a moft regular Building, Beautiful, Magnificent, and beyond all the Modern Works of its Kind in *Europe*, St. *Peter*'s at *Rome*, as above, only excepted.

It is true, St. *Peter*'s, befides its Beauty in Ornament and Imagery, is beyond St. *Paul*'s in its Dimenfions, is every way larger; but it is the only Church in the World that is fo; and it was a merry Hyperbole of Sir *Chriftopher Wren*'s, who, when fome Gentlemen in Difcourfe compared the Two Churches, and in Compliment to him, pretended to prefer St. *Paul*'s, and when they came to fpeak of the Dimenfions, fuggefted, that St. *Paul*'s was the biggeft: *I tell you*, fays Sir *Chriftopher*, *you might fet it in St*. Peter's, *and look for it a good while, before you could find it.*

The City as 'the Center of Commerce and Wealth'

Having thus fpoken of the City and adjacent Buildings of *London*, and of the Particulars which I find chiefly omitted by other Writers, I have not Room here to enter into all the Articles needful to a full Defcription: However, I fhall touch a little at the Things moft deferving a Stranger's Obfervation.

Suppofing now, the whole Body of this vaft Building to be confidered as one City, *London*, and not concerning myfelf or the Reader with the Diftinction of its feveral Jurif-dictions; we fhall then obferve it only as divided into Three, *viz.* the City, the Court, and the Out-Parts.

The City is the Center of its Commerce and Wealth.

The Court of its Gallantry and Splendor.

The Out-parts of its Numbers and Mechanicks; and in all thefe, no City in the World can equal it.

Between the Court and City, there is a conftant Communication of Bufinefs to that degree, that nothing in the World can come up to it.

As the City is the Center of Bufinefs; there is the *Cuftom-houfe*, an Article, which, as it brings in an immenfe Revenue to the Publick, fo it cannot be removed from its Place, all the vaft Import and Export of Goods being, of Neceffity, made there; nor can the Merchants be removed, the River not admitting the Ships to come any farther.

Here, alfo, is the *Excife* Office, the *Navy* Office, the *Bank*, and almoft all the Offices where thofe vaft Funds are fixed, in which fo great a Part of the Nation are concerned, and on the Security of which fo many Millions are advanced.

The original EXCISE OFFICE in London was situated in Smithfield from 1643, when excise duty was first introduced into this country. In 1647, what was called ' the new Excise House,' indicating an earlier one still, was ordered to be demolished. At one time the office was in Old Cockaine House, of which, although not improbably in Broad Street, the actual site is not known. Delaune in his *Angliæ Metropolis* speaks of it in 1690 as being in that thoroughfare, and as ' not only a convenient but a very stately and magnificent house fit to receive an ambassador or foreign prince.' Later it occupied Sir John Frederick's house in what is now Frederick Place, Old Jewry (so named from Sir Christopher Frederick, surgeon to James I); but when exactly the change of domicile occurred is not recorded. Here it remained till 1768.

Defoe speaks more fully of the Bank further on, and we leave any remarks on that institution till then. But the NAVY OFFICE requires a few words here. This headquarters of the senior service will always be notable because of the connection of Pepys with it. It was situated in Seething

PLATE XIX

THE OLD NAVY OFFICE IN CRUTCHED FRIARS
From a print by Thomas Taylor, 1714

PLATE XX

ONE OF THE MANY PICTORIAL SATIRES ON THE SOUTH SEA BUBBLE

From a contemporary print by Thos. Bowles

Lane, adjoining a house (which, by the way, belonged to it) inhabited at one time (1660-1669) by the diarist. Strype, writing in 1720, calls the street 'a place of no great account,' but adds that ' amongst the inhabitants are some merchants '; in his day the chief entrance to the Navy Office was in Crutched Friars, Delaune, indeed, giving this street as its address.

With regard to the Staff employed and their respective duties and rates of pay, the following extract from Delaune gives some interesting details:

' *Of the* NAVY OFFICE *where the whole Business concerning the King's Ships of War is managed :* *It is kept in* CROUTCHED-FRYERS

' First there is the *Treasurer* of the Navy; his Office is to receive out of the *Exchequer*, by Warrant from the Lord-Treasurer of *England*, and to pay all Charges of the Navy, by Warrant from the principal Officers of the Navy, for which he had formerly Sallary, 200*l.* 13*s.* 4*d.* besides 3*d.* in the pound for all Money paid by him, but hath now an honourable allowance certain from His Majesty in lieu thereof, viz. 3,000*l. per annum.*

' Next the *Comptroller* of the Navy; whose Office is to attend to controll all payments of Wages, to know the Market-Rates of all Stores belonging to Shipping, to examine and audit Treasurers, Victuallers, and Store-keepers Accounts, his Sallary is 500 *l.* yearly.

' *Surveyor* of the Navy, whose Office is Generally to know the state of all Stores, and see the Wants supplied; to find the Hulls, Masts and Yards, and estimate the Value of Repairs, by indenture to charge all *Boatswains* and *Carpenters* of His Majesty's Navy, with what Stores they Receive, and at the end of each Voyage, to state and audit their Accounts, his Sallary is 490 *l.*

' *Clerk* of the *Acts*, whose Office is to Record all Orders, Contracts, Bills, Warrants, and other business transacted by the principal Officers and Commissioners of the Navy, etc., the Sallary of the *Commissioners* of the Navy is 500 *l.* yearly to each. There are two *Commissioners* whose particular work is to be at *Portsmouth* and *Chatham*, always in readiness to give orders for the better Management of His Majesty's Affairs in his Yards or Store-houses there; Sallary to each is 350 *l.* yearly.

' Each of these Officers above-named have two *Clerks*, and some of them more, all paid by the Treasurer of the Navy, all hold their places by Patent from the *King*, and most of them during pleasure.'

'THAT PRODIGIOUS PAPER COMMERCE, CALLED STOCK-JOBBING'

Here are the *South Sea* Company, the *Eaft India* Company, the *Bank*, the *African* Company, *&c.* whofe Stocks fupport that prodigious Paper Commerce, called *Stock-Jobbing*; a Trade, which once bewitched the Nation almoft to its Ruin, and which, tho' reduced very much, and recover'd from that terrible Infatuation which once overfpread the whole Body of the People, yet is ftill a Negotiation, which is fo vaft in its Extent, that almoft all the Men of Subftance in *England* are more or lefs concerned in it, and the Property of which is fo very often alienated, that even the Tax upon the Transfers of Stock, tho' but Five Shillings for each Transfer, brings many Thoufand Pounds a Year to the Government; and fome have faid, that there is not lefs than a Hundred Millions of Stock transferred forward or backward from one Hand to another every Year, and this is one thing which makes fuch a conftant Daily Intercourfe between the Court Part of the Town, and the City.

Defoe's remarks here have, of course, reference to the South Sea and other analogous schemes which but for the wise measures taken by Sir Robert Walpole would, indeed, have landed this country in bankruptcy. The South Sea Bubble, as it is called, was inaugurated in 1711 on the suggestion of the Earl of Oxford. The idea, shortly stated, was that a floating debt of £10,000,000, not provided for by Parliament, should be funded, the purchasers to become stockholders in a corporation known as The South Sea Company, which was to enjoy a monopoly of trade with Spanish South America. Spain refusing to enter into a commercial treaty with England really made the proposal worthless; but the gullibility of the people and the activity and resource of the jobbers resulted in the scheme prospering to such an extent that shares nominally worth £100 rose to the fictitious price of over £1,000. Many made fortunes, far more were ruined, not only in the parent company but in numbers of subsidiary ones, some of which could only have been started on the basis of popular infatuation, so absurd and impossible were they. Among the ' Bubbles ' to which this South Sea mania gave rise were projects for ' Making Butter from Beech Trees '; ' Making deal boards of Sawdust '; ' Fattening Hogs '; ' Rendering quicksilver malleable '; ' Fishing for wrecks on the Irish Coast '; ' A scheme to learn men to cast nativities,' and a host of other schemes equally fantastic and visionary. During this craze money became at one time so cheap that Spence, in his *Anecdotes*, tells us that in what was called *par excellence* ' the South Sea Year ' (1720) a haunch of venison cost from £3 to £4. When Sir Isaac Newton was once asked as to the probabilities of a continuance of increase in the South Sea Stock, he replied that he could not ' calculate ' the madness of the people. We have reproduced a specimen of one of the numerous satirical prints to which the scandals of the South Sea Bubble gave rise. It was, in fact, this episode in our national history which gave the first great impetus to the development of pictorial satire in England, and which reached its zenith with Rowlandson and Gillray.

HENCE ' THE CONFLUX OF THE NOBILITY AND GENTRY TO LONDON '

This is given as one of the principal Caufes of the prodigious Conflux of the Nobility and Gentry from all Parts of *England* to *London*, more than ever was known in former Years, *viz.* That many Thousands of Families are fo deeply concerned in thofe Stocks, and find it fo abfolutely neceffary to be at Hand to take the Advantage of buying and felling, as the fudden Rife or Fall of the Price directs, and the Lofs they often fuftain by their Ignorance of Things when abfent, and the Knavery of Brokers and others, whom, in their Abfence, they are bound to truft, that they find themfelves obliged to come up and live conftantly here, or at leaft, moft Part of the Year.

This is the Reafon why, notwithftanding the Encreafe of new Buildings, and the Addition of new Cities, as they may be called, every Year to the old, yet a Houfe is no fooner built, but 'tis tenanted and inhabited, and every Part is crouded with People, and that not only in the Town, but in all the Towns and Villages round, as fhall be taken Notice of in its Place.

' TO RETURN AGAIN BY THE NATURE OF THE THING TO THEIR COUNTRY SEATS WHEN THE PUBLICK DEBTS ARE PAID OFF '!

But let the Citizens and Inhabitants of *London* know, and it may be worth the Reflection of fome of the Landlords, and Builders efpecially, that if Peace continues, and the publick Affairs continue in honeft and upright Management, there is a Time coming, at leaft the Nation hopes for it, when the publick Debts being reduced and paid off, the Funds or Taxes on which they are eftablifh'd, may ceafe, and fo Fifty or Sixty Millions of the Stocks, which are now the folid Bottom of the *South-Sea Company, Eaft-India Company, Bank,* &c. will ceafe, and be no more; by which the Reafon of this Conflux of People being removed, they will of Courfe, and by the Nature of the Thing, return again to their Country Seats, to avoid the expenfive living at *London*, as they did come up hither to fhare the extravagant Gain of their former Bufinefs here.

WHAT WILL THEN BE THE CONDITION OF THIS ' OVERGROWN CITY '

What will be the Condition of this overgrown City in fuch a Cafe, I muft leave to Time; but all thofe who know the temporary Conftitution of our Funds, know this, 1. That even, if they are to fpin out their own Length, all thofe Funds which were given for Thirty-two Years, have already run out one Third, and fome of them almoft half the Time, and that the reft will foon be gone: 2. That as in Two Years more, the Government which receives Six *per Cent.* and pays but Five, and will then pay but Four *per Cent.* Intereft, will be able every Year to be paying off and leffening the publick Debt, 'till, in Time, 'tis to be hoped, all our Taxes may ceafe, and the ordinary Revenue may, as it always ufed to do, again fupply the ordinary Expence of the Government.

Then, I fay, will be a Time to expect the vaft Concourfe of People to *London,* will feparate again and difperfe as naturally, as they have now crouded hither: What will be the Fate then of all the fine Buildings in the Out Parts, in fuch a Cafe, let any one judge.

It is amusing to read in the light of subsequent financial history Defoe's ingenuous remarks forecasting the probable results of the paying off of the Public Debt. He had witnessed as the first fruits of the initiation of a Banking system and Joint Stock enterprise the madness and collapse of the first great Stock Exchange 'Boom' in history, and this would appear to have blinded his usually clear outlook in matters of Commerce and Finance.

'FORMERLY GREAT EMULATION BETWEEN THE COURT END OF THE TOWN AND THE CITY'

There has formerly been a great Emulation between the Court End of the Town, and the City; and it was once ferioufly propofed in a certain Reign, how the Court fhould humble the City; nor was it fo impracticable a Thing at that Time, had the wicked Scheme been carried on: Indeed it was carried farther than confifted with the Prudence of a good Government, or of a wife People; for the Court envy'd the City's Greatnefs, and the Citizens were ever jealous of the Court's Defigns: The moft fatal Steps the Court took to humble the City, and which, as I fay, did not confift with the Prudence of a good Government, were, 1. The fhutting up the *Exchequer,* and 2. The bringing a *Quo Warranto* againft their Charter; but thefe Things can but be touch'd at here; the City has outliv'd it all, and both the Attempts turn'd to the Difcredit of the Court Party, who pufhed them on:

In 1672 Charles II, at the end of his financial resources during a long prorogation of Parliament, took the drastic step of closing the Exchequer, and suspending, under the minister Clifford's advice, the payment of either principal or interest on loans borrowed in the City. This step caused bankruptcy among half the goldsmiths (the bankers of that period) in London, Sir Robert Vyner, who had greatly assisted Charles II with loans, being one of those specially affected.

The Quo Warranto Act was originally passed in 1289. By it a writ could be served on a person for the purpose of enquiring by what authority he held a particular office. Charles II directed such an Act against the Corporation of London in 1683, and the Court of King's Bench declared the forfeiture of the City's Charter. This decision was reversed seven years later, under William and Mary.

BUT NOW 'PERFECT EQUALITY AND GOOD UNDERSTANDING'

But the City, I fay, has gained the Afcendant, and is now made fo neceffary to the Court (as before it was thought rather a Grievance) that now we fee the Court itfelf the Daily Inftrument to encourage and increafe the Opulence of the City, and the City again, by its real Grandeur, made not a Glory only, but an Affiftance and Support to the Court, on the greateft and moft fudden Emergencies.

Nor can a Breach be now made on any Terms, but the City will have the Advantage; for while the Stocks, and Bank, and trading Companies remain in the City, the Center of the Money, as well as of the Credit and Trade of the Kingdom, will be there.

Nor are thefe Capital Offices only neceffarily kept in the City, but feveral Offices belonging to the publick *Oeconomy* of the Adminiftration, fuch as the *Poft Office,* the *Navy,* the *Victualling*, and the *Pay Offices*, including the *Ordnance Office*, which is kept in the *Tower*. In a Word, the Offices may, indeed, be faid to be equally divided.

The City has all thofe above-mentioned, and the Court has the *Admiralty*, the Exchequer, and the *Secretaries of State's Offices*, with thofe of the *Pay-Mafters of the Army*, &c.

Befides thefe, the *Council*, the *Parliament*, and the *Courts of Juftice*, are all kept at the fame Part of the Town; but as all Suits among the Citizens are, by Virtue of their Privileges, to be try'd within the Liberty of the City, fo the Term is obliged to be (as it were) adjourned from *Weftminfter-Hall* to *Guild-Hall*, to try Caufes there; alfo Criminal Cafes are in like Manner tried Monthly at the *Old Baily*, where a fpecial Commiffion is granted for that Purpofe to the Judges; but the Lord Mayor always prefides, and has the Chair.

AND 'PUBLICK CREDIT GREATLY RAISED AND ALL THE KING'S BUSINESS DONE WITH CHEARFULNESS'

The Equality, however, being thus preferved, and a perfect good Underftanding between the Court and City having fo long flourifhed, this Union contributes greatly to the flourifhing Circumftances of both, and the publick Credit is greatly raifed by it; for it was never known, that the City, on any Occafion, was fo Affiftant to the Government, as it has been fince this general good Agreement. No Sum is fo great, but the *Bank* has been able to raife. Here the *Exchequer* Bills are at all Times circulated, Money advanced upon the Funds as foon as laid, and that at moderate Intereft, not incroaching on the Government, or extorting large Intereft to eat up the Nation, and difappoint the Sovereign, and defeat his beft Defigns, as in King *William*'s Time was too much the Practice.

By this great Article of publick Credit, all the King's Bufinefs is done with Chearfulnefs, Provifions are now bought to victual the Fleets without Difficulty, and at reafonable Rates. The feveral Yards where the Ships are built and fitted out, are currently paid: The Magazines of Millitary and Naval Stores kept full: In a Word, by this very Article of publick Credit, of which the Parliament is the Foundation (and the City, are the Architectures or Builders) all thofe great Things are now done with Eafe, which, in the former Reigns, went on heavily, and were brought about with the utmoft Difficulty.

OF OTHERS BESIDES THE CITY COMPANIES AND PUBLICK OFFICES

But, to return to the City; Befides the Companies and publick Offices, which are kept in the City, there are feveral particular Offices and Places, fome built or repaired on Purpofe, and others hired and beautified for the particular Bufinefs they carry on refpectively: As,

'SOCIETIES OF ENSURERS'

Here are feveral great Offices for feveral Societies of Enfurers; for here almoft all Hazards may be enfured; the Four principal are called, 1. *Royal Exchange Enfurance*: 2. *The London Enfurers*: 3. *The Hand in Hand Fire Office*: 4. *The Sun Fire Office*.

In the Two firft of thofe, all Hazards by Sea are enfured, that is to fay, of Ships or Goods not Lives; as alfo Houfes and Goods are enfured from Fire.

In the laft, only Houfes and Goods.

In all which Offices, the *Premio* is fo fmall, and the Recovery, in cafe of Lofs, fo eafy and certain, where no Fraud is fufpected, that nothing can be fhewn like it in the whole World; efpecially that of enfuring Houfes from Fire, which has now attained fuch an

PLATE XXI

ADVERTISEMENT AND DESCRIPTION OF A NEW FIRE ENGINE INVENTED BY JOHN LOFTING, *circa* 1720

PLATE XXII

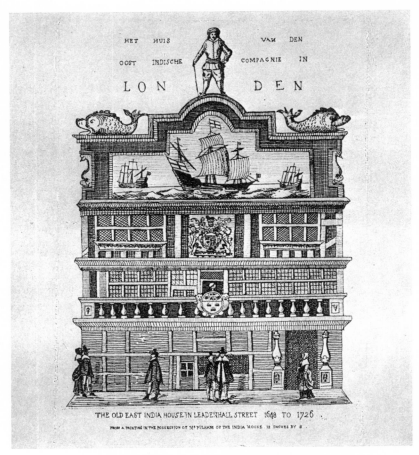

THE OLD EAST INDIA HOUSE
From a contemporary print, 1726

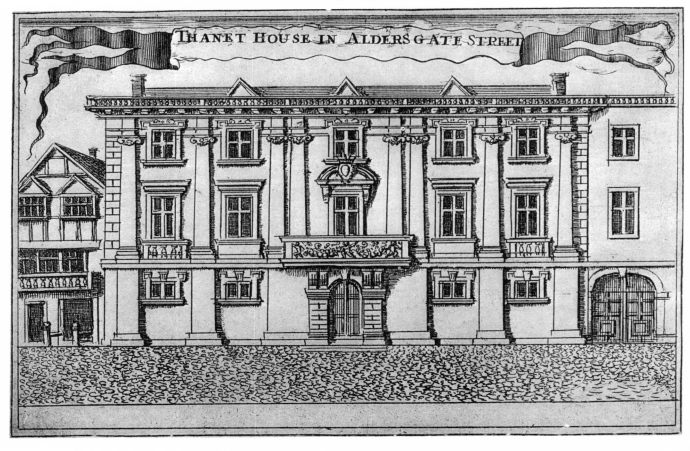

THANET (OR SHAFTESBURY) HOUSE, ALDERSGATE STREET, IN THE XVII CENTURY
From a print published by John Seller

universal Approbation, that I am told, there are above Seventy thoufand Houfes thus enfured in *London*, and the Parts adjacent.

The first quarter of the XVIII Century saw a very rapid development of the Insurance System, both Fire and Marine. Delaune, or rather the editor who re-issued that writer's original book on London, writes as follows in 1690, and it would appear, by comparing his figures with those given by Defoe, that within approximately thirty years the number of houses insured against fire had been multiplied nearly tenfold:

' This Ingenious and Usefull Invention was first put into practice about Eight years ago, and is now brought to great perfection, and has deservedly met with very considerable encouragement insomuch that there are now about 7,300 Houses Insured. The Rates of Insuring Houses from one Year to Eleven are, One Hundred Pounds on a Brick-House, is Six shillings for One year, Twelve Shillings for Two Years; Eighteen shillings for Three Years, (and double for Timber); and so in proportion for a Lesser sum: But if any Insure for Four Years, the Discount for paying down the Money, is Three Years and a Quarter; Five, for Seven; Seven, for Eleven Years Insurance. The Money Insured on the House, is to be paid as often as the House is Burnt or Demolish'd, by reason of Fire within the Term insured; But if damaged, then to be Repaired at the Charge of the Office.'

Of the four insurance offices mentioned by Defoe, three are still in existence, pre-eminent among the great Insurance Companies of the world. Some additional data on their origin and early struggles may be given.

I. The ROYAL EXCHANGE ASSURANCE CORPORATION was projected by one Case Billingsley, solicitor to the Mercers' Company, a man of varied interests who, besides being a member of the York Buildings Company for raising water from the Thames, invented a method for fixing the longitude at sea, which was approved by Newton and by some considered superior to Dr. Halley's system. In 1717 he was the prime mover in a scheme for opening subscriptions to inaugurate the Mercers' Marine Insurance Company. In 1718 Parliament was invoked to pass an Act of Incorporation. This was refused, whereupon the Company acquired an old Elizabethan charter of the ' Mines Royal and Mineral and Battery Works,' and adopted this title under which to begin insurance business. Their legal position being, however, uncertain, they made fresh attempts to obtain a definite charter, and finally succeeded, under the *ægis* of Lord Chetwynd and Lord Onslow and with the private concurrence of Sir Robert Walpole and Mr. Secretary Craggs (who had both obtained an interest in the project), by agreeing to make good a large deficiency in the Royal Civil List. They received their charter on May 4th, 1720, and needless to say the Royal assent was willingly given.

Unfortunately this was the year of the bursting of the South Sea Bubble, and as the Royal Exchange Assurance held much of its stock, the company found itself in a critical position. However, a further Act of Parliament relieved them of their liabilities in this direction, and they were enabled to ride into the smooth waters in which they have ever since remained. The Company began its activities with marine insurance, and later on, fire and life assurances were added. From the first it was identified with the London Assurance Corporation, but has always regarded itself as the senior, as there is a tradition that its charter was sealed half an hour before that of its partner. From its inauguration it had its headquarters in the Royal Exchange itself and here in the rebuilt structure it still remains. A fire-mark was affixed to such buildings as were insured by it, for which half-a-crown was charged.

In those days each Insurance Company had its own brigade, there being no public ones, and the only means of combating fires were small hand pumps fixed on wheeled carriages with hoses, buckets and tools, which were kept in churches and were often difficult to get at owing to the churches being frequently locked up. In the case of the Royal Exchange Assurance, we find that within a few weeks of the granting of its charter it had engaged the services of thirty-five water-men and twenty-one porters, who were ordinarily employed at the various wharves or ' stairs ' on the river. In the minute book of the company their names and addresses are set down (as for example: ' Thomas Hopping plys at Billingsgate ') in order that they could be called upon in need. They wore yellow uniforms lined with pink when on fire duty, and had, for the rank and file, silver badges, and for the foreman, a silver gilt one, on the left arm. These Brigades used to have periodical processions through the City from 1721 onwards.

II. The COMPANY OF LONDON ENSURERS was projected by that very versatile man, Charles Povey, as a sort of country branch to his other office, the Sun (*vide infra*), and was founded in

1709; but this Company appears eventually to have become part and parcel of the parent company. The 'London Ensurers' mentioned by Defoe is, therefore, probably that which Mr. Relton (in his exhaustive work on the Fire Insurance Companies) says had, in 1714, 'a sufficiently good reputation to induce Mr. William Adams to set up an office under that name,' of which this authority adds, 'we know nothing further of the scheme.'

III. The HAND-IN-HAND COMPANY was founded in 1696, under various more cumbersome titles for which, in 1706, its present designation was substituted. Its original founders numbered no fewer than one hundred. Its Deed of Settlement is dated November 12th, 1696, and it was enrolled in the Court of Chancery on January 23rd, 1698. Its office (*circa* 1708) is believed to have been at the Crown Coffee-house, behind the Royal Exchange; but later it took a new one in Angel Court, Snow Hill, in a house that had once been the residence of Sir Thomas Davis, Alderman. This insurance office has the distinction—perhaps unique—of being mentioned in poetry, for Cowper, in his *Friendship*, speaks of 'Hand in Hand Insurance plates.'

IV. Of the SUN FIRE INSURANCE OFFICE much interesting data is preserved. It was founded in 1710, and was evolved by Charles Povey, of the Traders' Exchange House, Hatton Garden, who shortly after formed, as we have said above, the London Ensurers as a sort of country branch. The success of the new office may be judged by the fact that in 1720 the amount insured was no less than ten millions. In 1713 an original share was worth £60; in 1714, £175; in 1715, £500; and in 1720, 1,000 guineas were offered for one, but there were no sellers. Extracts from the minute book of the Company reveal many interesting sidelights on contemporary manners and customs, apart from their special bearing on the annals of the company itself. Here is one indicating that political passions were easily excited in the year in which George I came to the throne. 'Dec. 1714. Whereas it has been thought convenient (for the prevention of Feuds and Quarrells which may happen or arise by the drinking of healths or talking of any party matter at any Dinner or General Court Days or at any other Meeting or Meetings), it is therefore thought fit and ordered that no health or healths be drank at any such Dinners or Meeting (other than Prosperity to the office and ourselves) nor any party matter argued.'

In common with many other similar ventures, the Sun Office issued its own paper, the *British Mercury*, in 1710 (it had been preceded by the *General Remarks on British Trade*, originated by the indefatigable Povey in 1705). Later it was superseded by the better known *Historical Register* in 1716; and one entry in the minute book reads thus: 'April 14th, 1710: Ordered that Forty Shillings be paid to Mr. Aaron Hill for writing three Mercurys,' Aaron Hill (1685-1750) being the well-known literary hack of the period, whose verses on the demolition of St. Martin's-in-the-Fields are included in his collected works. The *Historical Register* ceased publication in 1738.

With regard to those employed as firemen by the Sun Office, we read that 'thirty lusty able-bodied firemen' were in the service 'cloath'd in blue liveries and having silver badges with the Sun Mark upon their arms,' and also twenty able Porters, 'who are always ready to assist in quenching fires and removing goods, having given Bonds of their Fidelity.' Defoe later on refers to these '*firemen-watermen*,' who were, in virtue of their calling as firemen, exempt from the Press-gang, 'the Treasurer having procur'd a general Protection from the Admiralty Office for the Watermen belonging to ye office.' (Committee Minute, Feb. 2, 1726.) The Company's headquarters were first in the Traders' Exchange office, Hatton Garden; then in a room in Paul's Coffee House. In 1711 it removed to Mr. Garraway's 'near the Royal Exchange,' having two rooms on the first floor. There were various changes of venue till 1721, when a house in the Stocks Market was taken and occupied till 1726. The Company then became the tenants of the Bank 'in the new street, Bank Street' (Threadneedle Street). And there it seems to have remained till 1838, when the directors bought St. Bartholomew's Church (re-erected in Moorfields) and some houses in Threadneedle Street, and built the present offices on the site.

The *Eaſt-India Houſe* is in *Leadenhall-Street*, an old, but ſpacious Building; very convenient, though not beautiful, and I am told, it is under Conſultation to have it taken down, and rebuilt with additional Buildings for Warehouſes and Cellars for their Goods, which at preſent are much wanted.

PLATE XXIII

MERCERS' HALL AND CHAPEL, where the Bank of England started in 1694
From a print published by John Seller

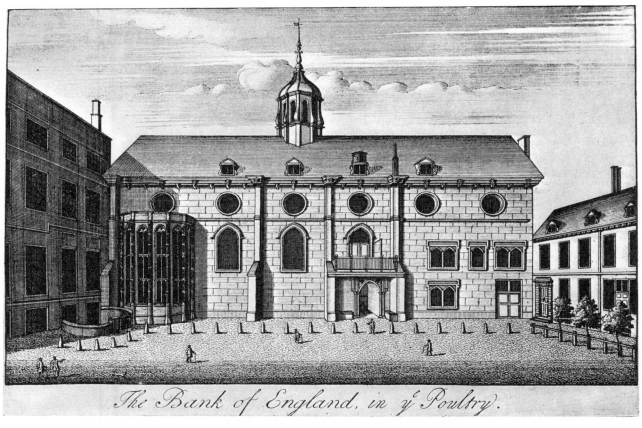

OLD GROCERS' HALL, used as the offices of the Bank of England from 1695 to 1734
From a contemporary print

Plate XXIV

THE GENERAL POST OFFICE, LOMBARD STREET, IN 1710
Formerly Sir Robert Viner's House
From a contemporary print by Sutton Nicholls

The *African Company*'s Houfe is in the fame Street, a very handfome, well-built, and convenient Houfe, and which fully ferves for all the Offices their Bufinefs requires.

The new East India House of which Defoe here speaks was erected in 1726, and completed four years later. The illustration shows the bizarre frontage and decoration of the old ' House,' dating from 1648. The new building was planned by Theodore Jacobsen, who afterwards designed the Foundling Hospital and Haslar Hospital. This exiguous structure by continual additions at last materialised into the ample proportions of the great East India House which dominated Leadenhall Street till the 'sixties of the last century, when ' John Company's ' business was wound up and transferred to the Crown after the Indian Mutiny.

The ' AFRICAN or GUINEY COMPANY,' as Delaune styles it, was instituted in 1672, and when Hatton wrote in 1708, Prince George of Denmark was its Governor. This was the fourth ' African Company,' to which exclusive rights had been granted for trading to Guinea. This last one, like its predecessors incorporated by James I and Charles I, failed to maintain its monopoly against the competition of private traders, and was finally dissolved by Act of Parliament in 1821.

THE BANK OF ENGLAND KEPT IN GROCER'S HALL

The *Bank* is kept in *Grocer's Hall*, a very convenient Place, and, confidering its Situation, fo near the *Exchange*, a very fpacious, commodious Place.

Here Bufinefs is difpatch'd with fuch Exactnefs, and fuch Expedition and fo much of it too, that it is really prodigious; no Confufion, nobody is either denied or delayed Payment, the Merchants who keep their Cafh there, are fure to have their Bills always paid, and even Advances made on eafy Terms, if they have Occafion. No Accounts in the World are more exactly kept, no Place in the World has fo much Bufinefs done, with fo much Eafe.

The BANK OF ENGLAND had been established in 1694, and carried on its business for the first few months in the Mercers' Hall before it moved to Grocers' Hall, which it rented till 1734, when it acquired premises of its own, built on the site of the residence of its first Governor, Sir John Houblon. Its occupation of Grocers' Hall is commemorated in a verse of one of the numerous lampoons in which its early days and difficulties were derided by the detractors and opponents of the scheme of a National Bank.

> ' I'll have a law made,
>   None shall set up the trade
> To borrow or lend money,
>   But they at Grocers' shop,
>   Who are at full stop,
> And neither pay all, nor any.'

Defoe's enthusiastic references to the vast improvement in ' Publick Credit ' and the facilities which the Government enjoyed for raising money at moderate interest in the City as compared with the difficulties in ' King William's time,' were written approximately thirty years after the incorporation of the Bank of England. These thirty years had seen the Bank grow from its small beginnings until, as our author says, ' No sum is so great, but the Bank is able to raise.' It is interesting to compare these words with those used by William Paterson, when he originated the first scheme for establishing the Bank, ' for the purpose of supplying the exigences of Government, and to save the ministerial people the disgrace of stooping so frequently to solicitations to the London Common Council, for the borrowing of only one or two hundred thousand pounds upon the credit of the Land Tax; as the Common Council did to the private inhabitants of their wards, going from house to house for the loan of the money.'

THE EXCISE OFFICE

In the next Street (the *Old Jury*) is the *Excife Office*, in a very large Houfe, formerly the Dwelling of Sir *John Frederick*, and afterwards, of Sir *Jofeph Hern*, very confiderable Merchants. In this one Office is managed an immenfe Weight of Bufinefs, and they have in Pay, as I am told, near Four thoufand Officers: The whole Kingdom is divided by them into proper Diftricts, and to every Diftrict, a Collector, a Supervifor, and a certain Number of Gaugers, called, by the vulgar Title Excife Men.

Nothing can be more regular, than the Methods of this Office, by which an Account of the whole Excife is tranfmitted from the remoteft Parts of the Kingdom, once every Six Weeks, which is called a Sitting, and the Money received, or Profecutions commenced for it, in the next Sitting.

Under the Management of this Office, are now brought, not only the Excife upon Beer, Ale, and other Liquors, as formerly, but alfo the Duties on Malt and Candles, Hops, Soap, and Leather, all which are managed in feveral and diftinct Claffes, and the Accounts kept in diftinct Books; but, in many Places, are collected by the fame Officers, which makes the Charge of the Collection much eafier to the Government: Nor is the like Duty collected in any Part of the World, with fo little Charge, or fo few Officers.

THE SOUTH-SEA HOUSE

The *South-Sea Houfe* is fituate in a large Spot of Ground, between *Broad-Street* and *Threadneedle-Street*, Two large Houfes having been taken in, to form the whole Office; but, as they were, notwithftanding, ftraighten'd for Room, and were obliged to fummon their General Courts in another Place, *viz.* At *Merchant-Taylors Hall*; fo they have now refolved to erect a new and compleat Building for the whole Bufinefs, which is to be exceeding fine and large, and to this End, the Company has purchafed feveral adjacent Buildings, fo that the Ground is inlarged towards *Threadneedle-Street*; but, it feems, they could not be accommodated to their Minds on the Side next *Broad-Street*, fo we are told, they will not open a Way that Way, as before.

As the Company are enlarging their Trade to *America*, and have alfo engaged in a new Trade, namely, That of the *Greenland* Whale Fifhing, they are like to have an Occafion to enlarge their Offices. This Building, they affure us, will coft the Company from Ten to Twenty thoufand Pounds, that is to fay, a very great Sum.

THE POST OFFICE

The *Poft Office*, a Branch of the Revenue formerly not much valued, but now, by the additional Penny upon the Letters, and by the vifible Increafe of Bufinefs in the Nation, is grown very confiderable. This Office maintains now, Pacquet Boats to *Spain* and *Portugal*, which never was done before: So the Merchants Letters for *Cadiz* or *Lisbonne*, which were before Two and Twenty Days in going over *France* and *Spain* to *Lisbonne*, oftentimes arrive there now, in Nine or Ten Days from *Falmouth*.

Likewife, they have a Pacquet from *Marfeilles* to *Port Mahone*, in the *Mediterranean*, for the conftant Communication of Letters with his Majefty's Garrifon and People in the Ifland of *Minorca*.

They have alfo a Pacquet from *England* to the *Weft-Indies*; but I am not of Opinion, that they will keep it up for much Time longer, if it be not already let fall.

This Office is kept in *Lombard-Street*, in a large Houfe, formerly Sir *Robert Viner*'s, once a rich Goldfmith; but ruined at the fhutting up of the *Exchequer*, as above.

The POST OFFICE* was first organised as a Government Service under Cromwell. Charles II confirming the Protector's regulations, settled the revenues from it on his brother James, Duke of York. But in 1680 an Inland ' Penny Post ' was instituted by Robert Murray, one of the clerks in the Excise Office, and William Dockwra. These whilom partners having quarrelled, however, they each set up a separate office, the former at Mr. Hall's coffee house in Wood Street, the latter in Lime Street, in Dockwra's own house, and so profitable did they prove that the Duke of York tried to obtain possession of them as an addition to the income he already enjoyed from the foreign post. In course of time (1682) the ' Penny Post ' was incorporated with the official

* An elaborate account of the early methods of the Post Office is given by Delaune in his *Present State of London* (1681), from which extracts are given in the Appendix.

one, and Dockwra was made Comptroller, being, however, dismissed on account of mismanagement, by the Lords of the Treasury, in 1698. It is interesting to know that Dockwra was the first to stamp letters with the date and hour of despatch from his office.

The house occupied by the Post Office in Lombard Street is described by Strype as being ' a very large and curious building, with good rooms,' and our illustration shows the general appearance of the courtyard of London's first G.P.O. with the clerks sitting at the open counters at the windows.

THE 'MODERN CONTRIVANCE' OF THE PENNY POST

The *Penny Poft*, a modern Contrivance of a private Perfon, one Mr. *William Dockwra*, is now made a Branch of the general Revenue by the *Poft Office*; and though, for a Time, it was fubject to Mifcarriages and Miftakes, yet now it is come alfo into fo exquifite a Management, that nothing can be more exact, and 'tis with the utmoft Safety and Difpatch, that Letters are delivered at the remoteft Corners of the Town, almoft as foon as they could be fent by a Meffenger, and that from Four, Five, Six, to Eight Times a Day, according as the Diftance of the Place makes it practicable; and you may fend a Letter from *Ratcliff* or *Limehoufe* in the *Eaft*, to the fartheft Part of *Weftminfter* for a Penny, and that feveral Times in the fame Day.

Nor are you tied up to a fingle Piece of Paper, as in the *General Poft-Office*, but any Packet under a Pound weight, goes at the fame Price.

I mention this the more particularly, becaufe it is fo manifeft a Teftimony to the Greatnefs of this City, and to the great Extent of Bufinefs and Commerce in it, that this Penny Conveyance fhould raife fo many Thoufand Pounds in a Year, and employ fo many poor People in the Diligence of it, as this Office employs.

We fee nothing of this at *Paris*, at *Amfterdam*, at *Hamburgh*, or any other City, that ever I have feen, or heard of.

THE CUSTOM HOUSE

The *Cuftom Houfe* I have juft mentioned before, but muft take up a few Lines to mention it again. The Statelinefs of the Building, fhewed the Greatnefs of the Bufinefs that is tranfacted there: The *Long Room* is like an *Exchange* every Morning, and the Croud of People who appear there, and the Bufinefs they do, is not to be explained by Words, nothing of that Kind in *Europe* is like it.

Yet it has been found, that the Bufinefs of Export and Import in this Port of *London*, is fo prodigioufly increafed, and the feveral new Offices, which they are bound to erect for the managing the additional Parts of the Cuftoms, are fuch, that the old Building, though very fpacious, is too little, and as the late Fire burnt or demolifh'd fome Part of the *Weft* End of the *Cuftom Houfe*, they have had the Opportunity in rebuilding, to enlarge it very much, buying in the Ground of fome of the demolifhed Houfes, to add to the *Cuftom Houfe*, which will be now a moft glorious Building.

THE SEVENTEEN KEYS OR WHARFS BETWEEN THE TOWER STAIRS AND LONDON BRIDGE

The Keys, or Wharfs, next the River, fronting not the *Cuftom Houfe* only, but the whole Space from the *Tower* Stairs, or Dock, to the Bridge, ought to be taken Notice of as a publick Building; nor are they lefs an Ornament to the City, as they are a Teftimony of the vaft Trade carried on in it, than the *Royal Exchange* itfelf.

The Revenue, or Income, brought in by thefe Wharfs, inclufive of the Warehoufes belonging to them, and the Lighters they employ, is faid to amount to a prodigious Sum; and, as I am told, feldom fo little as Forty thoufand Pounds *per Annum*: And abundance of Porters, Watchmen, Wharfingers, and other Officers, are maintained here by the

Bufinefs of the Wharfs; in which, one Thing is very remarkable, That here are Porters, and poor working Men, who, though themfelves not worth, perhaps, Twenty Pounds in the World, are trufted with great Quantities of valuable Goods, fometimes to the Value of feveral Thoufand Pounds, and yet 'tis very rarely to be heard, that any Loss or Embezzlement is made. The Number of thefe Keys extending, as above, from the Bridge to the *Tower Dock*, is Seventeen.

As may be seen in our maps and plans, the foreshore from Millbank to Wapping was dotted with wharves and quays except where Whitehall Palace, Somerset House, and the Temple Gardens intervened. The more important were, however, the ' Seventeen Keys,' between the Bridge and the Tower, of which many still remain. The following is a contemporary summary of the chief London Docks between Whitehall and Limehouse.

'These *Docks* or Harbours are cut into the Land without farther Current, and are usefull for the convenient lying of *Vessels, Houys, Lighters, Barges, Boats,* Etc. in order to the convenient Delivery of Provision, as *Victual, Fuel,* Etc. to the adjacent Inhabitants. They are in number very many.—Some of the chief are, *Scotland-Dock,* adjoining *to White-Hall;—White-Fryars-Dock; Puddle-Dock,* at the West-end of *Thames-Street;—Queen-Hith-Dock,* a place of much Trade for ground *Corn,* or *Meal,* which is brought out of the West-Country thither in great Quantities; *Billingsgate-Dock,* a place of great Trade, and where Ships of considerable Burthen may Harbour; —*Sabbs-Dock, Tower-Dock, St. Katherines-Dock. . . Hermitage-Dock, . . . Execution-Dock:* which though it be of later years fitted up, retains to this day the former Name which it received because it was the only place for Executing *Pyrates* and *Sea-Robbers,* which is usually done by Hanging them on a Gibbet erected at Low-water mark—*Limehouse-Dock.* And on the South-shoar are *Clink-Dock* and *St. Saviours-Dock*—There are, besides these, many *Docks* for private use; as for Repairing of Ships and Vessels, which we omit.'

The Markets 'Great and Very Many'

From thefe publick Places, I come next to the Markets, which, in fuch a Mafs of Building, and fuch a Collection of People, and where fuch Bufinefs is done, muft be great, and very many. To take a View of them in particular:

Firft, *Smithfield* Market for living Cattle, which is, without Queftion, the greateft in the World; no Defcription can be given of it, no Calculation of the Numbers of Creatures fold there, can be made. This Market is every *Monday* and *Friday.*

There is, indeed, a Liberty taken by the Butchers, to go up to *Iflington,* and to *Whitechapel,* and buy of the Country Drovers, who bring Cattle to Town; but this is called Foreftalling the Market, and is not allowed by Law.

There is alfo a great Market, or rather Fair for Horfes, in *Smithfield* every *Friday* in the Afternoon, where very great Numbers of Horfes, and thofe of the higheft Price, are to be fold Weekly.

The Flefh Markets are as follow:

Leaden-Hall, Honey-Lane, Newgate, Clare, Shadwell, Southwark, Weftminfter, Spittle Fields, Hoxton (forfaken) Brook, Bloomsbury, Newport, St. *James's, Hungerford.*

N.B. At all thefe Markets, there is a Part fet by for a Fifh Market, and a Part for an Herb Market; fo that when I fay afterwards, there are Fifh Markets, and Herb Markets, I am to be underftood, fuch as are wholly for Fifh, or for Herbs and Fruit. For Example,

SPECIAL MARKETS

Fish Markets	*Billingsgate, Fishstreet Hill,* and *Old Fishstreet.*
Herb Markets	*Covent Garden, and Stocks Market.*
N.B. Cherry Market, and Apple Market	At the Three *Cranes.*
Corn Markets	*Bear Key, and Queen Hith.*
Meal Markets	*Queen Hith, Hungerford, Ditch-Side,* and *Whitecrofs-Street.*
Hay Markets	*Whitechapel, Smithfield, Southwark,* the *Hay-Market-Street, Westminster,* and *Bloomsbury.*
Leather Market	*Leaden Hall.*
Hides and Skins	*Leaden Hall,* and *Wood's Clofe.*
Coal Markets	*Billingsgate, Room Land.*
Bay Market	*Leaden Hall.*
Broad Cloth Market	*Blackwell Hall.*

N.B. The laft Three are, without Doubt, the greateft in the World of thofe Kinds.
Bubble Market — *Exchange Alley.*

Thefe Markets are fo confiderable in themfelves, that they will merit a longer and more particular Defcription, than I have Room for in this Place. I fhall, however, briefly mention them again in their Order.

FOURTEEN 'FLESH MARKETS' OR MARKETS FOR PROVISIONS

Of the Fourteen Flefh Markets, or Markets for Provifions, Seven of them are of antient ftanding. Time out of Mind: But the other Seven are erected fince the Enlargement of Buildings mentioned above. The old ones are, *Leaden-Hall, Honey-Lane, Newgate Market, Southwark, Clare,* St. *James*'s, and *Westminster*; and thefe are fo confiderable, fuch Numbers of Buyers, and fuch an infinite Quantity of Provifions of all Sorts, Flefh, Fifh, and Fowl, that, efpecially of the Firft, no City in the World can equal them. 'Tis of the firft of thefe Markets, that a certain *Spanish* Ambaffador faid, There was as much Meat fold in it in one Month, as would fuffice all *Spain* for a Year.

LEADEN-HALL

This great Market, called, *Leaden-Hall,* though ftanding in the Middle of the City, contains Three large Squares, every Square having feveral Outlets into divers Streets, and all into one another. The Firft, and Chief, is called, The *Beef Market,* which has Two large Gates, one into *Leaden Hall Street,* one into *Gracechurch Street,* and Two fmaller, *viz.* One by a long pav'd Paffage leading into *Limeftreet,* and one under a Gateway from the Second Square. In this Square, every *Wednefday* is kept a Market for raw Hides, tann'd Leather, and Shoemakers Tools; and in the Warehoufes, up Stairs on the *Eaft* and *South* Sides of the Square, is the great Market for *Colechefter* Bayes.

The Second Square is divided into Two *Oblongs,* in the firft is the Fifh Market, and in the other, a Market for Country Higlers, who bring fmall Things, fuch as Pork, Butter, Eggs, Pigs, Country drefs'd, with fome Fouls, and fuch like Country Fare.

The *North* Part of the Fifh Market, the Place being too large for the Fifhmongers Ufe, are the Stalls of the Town Butchers for Mutton and Veal, the beft and largeft of which, that *England* can produce, is to be bought there, and the *East* Part is a Flesh Market for Country Butchers.

The Third, and last Square, which is also very large, is divided into Three Parts: Round the Circumference, is the Butter Market, with all the Sorts of Higglary Goods, as before: The *South* Part is the Poultry Market, and the Bacon Market, and the Center is an Herb Market.

All the other Markets follow the same Method in Proportion to the Room they have for it; and there is an Herb Market in every one; but the chief Markets in the whole City for Herbs and Garden-stuff, are the *Stocks* and *Covent Garden*.

TWO CORN MARKETS—' MONSTERS FOR MAGNITUDE '

There are but Two Corn Markets in the whole City and Out Parts; but they are Monsters for Magnitude, and not to be matched in the World. These are *Bear Key*, and *Queen Hith*: To the first comes all the vast Quantity of Corn that is brought into the City by Sea, and here Corn may be said, not to be sold by Cart Loads, or Horse Loads, but by Ship Loads, and, except the Corn Chambers and Magazines in *Holland*, when the Fleets come in from *Dantzick* and *England*, the whole World cannot equal the Quantity bought and sold here.

This is the Place whither all the Corn is brought, which, as I have observed, is provided in all the Counties of *England*, near the Sea Coast, and Shipp'd for *London*, and no Quantity can be wanted, neither for home consumption, or for Foreign Exportation, but the Corn Factors, who are the Managers of this Market, are ready to supply it.

The other, which I call a Corn Market too, is at *Queen Hith*; but this Market is chiefly, if not wholly, for Malt; as to the whole Corn, as the Quantity of Malt brought to this Market is prodigious great, so I must observe too, that this Place is the Receiver of all the Malt, the Barley of which, takes up the Ground of so many Hundred thousand Acres of Land in the Counties of *Surrey*, *Bucks*, *Berks*, *Oxford*, *Southampton*, and *Wilts*, and is called *West* Country Malt.

It is true, there is a very great Quantity of Malt, and of other Corn too, brought to some other Places on the River, and sold there, *viz*. To *Milford Lane*, above the Bridge, and the *Hermitage*, below the Bridge; but this is but, in general, a Branch of the Trade of the other Places.

QUEEN HITH—' A MARKET FOR MEAL AS WELL AS MALT '

It must not be omitted, that *Queen Hith* is also a very great Market for Meal, as well as Malt, and, perhaps, the greatest in *England*.

The Vessels which bring this Malt and Meal to *Queen Hith*, are worth the Observation of any Stranger that understands such Things. They are remarkable for the Length of the Vessel, and the Burthen they carry, and yet the little Water they draw; in a Word, some of those Barges carry above a Thousand Quarter of Malt at a Time, and yet do not draw Two Foot of Water. N.B. *A Thousand Quarter of Malt must be granted to be, at least, a Hundred Tun Burthen.* Note also, *Some of these large Barges come as far as from* Abbington, *which is above One hundred and Fifty Miles from* London, *if we measure by the River*.

THE COAL MARKET AT BILLINGSGATE

The next Market, which is more than ordinary remarkable, is the Coal Market at *Billingsgate*. This is kept every Morning on the broad Place just at the Head of *Billingsgate Dock*, and the Place is called *Room Land*; from what old forgotten Original it has that Name, History is silent. I need not, except for the Sake of Strangers, take Notice, that the City of *London*, and Parts adjacent, as also all the *South* of *England*, is supplied with Coals, called therefore Sea-Coal, from *Newcaftle upon Tine*, and from the Coaft of *Durham*, and *Northumberland*. This Trade is fo confiderable, that it is efteemed the great Nurfery of our beft Seamen, and of which I fhall have occafion to fay more in my Account of the *Northern* Parts of *England*. The Quantity of Coals, which it is fuppofed are, *Communibus Annis*, burnt and confumed in and about this City, is fuppofed to be about Five hundred thoufand Chalder, every Chalder containing Thirty-fix Bufhels, and generally weighing about Thirty hundred Weight.

All thefe Coals are bought and fold on this little Spot of *Room Land*, and, though fome-times, efpecially in cafe of a War, or of contrary Winds, a Fleet of Five hundred to Seven hundred Sail of Ships, comes up the River at a Time, yet they never want a Market: The Brokers, or Buyers of thefe Coals, are called Crimps, for what Reafon, or Original, is likewife a Myftery peculiar to this Trade; for thefe People are noted for giving fuch dark Names to the feveral Parts of their Trade; fo the Veffels they load their Ships with at *New Caftle*, are called *Keels*, and the Ships that bring them, are called *Cats*, and *Hags*, or *Hag Boats*, and *Fly Boats*, *and the like*. But of that hereafter.

The Increafe of this Confumption of Coals, is another Evidence of the great Increafe of the City of *London*; for, within a few Years paft, the Import of Coals was not, in the River of *Thames*, fo great by very near half.

THE 'CORN MEETERS' AND 'COAL MEETERS'

It muft be obferved, that as the City of *London* occafions the Confumption of fo great a Quantity of Corn and Coals, fo the Meafurement of them is under the Infpection of the Lord Mayor and Court of Aldermen, and for the Direction of which, there are allowed a certain Number of Corn Meeters, and Coal Meeters, whofe Places are for Life, and bring them in a very confiderable Income. Thefe Places are in the Gift of the Lord Mayor for the Time being, and are generally fold for Three or Four thoufand Pounds a Piece, when they fall.

They have abundance of poor Men employ'd under them, who are called, alfo, Meeters, and are, or ought to be, Freemen of the City.

This is, indeed, a Rent-charge upon the Buyer, and is a kind of Gabel,* as well upon the Coals as the Corn; but the Buyer is abundantly recompenfed, by being afcertained in his Meafure without any Fraud; fo that having bought his Coals or Corn, he is perfectly unconcerned about the Meafure, for the Sworn Meeters are fo placed between the Buyer and Seller, that no Injury can be offered, nor have I heard that any Complaint of Injuftice is ever made againft the Meeters, who are generally Men of good Character, are fworn to do Right, and cannot eafily do Wrong without being detected; fo many Eyes being about them, and fo many feveral Perfons concerned in the Work, who have no Dependance one upon another.

Defoe's account of the various MARKETS existing in London in his day is so long and complete that it hardly seems necessary to add anything to his description. They are all indicated on our Map, but a few notes may be added in regard to them, especially concerning some of the lesser known and no longer existing ones.

SMITHFIELD has gradually been so enlarged in space and developed in activity that the very name of the area it occupies connotes to most of us the market itself and little more. But it is to-day no longer a 'market for living cattle' as it was in Defoe's time, when, in 1668, Mr. Pepys went there to buy a pair of horses, without success, and records 'instances of craft and cunning' of which his innocent mind had not hitherto dreamed. The last market of this kind was held here in 1855, when the Metropolitan Cattle Market was opened, on what had once been known as Copenhagen Fields which, while Defoe was writing, was open ground with Copenhagen House, a small country tavern, standing on an eminence in their midst.

* From the French tax known as the Gabelle.

LEADENHALL had been a market from time immemorial, but its buildings, including the old Leaden Hall, from which it took its name, were destroyed in the Great Fire. Strype gives the following description of the place as it was known to Defoe: ' Leadenhall is a very large building of free-stone containing within it three large courts and yards, all encompassed with buildings; wherein is kept a market, one of the greatest, the best, and the most general for all provisions, in the City of London, nay of the kingdom; and if I should say of all Europe, I should not give it too great a praise'; while Gay, in his *Trivia*, recommends it specially as the spot where the best beef was to be obtained in those days.

HONEY LANE MARKET, which was the smallest in London, was formed on the site of Allhallows Church, destroyed in the Great Fire. Honey Lane adjoins Cheapside, and it was so called, according to Stow, indulging in one of his etymological guesses, ' not of sweetness thereof, being very narrow and somewhat dark, but rather of often washing and sweeping to keep it clean.'

NEWGATE MARKET was situated between Newgate Street and Paternoster Row, and Ivy and Warwick Lanes. It was entered by West Hart Street from Warwick Lane, and by Little Ivy Lane from Ivy Lane, and could also be approached from Paternoster Row and Newgate Street, in which latter thoroughfare it was held prior to the Great Fire. It gradually increased in importance and popularity, and indeed survived till after the middle of the last century.

CLARE MARKET, to which frequent references are made in *The Tatler*, is described as being ' very considerable and well served with provisions, both flesh and fish; for beside the butchers in the shambles, it is much resorted unto by the country butchers and higglers. . . . The toll belongs to the Duke of Newcastle as ground landlord thereof.' It occupied ground between Lincoln's Inn Fields and the Strand, close to Portugal Street and Vere Street, and the Duke of Newcastle, who, by the way, lived at the north-west corner of the Fields, erected a chapel near the market for the use of the butchers there. In its early days the place was called the New Market. The Kingsway-Aldwych scheme has altered all this neighbourhood, and Clare Market is now almost a forgotten name, although during the eighteenth century it bulked prominently in the news-sheets and even in the literature of the period. The quaint little structure, miscalled Dickens's Old Curiosity Shop, in Portugal Street, is a relic of these days.

SHADWELL MARKET, on Rocque's plan, is shown to be of considerable size, with two northern approaches, Peal Alley and Market Hill, from Ratcliffe Highway, and as being more or less open on the south at what was called Middle Shadwell. WESTMINSTER MARKET cannot even boast of having caught the attention of the cartographer, but it was probably situated in one of the open spaces contiguous with Horseferry Road, as the southern continuation of that thoroughfare was known as Market Street; the street-market still existing in Strutton (it should properly be Stourton) Ground is possibly a lineal descendant of the original market.

SPITALFIELDS MARKET stood in the centre of four streets: Lamb Street from Spital Square, Crispin Street on the west; Red Lyon Street on the east, and Paternoster Row on the south. It was of considerable size, and the wares exposed there supplied chiefly the weavers from France who lived in the neighbourhood. It has been greatly enlarged of recent years and is to-day one of London's chief Markets.

Against HOXTON MARKET, Defoe has set the word ' forsaken,' and no records appear to exist of its size, character or position.

Those in the west are BROOK MARKET, of which nothing seems to be known; BLOOMSBURY MARKET, founded in 1662, and first known as Southampton Market, a place of so small account, even in Strype's time, that the inhabitants of the district used to go elsewhere for their provisions, as he remarks; NEWPORT MARKET, where Orator Henley was wont to disport his eloquence, which may perhaps survive in the present-day street markets of Soho; and ST. JAMES'S MARKET (still existing in name), a kind of outcome of St. James's Fair, instituted in 1664 to serve the new houses being erected by Henry Jermyn, Earl of St. Albans, in St. James's Square, much as the later Shepherd's Market (1735) was formed for the use of Mr. Shepherd's tenants in that locality. Pepys knew and visited it, and Gay recommends it for its veal. In a large room over the central portion, Richard Baxter used to preach. Strype speaks of it as being of importance and much resorted to on account of the excellent provisions to be obtained there. When Waterloo Place and Lower Regent Street came into existence, St. James's Market was swept away.

Hungerford Stairs and Suspension Bridge perpetuated the name of the adjacent HUNGERFORD MARKET where Charing Cross Station now stands. The market was originally built, as stated above, in 1680 on the site of old Hungerford House, Sir Stephen Fox and Sir Christopher Wren having (1685) an interest in it. In its early days it was known as the Exchange, and so appears in the rate

PLATE XXV

THE OLD STOCKS MARKET
ON THE SITE OF THE MANSION HOUSE
From the original oil painting by Josef Van Aken, circa 1730.

PLATE XXVI

Where Great Belinus held his Court of Old ___
Oisters are now obstreperously Sold ___
Where Bows were made to Ministers of State ___
The Populace now purchase Ling and Skate ___

And where the Courtier's smiling Face portended,
Deceit to those who thought they were befriended;
You may, if Prudence is your cautious guide ___
Procure the produce of the oceans Pride ___

THE
Wonders of ye Deep,
often attempted, and
never performed, but by
Arnold Vanhaecken
1762.

But Ah! beware, when you your Beard would grace,
To rouse the Elevation of that place ___
For else, while bargaining for Prawns & Shrimps,
You'll hear your self proclaimed a thousand Pimps.

Consider likewise when you e're resort ___
To this fam'd Market that was once a Court:
Our gracious Court with a propitious hand ___
Diffuses plenteous Markets through the Land.

THE VIEW AND HUMOURS OF BILLINGSGATE

From the picture by A. Vanhaecken.

books. The Sir Edward Hungerford, who was originally responsible for the venture, died in 1711. It appears that at first the market was a success, and, indeed, so late as 1831, it was thought worth while to rebuild it; but by 1860 it had all been cleared away and the new railway station begun.

In the list of produce supplied by the various markets, given by Defoe, we find the names of some other lesser known centres and at least one famous one. This last is BILLINGSGATE which has been from very early times the chief fish emporium of the City. It was during Defoe's day (1699) that it was made, by Act of Parliament, 'a free and open market for all sorts of fish.' Billingsgate has long been synonymous for freedom of language, and in the prose and poetical writings of the late seventeenth and eighteenth centuries frequent references to this are to be found. A print by A. Vanhaecken, dated 1762, shows what the buildings, and incidentally the very varied frequenters, were like a few years after, and probably not much altered since, Defoe's time.

In the days of old London Bridge, FISH STREET HILL led immediately on to it, the position of the present bridge being some way to the west, and off this hill was the market, obviously, however, a small one, as Rocque does not mark it on his plan. *Old* Fish Street, which Strype calls 'a pleasant and considerable street,' is now absorbed in Queen Victoria Street and Knightrider Street, but was once an important centre of the fish trade; and it is probable that the market mentioned by Defoe was held here. John Locke, in *Certain Directions to a Foreigner Visiting London* (1699), recommends that supposititious person to 'eat fish in Fish Street,' as indicating the best spot for such fare.

The STOCKS MARKET was on the site now occupied by the Mansion House. Before the Great Fire it provided meat and fish, but when rebuilt was given over to vegetables. In its centre stood the famous statue of Charles II erected by Sir Robert Vyner, and exactly what the place looked like to Defoe (1730) may be seen from Josef Van Aken's contemporary oil painting. Just seven years after this picture was completed, the market was removed to what is now Farringdon Street, and became known as Fleet Market, to which we have referred elsewhere.

'THE THREE CRANES' where, Defoe tells us, the apple and cherry market was held, was the name applied to a Street, a Wharf and a Tavern, close to the site of the present Southwark Bridge, on account according to Stow 'not onely of a signe of three Cranes at a Taverne doore, but rather of three strong Cranes of Timber placed on the Vintrie wharfe by the Thames side to crane up wines there.' It seems that originally there was but one Crane here, as in Cavendish's *Life of Wolsey* only one is mentioned, and the tavern was then known as 'The Crane.' The place enters into literature through Ben Jonson's reference to it in his plays, and also through Scott, in *Kenilworth*, calling it 'the most topping Tavern in London.' Pepys hardly found it so, however, for in January, 1662, he speaks of having 'a sorry poor dinner here in a narrow doghole of a room.'

Such places as QUEENHYTHE, off Thames Street, and BEAR KEY, close to the Custom House, were wharves for the reception of produce brought by boat up the Thames, and although goods were sold there, the former can hardly be regarded as a regular market such as most of those before particularised. Of the latter, however, Delaune tells us that it was 'between Sab's Dock and Porters-Key,' and was 'the usual place or Chief Market for Corn, chiefly on Mondays, Wednesdays and Fridays, which are the Market-days, where great quantities of all kind of grain are bought and sold by small examples, commonly called *Samples*, whether it be lying in Granaries or Ships, and it (viz. Bear-Key) is the principal place where the *Kentish* and *Essex* Corn Vessels do lie.'

DITCH-SIDE it is difficult to identify, unless it was a small market by Fleet-Ditch or in Houndsditch, as the name might imply. WHITECROSS STREET was for long a resort of costermongers whose wares were no doubt exposed for sale in it. WOODS CLOSE was off Church Street, Bethnal Green; while BLACKWELL (or more correctly Bakewell) Hall is described by Hatton as 'a spacious building on the east side of Guild Hall Yard, or on the west side of Bazing Hall Street.' The market held here, for woollen fabrics, etc., had been established by the Corporation in the reign of Richard II. Hatton gives details of the rents and payments of those doing business here, and on stockings and blankets alone a revenue of over £1,000 a year was then (1708) obtained.

Defoe closes his list of markets by the words 'Bubble Market, Exchange Alley.' This was, of course, the famous centre for gambling in South Sea and other stocks, situated off Cornhill. In it was Jonathan's Coffee House where the first business was transacted; this, however, overflowed into the alley until the nuisance became so great that the Exchange Coffee House was taken for the purpose, and a charge made for its use. The literature of the period, both poetical and prose, is full of allusions to this focus of stock-jobbing during the years of the Bubble madness, Gay being among those who first won and then lost a large sum here. Swift refers to the place as one of 'dreadful name,' in his *South Sea Project* published in 1721.

Defoe's account of the various markets existing in London in his day can be supplemented by the rules governing them, which were both drastic and salutary, as given by Stow.

'The Laws of the Market.

' 1. In all the *markets* of this City, no Victual shall be sold but by the Price set by the *Mayor* of this City.

' 2. No Man shall Forestall any Victual coming to the *Market;* as for to Buy in any *Inn* or other privy place, or yet coming to the *Market*, whether it be found in the hands of the Buyer, or of the Seller, under pain of Forfeiture of the same: And no *Inn-holder* shall suffer any thing to be sold in his House, upon pain of Forfeiture of Forty Shillings.

' 3. No man shall *regrate* any Victuals which is in the *Market*, or buy any Victual to *ingrate* in the Market, so that the Commons can or may have any part of such Victual, as in especial such as be known for *Hucksters* or other people occupying their Living by such Victuals as they would so *ingross*, under pain of forfeiture of such Victuals so *regrated:* Provided always that any Steward, for any Noble Feast, may buy or *ingrate* such Victual as is convenient for the same Feast.

' 4. No *Butter* shall be sold but according to the Weight, for the time of the year allowed.

' 5. No *Poulterers* shall deceivably occupy the Market to sell any stale Victual, or such as be *Poulterers* of the City, for to stand in strange Cloathing so to do, under pain of *forty shillings*, and the forfeiture of such Victual *forty shillings*.

' 6. No *Hucksters* shall stand or sit in the Market, but in the *lower place*, and the ends of the Market, to the intent they may be perfectly known, and the *stranger-market-people* have the preheminence of the Market, under pain of *three shillings four pence*, if the *Hucksters* disobey the same.

' 7. No *unwholsome* or stale Victual shall be sold under pain of *forty shillings*, and the forfeiture of the same Victuals.'

THE SHIPPING AND THE POOL

There is one great Work yet behind, which, however, ſeems neceſſary to a full Deſcription of the City of *London*, and that is the Shipping and the Pool; but in what Manner can any Writer go about it, to bring it into any reaſonable Compaſs? The Thing is a kind of Infinite, and the Parts to be ſeparated from one another in ſuch a Deſcription, are ſo many, that it is hard to know where to begin.

A COMPARISON WITH THE DUTCH

The whole River, in a Word, from *London-Bridge* to *Black Wall*, is one great *Arſenal*, nothing in the World can be like it: The great Building-Yards at *Schedam* near *Amſterdam*, are ſaid to out-do them in the Number of Ships which are built there, and they tell us, that there are more Ships generally ſeen at *Amſterdam*, than in the *Thames*.

As to the Building Part, I will not ſay, but that there may be more Veſſels built at *Schedam*, and the Parts adjacent, than in the River *Thames*; but then it muſt be ſaid;

1. That the *Engliſh* build for themſelves only, the *Dutch* for all the World.

2. That almoſt all the Ships the *Dutch* have, are built there, whereas, not one Fifth part of our Shipping is built in the *Thames*; but abundance of Ships are built at all the Sea-Ports in *England*, ſuch as at *New-Caſtle, Sunderland, Stockton, Whitby, Hull, Gainsborough, Grimsby, Lynn, Yarmouth, Alborough, Walderſwick, Ipſwich* and *Harwich*, upon the *Eaſt* Coaſt; and at *Shoram, Arundel, Brighthelmſton, Portſmouth, Southampton, Pool, Weymouth, Dartmouth, Plymouth*, beſides other Places, on the *South* Coaſt.

3. That we ſee more Veſſels in leſs Room at *Amſterdam*; but the ſetting aſide their Hoys, Bilanders and Schoots, which are in great Numbers always there, being Veſſels particular to their Inland and Coaſting Navigation; you do not ſee more Ships, nor near ſo many Ships of Force, at *Amſterdam* as at *London*.

PLATE XXVII

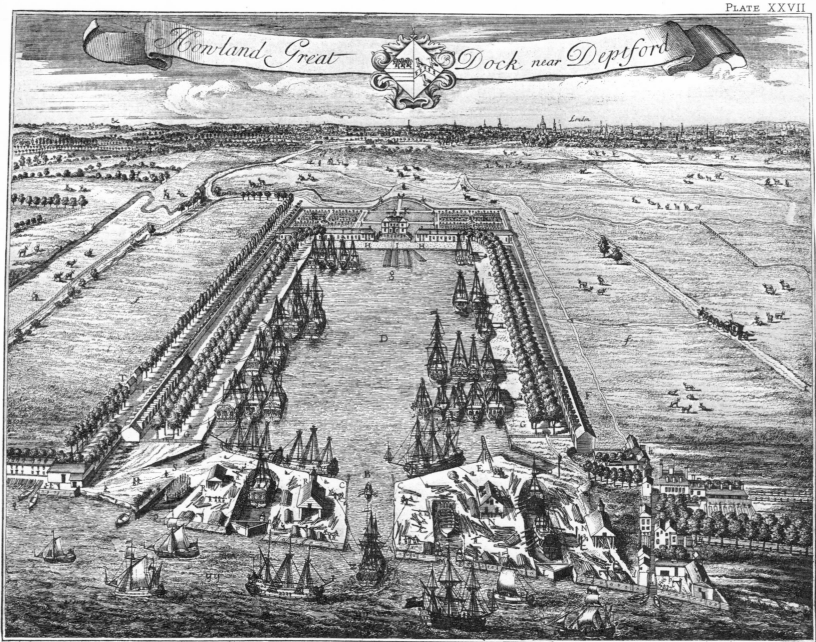

Howland Great Dock near Deptford

London

J. Badslade Delin.   J. Kip Sculp.

HOWLAND DOCK AT DEPTFORD

Engraved by J. Kip from a drawing by T. Badslade, 1717.

PLATE XXVIII

FIREMEN AND FIRE FIGHTING METHODS OF THE XVIII CENTURY

As illustrated in pictorial heading of an Insurance Policy

4. That you fee more Ships there in lefs Room, but, perhaps, not fo many Ships in the whole.

'ABOVE TWO THOUSAND SAIL OF ALL SORTS' IN THE POOL

That Part of the River of *Thames* which is properly the Harbour, and where the Ships ufually deliver or unload their Cargoes, is called the *Pool*, and begins at the turning of the River out of *Lime-houfe* Reach, and extends to the *Cuftom-houfe-Keys*: In this Compafs I have had the Curiofity to count the Ships as well as I could, *en paffant*, and have found above Two thoufand Sail of all Sorts, not reckoning Barges, Lighters or Pleafure-Boats, and Yatchs; but of Veffels that really go to Sea.

It is true, the River or Pool, feem'd, at that time, to be pretty full of Ships; it is true alfo, that I included the Ships which lay in *Deptford* and *Black-Wall* Reaches, and in the Wet Docks, whereof, there are no lefs than Three; but 'tis as true, that we did not include the Men of War at the King's Yard and in the Wet Dock there at *Deptford*, which were not a very few.

What Defoe here says of the activity on the river in his day is borne out by other writers, as well as cartographers who are careful (see Rocque as an outstanding example) to indicate, by the numbers of ships they place in their plans, the amount of traffic of this kind then existing. The fact is the Thames was London's chief highway, and was used not only for commerce but for pleasure in a way which seems strange to us in these days when the splendid river is practically ignored for the latter purpose altogether. In those days were to be seen the royal barge conveying the Sovereign up and down the stream, and the Lord Mayor and Corporation being rowed to Westminster in their state barge, attended by those of the City Companies; while the river was dotted with pleasure wherries filled with people going to the various places of recreation on its banks, or visiting the *Folly* which was moored in the stream. The diaries and plays and novels of the period abound in references to this aspect especially of the Thames traffic and the interchange of broad banter and chaff between the occupants of the numerous craft on its surface. The licensed watermen of the period appear to have developed a talent for repartee not less vigorous and considerably coarser than that of the busmen and cabbies of the Victorian age, so familiar to us in the early volumes of *Punch*. The *Folly*, which resembled a large modern houseboat, may be described as a floating Music Hall of the period, and was usually moored near the Savoy. It is represented in our illustrations of Somerset House and the bird's-eye view of Whitehall Palace.

WET AND DRY DOCKS AND SHIPBUILDING YARDS

In the River, as I have obferved, there are from *Battle-Bridge* on the *Southwark* Side, and the *Hermitage-Bridge* on the City-Side, reckoning to *Black-Wall*, inclufive,

Three Wet Docks for laying up
Twenty Two Dry Docks for Repairing } Merchants Ships.
Thirty Three Yards for Building

This is inclufive of the Builders of Lighters, Hoys, &c. but exclufive of all Boat-Builders, Wherry-Builders, and above-Bridge Barge-Builders.

ENGLAND'S INEXHAUSTIBLE 'STORE-HOUSE OF TIMBER'

To enter into any Defcription of the great Magazines of all manner of Naval Stores, for the furnifhing thofe Builders, would be endlefs, and I fhall not attempt it; 'tis fufficient to add, That *England*, as I have faid elfewhere, is an inexhauftible Store-houfe of Timber, and all the Oak Timber, and generally the Plank alfo, ufed in the building thefe Ships, is found in *England* only, nay, and which is more, it is not fetched from the remoter Parts of

England, but thefe *Southern* Counties near us are the Places where 'tis generally found; as particularly the Counties of *Berks* and *Bucks*, *Surrey*, *Kent*, *Suffex*, *Effex* and *Suffolk*, and very little is brought farther, nor can all the Ship-building the whole Kingdom are able to build, ever exhauft thofe Counties, tho' they were to build much more than they do.

But I muft land, left this Part of the Account feems to fmell of the Tarr, and I fhould tire the Gentlemen with leading them out of their Knowledge.

It is hardly necessary to point out how entirely mistaken Defoe was in his estimate of the ' inexhaustible ' supply of timber in England for all its possible future requirements. He commits himself to the same false prophecy when dealing with the Sussex iron industry in another chapter of the *Tour* and the ' prodigious expense of wood ' required for its furnaces. Even before the century was out it began to be difficult to find adequate supplies of English timber of the requisite size and quality for England's Wooden Walls. As Mr. Cole points out in his introduction to the *Tour*, ' only the introduction of coal as a fuel for use in all the processes of the iron trades saved the woods of England from complete destruction.' Within our own generation the same word ' inexhaustible ' used to be applied even by experts to the world's available supply of timber for the world's future requirements. It is only to-day that it is realised how rapidly its available sources of supply are being depleted, with a timber famine in prospect before the end of the century unless adequate forest conservation methods are generally adopted. If Defoe erred in his calculations, at any rate he erred in good company.

' NO CITY SO WELL FURNISHED FOR EXTINGUISHING FIRES '

I fhould mention, for the Information of Strangers, *&c.* that the Buildings of this great City are chiefly of Brick, as many ways found to be the fafeft, the cheapeft, and the moft commodious of all other Materials; by fafe, I mean from Fire, and as by Act of Parliament, every Builder is bound to have a Partition Wall of Brick alfo, one Brick and Half thick between every Houfe, it is found to be, indeed, very helpful in cafe of Fire.

And as I am fpeaking of Fire and burning of Houfes, it cannot be omitted, That no where in the World is fo good Care taken to quench Fires as in *London*; I will not fay the like Care is taken to prevent them; for I muft say, That I think the Servants, nay, and Mafters too in *London*, are the moft carelefs People in the World about Fire, and this, no doubt, is the Reafon why there are frequently more Fires in *London* and in the Out-parts, than there are in all the Cities of *Europe* put them together; nor are they the more careful, as I can learn, either from Obfervation or Report, I fay, they are not made more cautious, by the innumerable Fires which continually happen among them.

And this leads me back to what I juft now faid, That no City in the World is fo well furnifhed for the extinguifhing Fires when they happen.

A WATER SUPPLY LAID EVERY WHERE IN LARGE TIMBER PIPES

1. By the great Convenience of Water which being every where laid in the Streets in large Timber Pipes, as well from the *Thames* as the *New-River*, thofe Pipes are furnifhed with a Fire Plug, which the Parifh Officers have the Key of, and when opened, let out not a Pipe, but River of Water into the Streets, fo that making but a Dam in the Kennel,* the whole Street is immediately under Water to supply the Engines.

' ADMIRABLE ' FIRE ENGINES

2. By the great Number of admirable Engines, of which, almoft, every Parifh has One, and fome Halls alfo, and fome private Citizens have them of their own, fo that no fooner

---

* This method of making a ' Dam in the Kennel ' is well illustrated in the accompanying heading of a contemporary Fire Policy.

does a Fire break out, but the Houfe is furrounded with Engines, and a Flood of Water poured upon it, 'till the Fire is, as it were, not extinguifhed only, but drowned.

'WATER-MEN' AS 'FIRE-MEN'

3. The feveral Enfurance Offices, of which I have fpoken above, have each of them a certain Sett of Men, who they keep in conftant Pay, and who they furnifh with Tools proper for the Work, and to whom they give Jack-Caps of Leather, able to keep them from Hurt, if Brick or Timber, or any thing not of too great a Bulk, fhould fall upon them; thefe Men make it their Bufinefs to be ready at Call, all Hours, and Night or Day, to affift in cafe of Fire; and it muft be acknowledged, they are very dextrous, bold, diligent and fuccefsful. Thefe they call *Fire-men*, but with an odd kind of Contradiction in the Title, for they are really moft of them *Water-men*.

WATER PUMPED UP FROM THE THAMES

Having mentioned, that the City is fo well furnifhed with Water, it cannot be omitted, that there are Two great Engines for the raifing the *Thames* Water, one at the Bridge, and the other near *Broken Wharf*; thefe raife fo great a Quantity of Water, that, as they tell us, they are able to fupply the whole City in its utmoft Extent, and to fupply every Houfe alfo, with a running Pipe of Water up to the uppermoft Story.

The methods instanced by Defoe as so admirable for the extinguishing of fires will seem to us archaic enough in view of modern appliances; but there is no doubt they were a great advance on earlier ones. During the reign of Charles II considerable advance was made in scientific matters in all directions, largely helped by the influence of the Royal Society, incorporated in 1662, and of the King himself, whose interest in such things is well known. The fire-engines of the period were hand-drawn affairs, and so continued till much later than Defoe's day, as may be seen by specimens in the London Museum and elsewhere. A contemporary wood-cut shows us two firemen dressed in their leather clothing wearing the helmets such as Defoe describes, and with pikes and hatchets in their hands; while Gay, in a passage of his *Trivia* (1716), describes a London fire in his day and the heroic efforts of the firemen to extinguish it. There is, by the way, a humorous allusion to the use of the New River in the case of fire, in *The Spectator* for September 22nd, 1714: 'A publick-spirited gentleman tells me that on the second of September at night the whole City was on Fire, and would certainly have been reduced to Ashes again by this Time, if he had not flown over it with the *New River* on his Back, and happily extinguished the Flames before they had prevailed too far.'

Defoe refers to the 'two great engines for raising water' then existing in the city: one at the bridge, i.e. London Bridge, and the other at Broken Wharf. The former occupied the arches under the north end of old London Bridge; while that at Broken Wharf, on the south side of Thames Street, nearly opposite Old Fish Street Hill ('so called from its having been broken and fallen into the Thames,' says Hatton, quoting Stow), was originally set up by one Bevis Bulmer, in 1594, for supplying Fleet Street and Cheapside with water. But the pipes in this instance were of lead, not, as Defoe states was the general rule, of wood. A detailed account of the Water Works at London Bridge is printed as an Appendix, reproduced from Matthews's *Hydraulia, An Account of the Water Works of London*, with a woodcut of the type of machine then in use.

AND BROUGHT TO ISLINGTON BY THE NEW RIVER AQUEDUCT

However, the *New-River*, which is brought by an Aqueduct or artificial Stream from *Ware*, continues to fupply the greater Part of the City with Water, only with this Addition by the way, that they have been obliged to dig a new Head or Bafin at *Iflington* on a higher Ground than that which the natural Stream of the River fupplies, and this higher Bafin they fill from the lower, by a great Engine worked formerly with Six Sails, now by many Horfes conftantly working; fo from that new Elevation of the Water, they fupply the higher Part of the Town with the fame Advantage, and more Eafe than the *Thames* Engines do it.

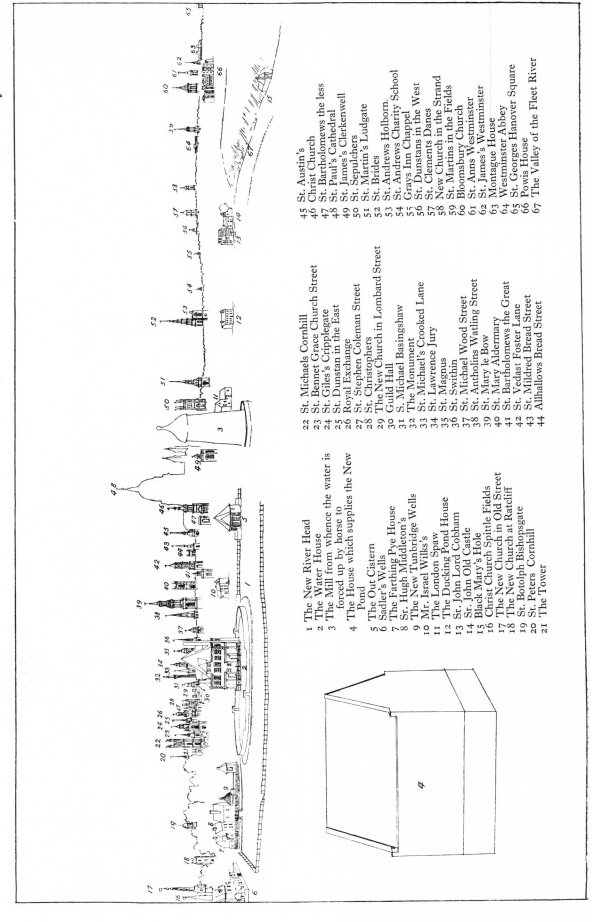

1 The New River Head
2 The Water House
3 The Mill from whence the water is
    forced up by horse to
4 The House which supplies the New
    Pond
5 The Out Cistern
6 Sadler's Wells
7 The Farthing Pye House
8 Sr. Hugh Middleton's
9 The New Tunbridge Wells
10 Mr. Israel Wilks's
11 The London Spaw
12 The Ducking Pond House
13 Sr. John Lord Cobham
14 Sr. John Old Castle
15 Black Mary's Hole
16 Christ Church Spittle Fields
17 The New Church in Old Street
18 The New Church at Ratcliff
19 St. Botolph Bishopsgate
20 St. Peters Cornhill
21 The Tower

22 St. Michaels Cornhill
23 St. Bennet Grace Church Street
24 St. Giles's Cripplegate
25 St. Dunstan in the East
26 Royal Exchange
27 St. Stephen Coleman Street
28 St. Christophers
29 The New Church in Lombard Street
30 Guild Hall
31 S. Michael Basingshaw
32 The Monument
33 St. Michael's Crooked Lane
34 St. Lawrence Jury
35 St. Magnus
36 St. Swithin
37 St. Michael Wood Street
38 St. Antholins Watling Street
39 St. Mary le Bow
40 St. Mary Aldermary
41 St. Bartholomews the Great
42 St. Vedast Foster Lane
43 St. Mildred Bread Street
44 Allhallows Bread Street

45 St. Austin's
46 Christ Church
47 St. Bartholomews the less
48 St. Paul's Cathedral
49 St. James's Clerkenwell
50 St. Sepulchers
51 St. Martin's Ludgate
52 St. Brides
53 St. Andrews Holborn
54 St. Andrews Charity School
55 Grays Inn Chappel
56 St. Dunstans in the West
57 St. Clements Danes
58 New Church in the Strand
59 St. Martins in the Fields
60 Bloomsbury Church
61 St. Anns Westminster
62 St. James's Westminster
63 Montague House
64 Westminster Abbey
65 St. Georges Hanover Square
66 Powis House
67 The Valley of the Fleet River

KEY TO A VIEW OF LONDON FROM NEAR ISLINGTON

PLATE XXIX

A PROSPECT OF THE NORTH SIDE OF LONDON FROM NEAR ISLINGTON

From a print by T.B (owles),1730.

PROPOSAL TO BRING WATER FROM THE COLNE AT ST. ALBANS

There was a very likely Propofal fet on Foot by fome Gentlemen, whofe Genius feem'd equal to the Work, for drawing another River, rather larger than that now running, and bringing it to a Head on fome rifing Grounds beyond *Mary le Bonne*.

This Water was propofed to be brought from the little *Coln* or *Cole* near St. *Albans*, and the River, called *Two Waters*, near *Rickmanfworth*, and as I have feen the Courfe of the Water, and the feveral Supplies it was to have, and how the Water-level was drawn for containing the Current, I muft acknowledge it was a very Practical Undertaking, and merited Encouragement; but it was oppofed in Parliament, and dropt for the prefent: This Defign was particularly calculated for fupplying thofe prodigious Additions of Buildings, which I have already defcrib'd at the *Weft* End of the Town.

OTHER SMALLER SUPPLIES

However, tho' this be laid afide, as alfo feveral Water-houfes in other Parts, particularly one at *Wapping*, one near *Battle-Bridge* in *Southwark*, and the famous one at *York-Buildings*, yet it cannot be denied, that the City of *London* is the beft fupplied with Water of any great City in the World, and upon as eafy Terms to its Inhabitants.

It seems impossible to identify the spot where the water-house at Wapping stood; the one at Battle Bridge, Southwark (not, of course, to be confounded with the better-known Battle Bridge, St. Pancras), was just to the west of Battle Bridge stairs connecting Tooley Street with the river; but the best known was that at York Buildings, between the Strand and the Thames, which is a prominent feature in so many eighteenth century pictures and prints. By a patent from Charles II, dated 1675, the York Waterworks were established here with the object of supplying the west end of London. Fifteen years later the building was burnt down, but re-erected in the following year, and an Act was then obtained for the incorporation of a company under the style of ' The Governor and Company of Undertakers for raising the Thames water in York Buildings.' Although heavy losses were incurred by the company it retrieved its position by using its charter for more extended purposes, and in 1719 the shares rose to a great premium. It was not till 1829 that the company was dissolved by Act of Parliament. The tall conical tower connected with the undertaking is a particularly prominent landmark in a drawing by Canaletto, dated 1747, and is to be seen, roughly indicated, in Thomas Sandby's water-colour drawing reproduced in this volume; it stood on the river bank at the south-west corner of Villiers Street, approximately where the Charing Cross railway bridge begins; the river in those pre-Embankment days coming a considerable way further up the foreshore than the spot where the District Station now stands.

' SEVERAL BEAUTIFUL CONDUITS '

There were formerly feveral beautiful Conduits of Running-Water in *London*, which Water was very fweet and good, and was brought at an infinite Expence, from feveral diftant Springs, in large leaden Pipes to thofe Conduits, and this was fo lately, that feveral of thofe Conduits, were re-built fince the Fire, as one on *Snow-Hill* and one at *Stockf-Market*, which ferves as a Pedeftal for the great Equeftrian Statue of King *Charles* II. erected there at the Charge of Sir *Robert Viner*, then Lord Mayor, and who was then an eminent Banker in *Lombard-ftreet*; but his Loyalty could not preferve him from being ruined by the common Calamity, when the King fhut up the *Exchequer*.

They tell us a merry Story of this Statue, how true it may be, let thofe teftify who faw it, if any fuch Witneffes remain, *viz*. That a certain famous Court Lady, I do not fay it was the D——fs of *Portfmouth*, being brought to Bed of a Son late in the Night, the next Morning this glorious Equeftrian Statue had a *Pillion* handfomely placed on it behind the Body of the K——, with a Paper pinned to the Trapping of the Pillion, with Words at length, *Gone for a Midwife*.

The origin of the statue is thus given by Pennant. Speaking of the Stocks Market he says: 'In it stood the famous equestrian statue, erected in honour of Charles II. by his most loyal subject Sir Robert Viner, Lord Mayor. Fortunately his lordship discovered one (made at Leghorn) of John Sobieski, trampling on a Turk. The good knight caused some alterations to be made and christened the Polish monarch by the name of Charles, and bestowed on the turbaned Turk that of Oliver Cromwell.'

BUT FEW STATUES AND THOSE 'NOT VERY VALUABLE'

It is fcarce worth while to give an Account of the Statues in this City, they are neither many, or are thofe which are, very valuable.

The Statue of King *Charles* II. in Marble, ftanding in the middle of the *Royal Exchange*, is the beft beyond Comparifon; one of the fame Prince, and his Father, ftanding in Two large Niches on the *South* Front of the fame Building, and being bigger than the Life, are coarfe Pieces compared to it.

The Statues of the Kings and Queens, Seventeen of which are already put up in the Infide of the *Royal Exchange*, are tolerable, but all infinitely inferior to that in the middle.

There is a Statue of Sir *Thomas Grefham*, the Founder of the *Royal Exchange*, which outdoes many of thofe Kings, only that it ftands in a dark Corner, and is little noticed; 'tis placed in a Nitch under the Piazza, in the *North Weft* Angle of the *Exchange*, juft regarding the *Turky* Walk, and he has a Bale of Silk lying by him.

The STATUES which embellished Jarman's Royal Exchange were apparently more or less copies of those which had been destroyed in Gresham's earlier building. We are told that in the former there was a series of sovereigns of this country from Edward the Confessor to Queen Elizabeth, and that those of her three immediate successors were from time to time added, that of Charles I having been overthrown after his execution with the unfortunately chosen inscription on the pedestal: 'Exit Tyrannus Regum ultimus.' In the later Exchange the statues ranged from Edward I to Charles II, and to these were added in Defoe's day one of George I by Rysbrack. Certain of the earlier ones were the work of Nicholas Stone who himself records having executed in 1625 four of them, for which he was paid £25 each, and one of Queen Elizabeth, which was afterwards removed to the Guildhall, for £30. Edward Pierce produced the famous one of Sir Thomas Gresham as well as one of Edward III for the old Exchange. Caius Gabriel Cibber was responsible for most of those in the new building, including one of Gresham; but that of Charles II was from the greater hand of Grinling Gibbon who, according to the fashion of the time, received a patent to have engravings made of it, and to sell them for his own benefit. This was the one to which Defoe refers as occupying the central site in the Quadrangle; the other of Charles II, and that of Charles I on the south front of the building, were by John Bushnell. This lesser-known sculptor had as a matter of fact been commissioned to execute the whole series of statues, but hearing that Cibber was making efforts to obtain the commission, he withdrew from what he probably realised would have been a hopeless competition.

There is another Equeftrian Statue, and but One, as I remember, within the City, and that is of King *James* the Firft on the *North* Front of one of the Gates of the City called *Alderfgate*: This was erected on the Occafion of that King's entring the City at that Gate when he arrived here from *Scotland*, to take the Crown after the Death of Queen *Elizabeth*; when that Statue was finely Painted and Gilded, which is not ufual, nor is the Gilding yet worn off; there are fome emblematick Figures remaining, which were then fuited to the Occafion of his triumphal Entry, and there was another Arch form'd for the Day at the Bars, where the Liberties of the City end, that Way which is now called *Gofwell-ftreet*, but that was taken down foon after.

51

SEVEN GATES AND FOUR POSTERNS

The Gates of the City are Seven, befides Pofterns, and the Pofterns that remain are Four, befides others that are demolifhed.

The Gates are all remaining, Two of them which were demolifhed at the Fire, being beautifully Re-built: Thefe are *Ludgate* and *Newgate*; the Firft a Prifon for Debt for Freemen of the City only, the other a Prifon for Criminals, both for *London* and *Middle-fex*, and for Debtors alfo for *Middlefex, being the County Gaol.*

Moregate is alfo re-built, and is a very beautiful Gateway, the Arch being near Twenty Foot high, which was done to give Room for the City Train'd Bands to go through to the *Artillery* Ground, where they Mufter, and that they might march with their Pikes advanc'd, for then they had Pikemen in every Regiment, as well in the Army as in the *Militia*, which fince that, is quite left off; this makes the Gate look a little out of Shape, the Occafion of it not being known. *Cripplegate* and *Bifhhopfgate* are very Old, and make but a mean Figure; *Aderfgate* is about One hundred and Twenty Years old, and yet being Beautified, as I have faid, on the Occafion of King *James*'s Entry, looks very handfome.

Aldgate was very Ancient and Decay'd, fo that *as Old as Aldgate*, was a City Proverb for many Years; but this Gate was Re-built alfo, upon the Triumphant Entry of K. *James I* and looks ftill very well; on the *Eaft* Side of this Gate are Two Statues in Stone, repre-fenting Two Men, from the Wafte upward, and in Armour, throwing down Two great Stones, fuppofing it to be on an Enemy affaulting the Gate, which I mention, becaufe fome time ago, one of thefe Men in Armour, whether tired with holding it fo long, or dreaming of Enemies affaulting the Gate, our Authors do not inform us; but he threw down the Stone, or rather let it fall, after having held it upwards of an Hundred Years; but, as it happened, it did no harm.

Moft of thefe Gates are given by the City to the chief of the Officers of the City to live in, and the Houfes are very convenient Dwellings.

LUDGATE and NEWGATE were each rebuilt in 1672 and used as prisons, but the former seems to have been a ' sponging house ' rather than a prison proper, and indeed even more like a sanctuary, as those unable to pay their debts voluntarily sought asylum from their creditors here. BISHOPSGATE became so dilapidated that it was taken down in 1731, when an even less imposing structure than Defoe's ' *mean figure* ' was substituted. ALDERSGATE, which he speaks of as being about one hundred and twenty years old, was hardly that, for it was erected in 1617, the gate by which King James entered the City in 1603 being the one described by Stow as having existed so far back as 1289. Pepys mentions (1660) seeing the ' limbs of some of our new traytors set upon Aldersgate,' and this was a use to which the other gates, especially Temple Bar, were frequently put. The general appearance of these gates as they stood before being swept away in the 'sixties of the 18th century is depicted in our map of the City.

TEMPLE BAR

Temple-Bar is the only Gate which is erected at the Extent of the City Liberties, and this was occafioned by fome needful Ceremonies at the Proclaiming any King or Queen of *England*, at which Time the Gates are fhut; the Herald at Arms knocks hard at the Door, the Sheriffs of the City call back, asking who is there? Then the Herald anfwers, *I come to Proclaim, &c.* according to the Name of the Prince who is to fucceed to the Crown, and repeating the Titles of *Great Britain, France* and *Ireland, &c*, at which the Sheriffs open, and bid them Welcome, and fo they go on to the *Exchange*, where they make the laft Proclamation.

This Gate is adorned with the Figures of Kings below, and Traytors above, the Heads of feveral Criminals executed for Treafon being fet up there; the Statues below are of

PLATE XXX

THIS VIEW SHOWS PRINCES STREET, THREADNEEDLE STREET, CORNHILL AND LOMBARD STREET CONVERGING ON
THE SITE OF THE PRESENT MANSION HOUSE AND THE CHURCH OF S? CHRISTOPHERS WHICH LATTER
WAS DEMOLISHED IN 1781 WHEN THE BANK OF ENGLAND WAS ENLARGED.

From a print by Sutton Nicholls, 1720.

Plate XXXI

THE TOWER OF LONDON IN 1715
From a print by Sutton Nicholls published in that year

Queen *Elizabeth* and King *James* I. King *Charles* I. and II. and this is the Fourth Statue of King *Charles* II. which is to be feen in the City of *London*, befides his Picture nobly done at full Length, which was fet up formerly in the *Guild-Hall*.

TEMPLE BAR possesses a history so long and varied that special volumes have been dedicated to its annals. One of these, in its sub-title, calls it ' The City Golgotha,' and notwithstanding the fact that the heads of criminals were once exposed on other prominent places such as Aldersgate and at the Southwark end of London Bridge, it is their exhibition on Temple Bar which has chiefly caught the imagination of Londoners, probably because that structure stood in a central position between the City and the West End.

Young Defoe may have been among the crowds which gazed at the remains there exposed of Sir Thomas Armstrong, who was hanged at Tyburn, in 1684, for complicity in the Rye-House Plot, and later still at those of Sir William Parkins and John Freind, executed for their share in the Assassination Plot of 1696. It was here, too, that Defoe later on in life was himself exposed in the Pillory in 1703 in connection with his famous pamphlet *The Shortest Way with the Dissenters*.

Without entering into the history of the earlier ' Bars ' which stood here, it will be sufficient to state that the one known to Defoe was that which Wren designed and which was set up during the years 1670-2. As a child he may certainly have dimly remembered the earlier one described by Stow, of which Strype says that it was ' a House of Timber, erected across the street, with a narrow gateway, and an entry on the south side of it under the house,' a structure which took the place of what was earlier but a chain stretched across the thoroughfare from posts placed there by the Knights Templar to indicate the City's jurisdiction outside the ancient walls. But such a building must have soon become obliterated from memory when the great architect designed and set up his beautiful entrance to the City. The new gate was embellished by four statues, those of James I and Anne of Denmark, on the east side, and those of Charles I and Charles II, on the west. John Bushnell was responsible for all of them, and they are considered the best things he produced. The decorative stone work on Temple Bar was from the hand of Joshua Marshall who executed the stone pedestal on which Hubert le Soeur's statue of Charles I, at Charing Cross, rests. Marshall, by the way, was Master Mason to the Crown, and it is more than probable that we owe the design of this exquisite pedestal to the genius of Grinling Gibbon.

In 1878, Temple Bar, being found in the way of increasing traffic, was condemned to be taken down. The demolition was completed in the following year, and the stones remained lying in Battersea Park for some ten years, when they were purchased by Sir Henry Meux who had the gate reconstructed as an entrance to Theobalds Park, Waltham Cross, at the end of 1888. Thus one of London's most interesting and outstanding relics was permitted to be set up far away from the City, instead of being re-erected on some spot in London itself.

PUBLIC GAOLS

There are in *London*, and the far extended Bounds, which I now call fo, notwithftanding we are a Nation of Liberty, more publick and private Prifons, and Houfes of Confinement, than any City in *Europe*, perhaps as many as in all the Capital Cities of *Europe* put together; *for Example*:

The *Tower*.	*King's Bench*.
Newgate.	The *Fleet*.
Ludgate.	*Bridewell*.
Marfhalfeas.	The *Dutchy*.
The *Gatehoufe*.	St. *Katherines*.
Two *Counters* in the City.	*Bale-Dock*.
One *Counter* in the Burrough.	*Little-Eafe*.
St. *Martin's le Grand*.	*New-Prifon*.
The *Clink*, formerly the Prifon to the *Stews*.	*New-Bridewell*.
Whitechapel.	*Tottil-Fields Bridewell*.
Finsbury.	Five Night Prifons, called *Round-houfes*, &c.

Tolerated PRISONS

Bethlem or *Bedlam*.

One hundred and Nineteen *Spunging Houfes*.

Fifteen private *Mad-Houfes*.

The King's *Meffengers-Houfes*.

The Serjeant at Arms's Officers Houfes.

The *Black Rod* Officers-Houfes.

Cum aliis.

Three *Peft-houfes*.

The *Admiralty* Officers-Houfes.

Tip-ftaffs Houfes.

Chancery Officers Houfes.

N.B. *All thefe private Houfes of Confinement, are pretended to be like little Purgatories, between Prifon and Liberty, Places of Advantage for the keeping Prifoners at their own Requeft, till they can get Friends to deliver them, and fo avoid going into Publick Prifons; tho' in fome of them, the Extortion is fuch, and the Accommodation fo bad, that Men choofe to be carried away directly.*

This has often been complained of, and Hopes had of Redrefs; but the Rudenefs and Avarice of the Officers prevails, and the Oppreffion is fometimes very great; *but that by the Way.*

'TO SUM UP MY DESCRIPTION'

In a Word; To fum up my Defcription of *London*, take the following Heads; There are in this great Mafs of Buildings thus called *London*,

Two Cathedrals.

Four Choirs for Mufick-Worfhip.

One hundred and Thirty Five Parifh Churches.

Nine New Churches unfinifhed, being part of Fifty appointed to be built.

Sixty Nine Chapels where the Church of *England* Service is perform'd.

Two Churches at *Deptford*, taken into the Limits now defcrib'd.

Twenty Eight Foreign Churches.

Befides Diffenters Meetings of all Perfuafions;

Popifh Chapels; and

One *Jews* Synagogue.

There are alfo, Thirteen Hofpitals, befides leffer Charities, call'd *Alms-houfes*, of which they reckon above a Hundred, many of which have Chapels for Divine Service.

Three Colleges.

Twenty-Seven publick Prifons.

Eight publick Schools, called *Free Schools*.

Eighty Three *Charity Schools*.

Fourteen Markets for Flefh.

Two for live Cattle, befides Two Herb-Markets.

Twenty Three other Markets, as defcrib'd.

Fifteen Inns of Court.

Four Fairs.

Twenty Seven Squares, befides thofe within any fingle Building, as the *Temple*, *Somerfet* Houfe, &c.

Five publick Bridges.

One Town-House, or *Guild-Hall*.

One *Royal Exchange*.

Two other *Exchanges* only for Shops.

One *Cuftom-houfe*.

Three *Artillery* Grounds.

Four *Peft-houfes*.

Two Bifhops Palaces;

and

Three Royal Palaces.

PLATE XXXII

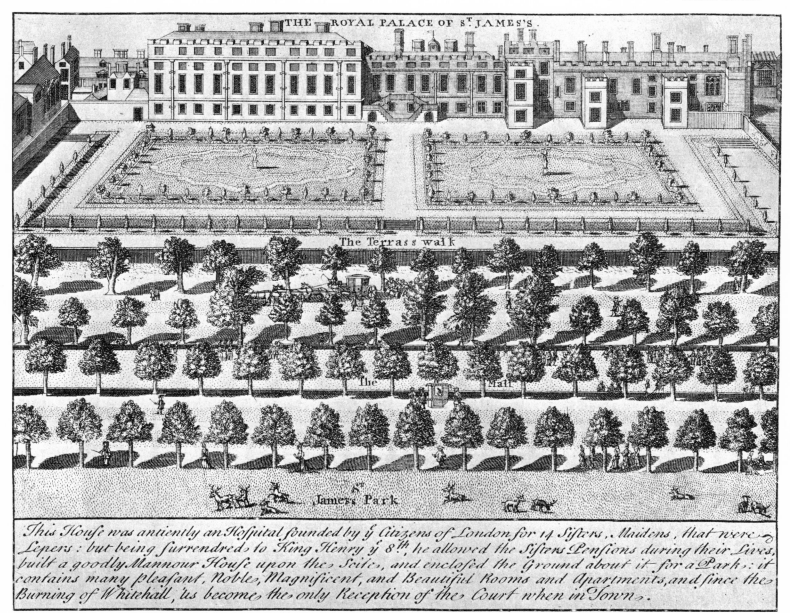

ST. JAMES'S PALACE

(Described by Defoe as " really mean ")

From a print published by John Bowles, 1725

PLATE XXXIII

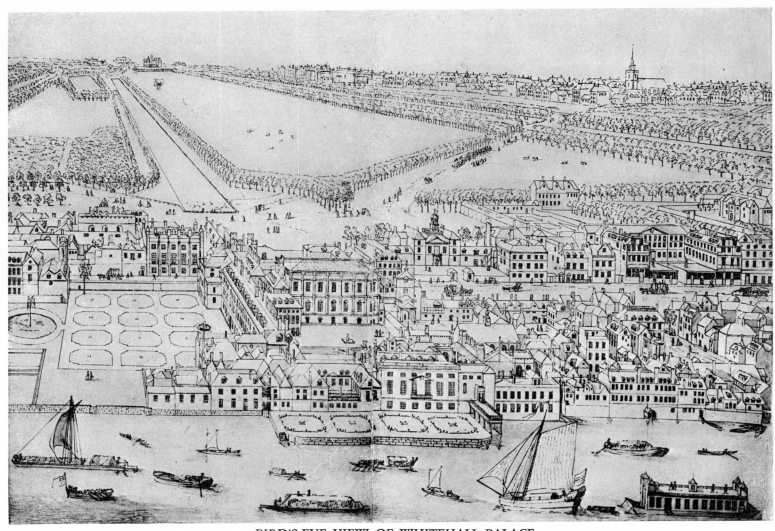

BIRD'S-EYE VIEW OF WHITEHALL PALACE

From an original drawing by Knyff, circa 1720

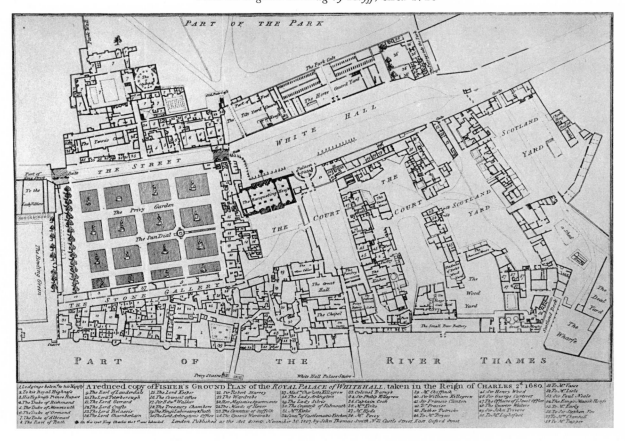

GROUND PLAN OF WHITEHALL PALACE 1680

NOTE.—Knyff's 'bird's-eye' shown above is not to be confounded with the better known but far less complete version of
the subject included by J. T. Smith in his *Antiquities of Westminster*

'The Court End of the Town'

Having dwelt thus long in the City, I mean properly called ſo, I muſt be the ſhorter in my Account of other Things. The Court End of the Town, now ſo prodigiouſly in-creaſed, as is ſaid before, would take up a Volume by itſelf, and, indeed, whole Volumes are written on the Subject.

THE KING'S PALACE OF ST. JAMES 'IS REALLY MEAN'

The King's Palace, tho' the Receptacle of all the Pomp and Glory of *Great Britain*, is really mean, in Compariſon of the rich Furniture within, I mean the living Furniture, the glorious Court of the King of *Great Britain*: The Splendor of the Nobility, the Wealth and Greatneſs of the Attendants, the Oeconomy of the Houſe, and the real Grandeur of the whole Royal Family, out-does all the Courts of *Europe*, even that of *France* itſelf, as it is now managed ſince the Death of *Lewis the Great*.

MANY PROJECTS TO REBUILD THE ANCIENT PALACE OF WHITEHALL

But the Palace of St. *James*'s is, I ſay, too mean, and only ſeems to be Honoured with the Court, while a more magnificent Fabrick may be erected, where the King of *England* uſually reſided, I mean at *White-Hall*.

The Ruins of that Old Palace, ſeem to predict, that the Time will come, when that *Phœnix* ſhall revive, and when a Building ſhall be erected there, ſuiting the Majeſty and Magnificence of the *Britiſh* Princes, and the Riches of the *Britiſh* Nation.

Many Projects have been ſet on foot for the re-building the Antient Palace of *White-hall*; but moſt of them have related rather to a Fund for raiſing the Money, than a Model for the Building: But as I once ſaw a Model for the Palace itſelf, know its Author, and when it was propoſed, and that I ſtill believe that Scheme will, at laſt, be the Ground-Plot of the Work itſelf, I believe it will not be diſagreeable to give a brief Account of the Deſign.

*   *   *   *   *   *   *

Defoe's 'Brief Account of the Design' is printed as an Appendix.

*   *   *   *   *   *   *

Defoe's period was not one which appreciated Gothic architecture, nor, indeed, was it greatly interested in the remains of the past at all, and our author has here some reason to complain of what he calls the meanness of ST. JAMES'S PALACE, as it was in his day. As we see it now, it possesses the picturesqueness which we have come to associate with the mellowness of old red-brick architecture, and we recognise in it a building instinct with innumerable historic memories. To Defoe and his contemporaries it was but an irregular structure little suitable and quite in-adequate for a Court. It must be remembered, too, that much of what we see to-day was not in existence in those times, the palace having been considerably added to in the reign of George II. Happily the beautiful and noble gateway still remains, perhaps the finest relic of the domestic architecture of the time of Henry VIII which is left to us in London.

The fact is, London has never been specially happy in its royal palaces. The first of them, the Tower, was after all rather a fortress than a residence; the next, at Westminster, was small, and had been allowed in Henry VIII's day to fall into decay; St. James's was, in its origins, merely a royal sporting lodge created by Henry out of a leper hospital, and even in the eighteenth century was so unimpressive that Fielding remarked of it, that it ' reflects no honour on the kingdom, and is the jest of foreigners'; Whitehall, by gradual accretions, had become a vast caravanserai, inchoate and formless; and in its early days Buckingham House was but a private house adapted to very modest royal requirements; while even in its rebuilt form as a palace, it seems to have been so unsatisfactory that the Duke of Wellington on one occasion remarked in the House of Lords, that the King of England was 'worse lodged than many private gentlemen.' Had the plans for a new Palace of Whitehall prepared by Inigo Jones for James I in 1619, after the destruction by fire of most of the original Tudor structure, been carried into effect, we might have possessed a royal palace worthy to compare with the finest Continental ones. All we have of that vast conception is the exquisite fragment of the Banqueting House. This luckily escaped destruction in the successive fires of 1691 and 1698 which reduced to the ruinous mass which Defoe here describes the Whitehall of Cromwell and the later Stuarts.

What this rabbit-warren of a Palace looked like in the days of Charles II and the extent of its area can be seen from the accompanying illustrations; what was to have been the general outline of the suggested new palace, of which the precincts were to include all St. James's Park and Spring Gardens and also Buckingham House and its gardens, in addition to a large area of the adjoining streets and buildings which were to be demolished, is indicated in the plans printed in the Appendix. Defoe speaks of having seen a model of this projected palace, and as being acquainted with the creator of the scheme, but he unfortunately does not give us the name of the latter; nor is the former known to exist. But some light is thrown on the matter in the following passage in Strype's edition of Stow:

'Whitehall now lies in Ruines, having been burnt down in the reign of King William. For want of rebuilding the same, Mr. Weedon, an ingenious gentleman, supposed the City of Westminster was damnified above £30 per cent in their Houses, Trades, and Properties. The same gentleman, therefore, of his own good Will for the reforming that most noble Palace, for the Honour and Benefit of the Queen, and her Kingdom, proposed in Print, That an Act of Parliament should be made for the Rebuilding of it, after the Manner of a Model or Plan of *Inigo Jones*, the famous *English* Architect in King *James* the *First's* time, who built the Banqueting House in *Whitehall*, and left a Plan for the whole Palace to be built suitable to it, that being reputed one of the best Buildings in *Europe*; which Plan, his late Majesty viewed and approved of: This Palace to be built after the said Plan, would amount to six hundred thousand pounds, and might be about seven years in building. He propounded, moreover, that the said Structure should extend from the north-east of the first *Scotland Yard*, and be continued to the North Side of the old *Palace-Yard*, at *Westminster*; and the common way to *Westminster* made to run next the Water-side; whereby the new Palace might front *St. James's Park* and the River.'

Strype gives details as to those who should be commissioned to superintend the work; and the means of raising the necessary money, etc. The scheme which Defoe sets forth, whatever its relation may be to that of the Mr. Weedon mentioned by Strype, which obviously dates back to the reign of Queen Anne, and from which it differs in many particulars, never materialised, it being manifestly on far too grandiose a scale ever to have been regarded as a practical proposition. The question of the various plans for a reconstruction of the Palace of Whitehall, generally identified with the name of Inigo Jones, is also dealt with in the Appendix.

This, indeed, is but an Embryo; but it muſt be confeſs'd, it would be a magnificent Building, and would very well ſuit the Grandeur of the *Britiſh* Court: Here a King of *Great Britain* would live like himſelf, and half the World would run over to ſee and wonder at it.

This whole Building, the Perſon projecting it, offered to finiſh, that is to ſay, all the Out-ſide Work, Maſonry and Bricklayers Work, with Plaiſterers, Glaſiers, Plumbers, Carpenters and Joyners Work, Carvers, Stone-Cutters, Copper Work, Iron Work, and Lead, including Balluſtrade and fine Gates, and, in a Word, the whole Palace, except Painting, Gilding, Gardening and Waterworks, for Two Millions Three hundred thouſand Pounds, the King giving Timber, but the Undertaker to cut it down, and bring it to the Place, the King giving the *Portland* Stone alſo, and bringing it by Water to the Place.

Alſo the King to lay in Four thouſand Blocks of *Italian* Marble of the uſual Dimenſions, the Builder to make all the Imagery that are to be made of Stone; but the King to be at the Charge of the Equeſtrian Statues in Braſs; the Builder to form all the Fountains and Baſins for the Water-Works; but all the Pipes, Vaſa, Buſts, and Statues in the Gardens, to be at the King's Expence.

Plate XXXIV

THE HOUSE OF LORDS IN 1755
From a contemporary print by B. Cole

THE HOUSE OF COMMONS IN 1741
From a contemporary print by B. Cole

These illustrations show the two Houses at a somewhat later date than that of Defoe, but represent them essentially as they were in his time, after Wren's alterations and the addition of a gallery to the "Commons," and as they practically remained until their destruction, by fire, in 1834. In the one King George II is shown on the throne with the Commons attending him; in the other Sir Robert Walpole (whose last year of office it was) is addressing the House, and Speaker Onslow is in the Chair.

Plate XXXV

WESTMINSTER HALL AND ADJOINING BUILDINGS

From a wash drawing, circa 1740

This drawing confirms Defoe's remarks as to the appearance of buildings at Westminster as exhibiting 'an air of venerable though ruined antiquity'

THE 'RUIN'D ANTIQUITY' OF THE OLD PALACE AT WESTMINSTER

But I return to the Defcription of Things which really exift, and are not imaginary: As the Court is now ftated, all the Officers and Places for Bufinefs are fcatter'd about.

The Parliament meets, as they ever did, while the Court was at *Weftminfter*, in the King's Old Palace, and there are the Courts of Juftice alfo, and the Officers of the *Exchequer*, nor can it be faid, however convenient the Place is made for them, but that it has a little an Air of venerable, tho' ruin'd Antiquity: What is the Court of *Requefts*, the Court of *Wards*, and the Painted Chamber, tho' lately Repair'd, but the Corps of the old *Englifh* Grandeur laid in State?

Before Henry VIII took possession of Wolsey's palace at Whitehall, on the Cardinal's fall in 1530, the old royal PALACE AT WESTMINSTER had been largely destroyed by a fire which occurred there eighteen years previously, and the king was, no doubt, glad enough to have an excuse for appropriating the splendid residence of his one-time favourite, which stood, as it were, midway between his official and grimmer palace in the Tower and the more rural one at St. James's. What remained from the fire of 1512 principally consisted of what was known as the Painted Chamber, the Star Chamber, St. Stephen's Chapel and Westminster Hall. In old days the Royal Court included the whole official machinery and personnel of Government, so to speak, which have long become separated from it, and thus around the sovereign's abode existed a congeries of buildings housing the Parliament, the Law Courts, the Exchequer, and other portions of what are now known as the Civil Service. The House of Lords, accommodated in what Strype calls ' a fair room,' was at the south end of Westminster Hall, formerly the old Court of Requests; but the House of Commons sat in what had been St. Stephen's Chapel, on the south of the Hall, with large gardens, now chiefly covered by Barry's immense pile, and partly by the famous Terrace overlooking the river. The Court of Exchequer immediately adjoined Westminster Hall on the east; and other offices, such as the Augmentation Court, etc., were domiciled in various adjacent buildings which had been either repaired or newly constructed since the fire of 1512.

The whole, it is true, was anciently the King's Palace or Royal Houfe, and it takes up full as much Ground as the New Palace, which I have given a Scheme of, would do, except only the Gardens and Parks, the Space before it, which is ftill called *Palace-yard*, is much greater than that which would be at the *North* Gate of the Palace of *White-hall*, as propofed. The Gardens, indeed, were not large, but not defpicable neither, being the fame where my Lord *Hallifax*'s Houfe and Gardens now are, and took up all the Ground which we fee now built upon between the River and the Old Palace, where the Tellers of the *Exchequer*, as well as the Auditor, have handfome Dwellings and Gardens alfo.

NEW PALACE YARD, to which Defoe presumably refers, was larger than the present one by which the House of Commons is entered, for Barry's plan of building impinged considerably on it. But both on the north and west of the Yard, where now are Bridge Street and Parliament Square, the ground was covered with small blocks and rows of buildings intersected by narrow streets. It would seem that when Defoe specifies Lord Halifax's house as occupying a portion of the gardens once attached to the Palace of Westminster, he refers to what had been that nobleman's official residence here in his capacity of Auditor of the Exchequer prior to his death in 1715.

In the following paragraphs our author bemoans the comparative meanness of all these public buildings which had been contrived out of what must, after all, have been in his day a more or less ruinous, although not unpicturesque, patchwork medley. And, incidentally, he hints at the danger of employing an incompetent architect in the work of reconstruction. Indeed, the Mr. Benson he names, who was Surveyor of the King's Buildings, was an insignificant and almost a ridiculous person for such a post—a post from which he had been permitted to oust no less a man than Wren himself, through the machinations of his patroness, the Duchess of Kendal (George I's mistress), on the death of Queen Anne in 1714. The story is that because Wren refused to give his consent to certain mutilations (for they were little else) of Hampton Court, which that preposterous lady desired, she obtained his post (not without receiving a *douceur* from

I

the recipient) for Benson, a man who did his best to spoil some part of the general effect of St. Paul's by adding a foolish flight of steps to the chief front, an addition which might have stultified a less noble work. They were removed in 1873.

But, alas! as I fay, tho' they feem now even in their Ruins, great; yet compared to the Beauty and Elegancy of Modern Living, and of Royal Buildings in this Age, what are they!

The Royal Apartments, the Prince's Lodgings, the great Officers Apartments, what are they now, but little Offices for Clerks, Rooms for Coffee-houfes, Auctions of Pictures, Pamphlet and Toy-fhops?

HOW SHORT OF THE DIGNITY OF KING, LORDS AND COMMONS!

Even St. *Stephen*'s Chapel, formerly the Royal Chapel of the Palace, but till lately beautify'd for the Convenience of the Houfe of Commons, was a very indifferent Place, old and decay'd: The Houfe of Lords is a venerable old Place, indeed; but how mean, how incoherent, and how ftraitned are the feveral Avenues to it, and Rooms about it? the Matted Gallery, the Lobby, the back Ways the King goes to it, how fhort are they all of the Dignity of the Place, and the Glory of a King of *Great Britain*, with the Lords and Commons, that fo often meet there?

Some Attempts were made lately, to have reftored the decrepid Circumftances of this Part of the Building, and Orders were given to Mr. *Benfon*, then Surveyor of the King's Buildings, to do his Part towards it; but it was directed fo ill, or underftood fo little, that fome thought he was more likely to throw the old Fabrick down, than to fet it to Rights for which Ignorance and Vanity, 'tis faid, fome have not fared as they deferv'd.

It is true, the Sitting of the Parliament is by the Order of the Houfes themfelves, accommodated as well as the Place will admit; but how much more Beautiful it would be in fuch a Building, as is above contrived, I leave to the Contriver to defcribe, and to other People to judge.

WESTMINSTER HALL

Come we next to *Weftminfter-Hall*; 'tis true, it is a very noble *Gothick* Building, Ancient, vaftly large, and the fineft Roof of its kind in *England*, being One hundred Feet wide; but what a wretched Figure does it make without Doors; the Front, a vaft Pinacle or Pedement, after the moft Ancient and almoft forgotten Part of the *Gothick* Way of Working; the Building itfelf, refembles nothing fo much as a great Barn of Three hundred Feet long, and really looks like a Barn at a Diftance.

Nay, if we view the whole Building from without Doors, 'tis like a great Pile of fomething, but a Stranger would be much at a Lofs to know what; and whether it was a Houfe, or a Church, or, indeed, a Heap of Churches; being huddled all together, with differing and diftant Roofs, fome higher, fome lower, fome ftanding *Eaft* and *Weft*, fome *North* and *South*, and fome one Way, and fome another.

Defoe, like most of his English contemporaries, not excluding the great Wren himself, had no love for gothic—hence his fulmination at the north front of WESTMINSTER HALL. What we should now consider a picturesque and, indeed, beautiful piece of architectural work, he regards as little less than an eye-sore. That the building does, indeed, remotely resemble in its general outlines a barn may be true enough, as is suggested in the contemporary distant view of its long roof from St. James's Park (reproduced in plate xxxvi); but an age that had little reverence for antiquity, unless it was the antiquity of classicism, did not care for the preservation of anything which, characteristic of its period as it may have been, did not fall in with its standard of beauty. Defoe's depreciatory comments are further justified by the fact that in those days all sorts of structures, including even stalls, had been permitted, and were for a considerable period still to be permitted, to stultify the frontage of Westminster Hall, as can be seen from old prints of that building as it was during even the latter part of the eighteenth century.

PLATE XXXVI

A view of Westminster Hall and the Abbey in St. James's Parke

From a view taken in 1670

The Clock Tower, on the left of the picture, was demolished in 1698, and its big bell 'Tom' was recast and re-hung in St. Paul's. This illustration bears out Defoe's description of the Hall as 'really looking like a barn at a distance'

WESTMINSTER HALL

From a drawing by Gravelot engraved by C. Mosley, circa 1720

This illustration represents the first day of Term. It is interesting as showing the milliners and booksellers carrying on their trades amid the business of the law courts

PLATE XXXVII

To BROWNE WILLIS Esq.
whose Grandfather Dr THOMAS WILLIS
the Celebrated Physician was many Years
an Inhabitant of this Parish,
& he bequeath'd to it a perpetual Legacy
for early Morning Prayers, and in the
Evening. This Prospect of the Old Church
was drawn & is humbly inscrib'd by
George Vertue a Native of the said Parish.

THE OLD CHURCH OF ST. MARTIN'S-IN-THE-FIELDS

Pulled down 1720 to make way for Gibbs's present structure   *From a print by G. Vertue*, circa 1720

THE OLD BROADWAY CHAPEL, WESTMINSTER
From a contemporary wash drawing

In those days WESTMINSTER HALL was the chief Law Court of London, and here and in the large annexe which was erected on the spot where the statue of Cromwell now stands, the legal business of the country was carried on till 1880, when the new Law Courts in the Strand were ready for occupation. That glorious structure, ' Rufus's Roaring Hall,' as it was once called, presented then a far gayer and more animated appearance than it does to-day. Its sides were lined with booths where all sorts of things from books to bodkins were on sale, the former at one time being sold by the poor scholars of Westminster School between school hours. It was a recognised lounging-place for others besides those who came to consult the lawyers who were to be seen walking about it in wig and gown, including those who used to sell themselves as witnesses and whose badge of their calling was a wisp of straw in their shoes. Defoe himself may well have seen it bright with the standards taken at Blenheim which were brought here in solemn procession, in 1704. There had been a precedent for such decoration of the place, for Strype tells us that, as a boy, he remembers seeing on one side hung up the flags taken by the victors at the Battle of Worcester, flags which, it is needless to say, were promptly taken down on the Restoration.

That noble hall—with one exception the largest in the world unsupported by pillars—cannot but strike the imagination, as one stands amidst its vast area, not only because of its proportions and its glorious roof, but because there is about it an aura of romance and tragedy. Rufus may have made the rafters ring with the boisterous merriment of his day when he and his vassals held wassail here; Richard II may have complacently gazed at the structure which he rebuilt; Peter the Great is related to have made his characteristic joke about the lawyers in its precincts, for, when on his visit to this country in 1698, he was shown over Westminster Hall and, observing a number of black-gowned figures moving about there, asked who they were; he was told they were lawyers; ' Lawyers!' he replied, ' I have only two in my country, and I think of hanging one of them when I return.' But it is other ghosts than these that chiefly fill it in imagination: Anne Boleyn sitting on ' a scaffold ' at her trial; Strafford deserted by the King he had served so well, that King being legally done to death beneath the banners taken at Naseby; the Seven Bishops being gloriously acquitted; Warren Hastings listening to the fulminations of Sheridan and Burke; and, as a contrast, George IV sitting in glory at the last great Coronation banquet to be held here, while young Dymoke rides in on horseback to throw down his gauntlet in challenge to any who should gainsay the new sovereign's title to the crown.

WESTMINSTER ABBEY—' BEGINS TO STAND ON NEW LEGS NOW '

The Abbey, or Collegiate Church of *Weftminfter*, ftands next to this; a venerable old Pile of Building, it is indeed, but fo old and weak, that had it not been taken in Hand fome Years ago, and great coft beftowed in upholding and repairing it, we might, by this Time, have called it a Heap, not a Pile, and not a Church, but the Ruins of a Church.

But it begins to ftand upon new Legs now, and as they continue to Work upon the Repairs of it, the Face of the whole Building will, in a fhort while, be intirely New.

Defoe's remarks on Westminster Abbey will have been written almost concurrently with the completion of Wren's repairs and with that great man's death in 1723. Before that time it had been permitted to fall into a more or less ruinous condition, but when Wren was appointed surveyor in 1698, he took it in hand, and, so far as he was permitted, repaired portions of it, such as the west towers then only reaching to the roof, and the façade generally. This took some ten years to complete, and owing to various causes was not actually begun till 1713. It was not till some years after Defoe's death that the completion of the towers was effected, either by Hawksmoor, guided perhaps by certain plans Wren had prepared for this purpose, or by James of Greenwich, who was appointed surveyor to the Abbey in 1725. What seems likely is that James superintended the carrying out of Hawksmoor's work, as in the year in which the latter died (March 25th, 1736), Ralph, in his *Critical Review of the Public Buildings*, remarks that ' there is a rumour that the Dean and Chapter still design to raise the towers!' The print of a View from Constitution Hill, dated 1735, reproduced in plate vi, shows one of the towers still unfinished.

This is the Repofitory of the *Britifh* Kings and Nobility, and very fine Monuments are here feen over the Graves of our Ancient Monarchs; the Particulars are too long to enter into here, and are fo many Times defcribed by feveral Authors, that it would be a vain Repetition to enter upon it here; befides, we have by no means any Room for it.

The Monarchs of *Great Britain* are always Crown'd here, even King *James* II. fubmitted to it, and to have it perform'd by a Proteftant Bifhop. It is obfervable, that our Kings and Queens make always Two Solemn Vifits to this Church, and very rarely, if ever, come here any more, *viz.* to be *Crown'd* and to be *Buried*.

'ROYAL ASHES' AND 'COMMON DUST'

Two Things I muft obferve here, and with that I clofe the Account of it.

1. 'Tis very Remarkable, that the Royal Vault, in which the *Englifh* Royal Family was laid, was filled up with Queen *Ann*; fo that juft as the Family was extinct above, there was no Room to have buried any more below.

2. It is become fuch a Piece of Honour to be buried in *Weftminfter-Abbey*, that the Body of the Church begins to be crowded with the Bodies of Citizens, Poets, Seamen and Parfons, nay, even with very mean Perfons, if they have but any way made themfelves known in the World; fo that in Time, the Royal Afhes will be thus mingled with common Duft, that it will leave no Room either for King or common People, or at leaft not for their Monuments, fome of which alfo are rather pompoufly Foolifh, than Solid and to the Purpofe.

How true the author's second remark is, is being realised to-day when there is scarcely space left even for the smallest mural tablet, much less for interments. Had Defoe been writing later he would no doubt have criticised far more severely the crowding of the Abbey with those terrific cenotaphs and statues which were subsequently set up there in such profusion and with such a disregard to space and the gothic beauty of the structure, and which to-day give the place the appearance of a statuary's yard. When our author remarks on the ' mean persons ' buried here, he seems to be re-echoing the utterance of Sir Godfrey Kneller who, on one occasion, exclaimed, ' By God, I will not be buried in Westminster Abbey. They do bury fools there.'

Defoe's reference to the ' Royal Vault ' is to the new one which was built at the east end of the south aisle after the death of Charles II, who was the last to be buried in the vault which had been prepared for Oliver Cromwell and was commonly known as ' Oliver's vault.' Later on, George II and Queen Caroline, and those members of the Hanoverian Royal family who lie in Westminster Abbey, were buried in a new vault under the centre of Henry VII's Chapel.

WESTMINSTER SCHOOL

Near to this Church is the Royal Free-School, the beft of its kind in *England*, not out-done either by *Winchefter* or *Eaton*, for a Number of eminent Scholars.

The Royal Free-School here referred to is, of course, WESTMINSTER SCHOOL, which had been founded by Queen Elizabeth, in 1560, as ' a publique schoole for grammar, rhetorick, Poetrie, and for the Latin and Greek languages.' A still more ancient school appears to have been in existence as an annexe to the Church of St. Peter and Elizabeth's foundation was in the nature of a revival of this. Among the illustrious who had been educated here and who lived during Defoe's day, were Wren and Lord Halifax, John Locke and Robert South, Bishop Atterbury, Cowley, Dryden, and Prior; while the famous Dr. Busby remained head master till his death in 1695, after he had thrashed half a century of recalcitrant scholars. It is interesting, too, to remember that the dormitory was designed by that very able amateur architect, the Earl of Burlington, in 1716, the very year in which the notorious Edmund Curll was whipped and tossed in a blanket by the Westminster boys for having pirated and printed, with a lively disregard to its latinity, one of Dr. South's discourses.

PRIVILEGES AND REVENUES OF THE DEAN AND CHAPTER

The Antiquities of this Church, for it is very Ancient, are publifhed by Two or Three feveral Authors; but are particularly to be feen in *Dugdale's Monafticon*. The Revenues of it were very great, and the Abbot fat as a Spiritual Peer in the Houfe of Lords. The Revenues are ftill very large, and the Dean is generally Bifhop of *Rochefter*; the Fate of the late Bifhop I defire to bury with him, who is gone to Oblivion. The Dean and Chapter have ftill great Privileges as well as Revenues, and particularly the Civil Government, or Temporal Jurifdiction of the City of *Weftminfter*, is fo far in them, that the *High-Steward* and the *High-Bailiff* are named by them abfolutely, without any Referve either to King or People. Their prefent *High-Steward* is the Earl of *Arran*, Brother to the late Duke of *Ormond*, and their *High-Bailiff*, is *William Morris*, Efq.

Defoe's 'several authors' probably refers to J. C. Crull's *Antiquities of the Abbey Church of Westminster*, 2 vols., 3rd edition, 1722, and J. Dart's similar work published in 1723. 'The late Bishop' is, of course, the famous Francis Atterbury, who was made Dean of Westminster and Bishop of Rochester in 1713 and banished as a Jacobite in 1723. He died in Paris in 1732.

THE NEW CHURCH OF ST. JOHN

Being got into this Part of *Weftminfter*, I fhall finifh it as I go, that I may not return; 'Tis remarkable, that the whole City, called properly, *Weftminfter*, and ftanding on the *S*. Side of the Park, is but One Parifh, and is the only City of One Parifh in *England*. There is now another great Church erected, or rather erecting, by the Commiffioners for building Fifty New Churches; but they have been ftrangely miftaken in the Situation, which is a fenny marfhy Ground, and it is not found fo able to fupport the Weight as, perhaps, they were told it would; I fay no more. The Building was very curious, efpecially the Roof; but the Towers are not fo beautiful as it is thought was intended, the Foundation not being to be trufted.

Defoe here notices one of the curious anomalies connected with the CITY OF WESTMINSTER, by which, until quite modern times, although a city, and so constituted by royal charter, it possessed no municipality, but was governed by an official known as the High Steward who was nominated by the Dean of Westminster, and by a High Bailiff, together with a Council of sixteen Burgesses and a similar number of so-called assistants.

The new church above referred to by our author is ST. JOHN'S, in Smith Square. This curious structure was designed by Thomas Archer, a pupil of Vanbrugh. Archer produced a good church in St. Philip's, Birmingham, and one not at all despicable in St. Paul's, Deptford, with its gracefully designed steeple. Unfortunately for his fame he is, however, best known by St. John's, which was begun in 1714 and finished in 1728. Walpole calls it a ' *chef d'œuvre* of absurdity'; while from Lord Chesterfield to Charles Matthews, humorous comparisons have been evoked by its strange outlines, the former likening it to an elephant on its back with its legs in the air; the latter saying that it reminded him of a dinner table in the same position. It was the second of the fifty churches ordered to be built in Queen Anne's reign, and is said to have cost the then considerable sum of £40,000.

The ' fenny marshy Ground ' on which it was erected, proved, as Defoe indicates, disastrous to the structure, for while it was in progress it began to sink, and this caused an alteration of Archer's original plans, a drawing showing which is in the Crowle-Pennant Collection labelled 'Mr. Archer's design for St. John's Church, Westminster, as it was resolved upon by the Commissioners.' This is so different from the completed work, as to show that the latter was an afterthought, necessitated by adverse circumstances; and so Archer hardly, perhaps, deserves all the ridicule that has been lavished on his production.

The Earl of *Peterborough*'s Houfe ftands at the Extremity of the Buildings, and is the Point of Meafurement for the Length of *London*, which from that Houfe to *Lime-houfe*, is reckoned Seven Miles and a Quarter, and fome Rods: This Houfe might have been a Monitor for the Builders of the New Church, for they tell us it has funk feveral Yards, fince it was firft built, tho' this I do not affirm.

There are Three Chapels of Eafe to St. *Margaret*'s in this Part of *Weftminfter*, befides that great Numbers of People go to the *Abbey*, fo that there is no Want of Churches. There is but One Meeting-houfe in this whole Part, which is called *Calamy*'s Meeting, and was formerly fupplied by Mr. *Stephen Lobb*, who, tho' a Diffenter, lived and died a Jacobite.

Of the three Chapels of Ease mentioned by Defoe, the Broadway Chapel was erected primarily through a benefaction of £400 left for the purpose by Dr. Darrell, Prebendary of St. Peter's, Westminster, in 1631. This proving far from sufficient, Sir Robert Pye, whose name is perpetuated in the neighbouring Pye Street where he lived, gave £500 to complete it; while Archbishop Laud contributed £1,000 as well as some stained glass windows. The chapel itself was completed in 1636, but its large burial ground had been used considerably earlier; indeed, the first burial recorded here ' in the new Chapell yard ' was on May 9th, 1627. Among others interred here were Sir William Waller, the Parliamentary leader, and Colonel Blood who stole the Crown from the Tower. Christ Church, erected in 1843, and its precincts mark approximately the old site.

The second chapel was in Queen's Square (now Queen Anne's Gate), and was intended chiefly for the use of the residents in the new houses, which were built there about the beginning of the eighteenth century. It was erected, according to Hatton, in 1706, and the Rate books indicate the importance of some of the residents, those for 1728 including the names of the Earls of Aylesford, Derby, and Warwick; the Bishops of Carlisle and Chichester; Lord Willoughby de Broke, Lord Windsor and Lady Winchelsea.

The third chapel cannot be identified with certainty, but may have been the one erected under the will of Mr. Emery Hill whose Almshouses in Rochester Row, instituted in 1708, were afterwards incorporated with the other local benefactions of Butler and Palmer, and are now housed in the new structure set up on the site of the original buildings in 1884. This of course was intended, primarily, for the use of the inmates of Hill's almshouses.

The *Cottonian* Library is kept here in an Ancient Building, near *Weftminfter-Hall* Gate; we were told it would be removed to the Royal Library, and then, that it would be removed to a Houfe to be built on purpofe; but we fee neither yet in hand. This is one of the moft valuable Collections in *Britain*, and, the *Bodleian* Library excepted, is, perhaps, the beft: It has in it fome Books and Manufcripts invaluable for their Antiquity; but I have not Room fo much as to enter upon giving an Account of the Particulars.

Defoe's remarks on the COTTONIAN LIBRARY may be supplemented by an extract from Strype who thus particularises the spot where Sir Robert Cotton's house once stood: ' In a passage out of Westminster Hall into the Old Palace Yard, a little beyond the stairs going up to St. Stephen's Chapel (now the Parliament House) on the left hand, is the house belonging to the ancient and noble family of the Cottons, wherein is kept a most inestimable library of manuscript volumes, famed both at home and abroad.' This was what Defoe calls an 'Ancient Building,' and Wren reported it to be in a very dilapidated state, when the Crown, which had already purchased the famous library, acquired it in 1707. Defoe would seem here to be at fault with his facts, for it is known that in consequence of the ruinous state of Cotton House the library had in 1712 been removed to Essex House, Strand, and it was not till eighteen years later that it was taken back to Westminster and placed in Ashburnham House, Little Dean's Yard, where in the following year (1731) a disastrous fire destroyed a large number of its treasures.

Some facts concerning the Cottonian Library may be not inappropriately given here. It was formed by Sir Robert Cotton (1571-1631), the noted antiquary and collector, who was the friend of such men as Bacon, Ben Jonson, Speed and Camden, and, indeed, most of the learned of his day. He was an omnivorous gatherer of all sorts of curiosities, but especially of manuscripts, and so large was the number of official documents accumulated by him that the Government regarded it as a source of danger, and Sir Robert having fallen into disfavour with the Court, an opportunity was sought and found to sequestrate his collections in 1629. Although he himself never regained possession of his treasures, his son was able to do so, and they remained in the family, which permitted, however, scholars to have access to them, till 1707, when the founder's grandson sold them to the nation. Such of the books as escaped the fire in 1731 are now in the British Museum, where some of the volumes may be seen bearing marks of the flames.

PLATE XXXVIII

His Majesty's Royal Banqueting House of Whitehal London. 1713.

This print by H. Terasson, shows the entrance to Whitehall Palace; the large weathercock traditionally watched by James II on the approach of the Dutch Fleet in 1688; and a low wall pierced with cannon to cover the approaches of Whitehall from the north

THE NORTH VIEW of the Entrance into St James: Park thro' Queens Square Westminster.   by Jn: Bowles

A contemporary drawing of the new gate (mentioned by Defoe) into St. James's Park, through Queen's Square
John Bowles, del.

PLATE XXXIX

A VIEW OF WHITEHALL SHOWING THE HOLBEIN GATE AND THE ORIGINAL 'HORSE GUARDS'

From a print by J. Kip, 1724.

'LONG, DARK, DIRTY' KING STREET

This Part of *Weftminfter* has but one Street, which gives it a Communication with *London*, and this is called *King-ftreet*, a long, dark, dirty and very inconvenient Paffage; but there feems to be no Remedy for it, for moft Paffengers get out of it through the *Privy Garden*, and fome by private Paffages into the Park, as at *Locket*'s, at the *Cock-Pit*, and the New Gate from *Queen's-Square*; but thefe are all upon Sufferance.

A reference to our detailed plan of this part of Westminster will show what a relatively inconvenient entry from London to Westminster existed in those days, and bears out what Defoe here remarks. By the creation of Parliament Street, *circa* 1756, this disability was, to some extent, removed, and the further widening of that street at its southern end in our own days has created the present splendid thoroughfare from Charing Cross to Parliament Square.

The PRIVY GARDEN which Defoe specifies is to-day represented, as regards a part of its area, by Whitehall Gardens, but was originally the private garden, laid out in the formal Dutch manner, attached to the royal residence.

The principal inlet into the Park was, as we are here told, next to LOCKET'S. This was the well-known eating-house kept by Adam Locket, which stood on the site of Drummond's Bank. Adam Locket died in 1688, but the house continued to be run by Edward Locket till 1702. Apparently the popularity of Locket's gradually decreased after the reign of Queen Anne; but its name, as we here see, survived as a landmark. It would appear by the inclusion of this place among those by which outlets could be obtained from King Street, that that thoroughfare then extended as far as the extreme north end of Whitehall.

The entrance to the Park by the COCKPIT was, no doubt, that now known as Cockpit Steps leading from Dartmouth Street, which perpetuates the name of the Earl of Dartmouth who was living in Queen Square in 1708. This Cockpit, a public one familiar to students of Hogarth from his prints of its interior (1758), is not to be confounded with the Cockpit which, originally a royal cockpit, was used as a sort of private theatre attached to the royal residence, and later on for Government offices. It was part and parcel of old Whitehall Palace and occupied ground on the Park side of that straggling structure, the present Treasury Passage running through a part of its site. How its name came to be applied generally to this section of the old Whitehall Palace is described below.

The NEW GATE from Queen's Square is that which is still used for access to Birdcage Walk; but all these entrances into the Park were then 'private,' as Defoe remarks, which the public were permitted, as now, to use 'on sufferance.'

From hence we come through Two very handfome, tho' Ancient Gates, into the open Palace before *White-Hall* and the *Banqueting-houfe*.

In Defoe's day KING STREET was divided, between Downing Street and the Horse Guards, by two gateways having between them a narrower highway than the portions outside these barriers. The more elaborate of these gateways was known as Holbein's Gate, and sometimes as the Whitehall Gate or the Cock-pit Gate. It was designed for Henry VIII by Holbein, hence, of course, its popular name, and its exact position was between Dover House and the west end of the Banqueting House. It was taken down in 1759. It was constructed in a chequer-work pattern of stones and flint and on each front were four terra-cotta busts. There was at one time some idea of re-erecting the gate at Windsor, but it came to nothing. In a recent exhibition of old furniture there were shown three coloured busts which are said to have adorned Holbein's Gate. They are attributed to Torrigiano, the great Italian sculptor, who executed the tomb of Henry VII in the Abbey. The annexed illustration shows the gate in its relation to the Banqueting House. Its companion gateway—the King's or King Street Gate, as it was indifferently called—is described by Smith, in his *Antiquities of Westminster*, as having four towers, and as being adorned on the south side 'with pilasters and an entablature of the Ionic order.' It is said to have been removed in 1723, in which case Defoe must have been referring to it only just before its destruction.

Having mentioned *White-Hall* already, I have nothing more to fay of it, but that it was, and is not, but may revive. There is, doubtlefs, a noble Situation, fit to contain a Royal Palace, equal to *Verfailles*; but I have given you my Thoughts on that Subject at large.

THE COCKPIT

Nor can I dwell here upon a Defcription of his Majefty's Court, or an Account of the Politicks managed there; it does not relate to this Work; let it fuffice to fay, His Majefty refides, efpecially all the Winter, at St. *James*'s; but the Bufinefs of the Government, is chiefly carried on at the *Cock-pit*: This is a Royal Building, was once Part of *White-hall*, firft the Duke of *Monmouth* lived in it, then Prince *George* of *Denmark* and his Princefs, afterwards Queen *Ann*, and fince the Fire at *White-Hall*, the *Treafury*, the *Secretary*'s Office, the *Council Chamber*, the *Board of Trade*, and the Lord *Chamberlain*, hold all their particular Offices here; and here there is alfo, a By-way out of *Duke-ftreet* into the Park.

When Defoe remarks that ' the Business of the Government is chiefly carried on at the Cockpit' and that the Duke of Monmouth once lived in it, he is not referring to the actual building known as the Cock-Pit, but that portion of the palace which abutted on it, and lay between it and King Street, on which thoroughfare the Duke's front windows looked. As a matter of fact, there was another set of apartments between these, which had been occupied, in Charles II's time, by the Duke of Albemarle whose lodgings also stretched to the Park on the south side of the Cockpit. The fact is the name became applied to all this quarter of the rambling Whitehall Palace, which accounts for the statement that it was used as a Government Office. One of the residential portions had been allotted to George Villiers, second Duke of Buckingham, in 1673, and he probably sold it to Sir Thomas Osborne, afterwards Duke of Leeds, as it is known that on the marriage of the Princess Anne with Prince George of Denmark, these apartments were purchased from the latter Duke and settled on the young couple. On the burning of Whitehall in 1697, this portion of the palace escaped, the Cockpit being used as a committee room for the Privy Council, and it was here that the Commissioners dealing with the Union of England and Scotland sat in 1705, and Guiscard stabbed Harley, Earl of Oxford, in 1711.

THE HORSE GUARDS

From thence we come to the Horfe Guards, a Building commodious enough, built on purpofe, as a Barrack for a large Detachment of the Horfe-Guards, who keep their Poft here, while attending on Duty; over it are Offices for Payment of the Troops, and a large Court of Judicature, for holding Councils of War, for Tryal of Deferters and others, according to the Articles of War.

When Defoe speaks of the HORSE GUARDS he is, of course, not referring to the present structure which did not come into being till 1751-3, when it was erected by John Vardy working on plans prepared by Kent who had died in 1748, subsequent additions being made during the years 1756-60. The previous Horse Guards had been built in 1641 ' for Gentlemen Pensioners who formed the Guard,' no standing army being in existence at that time.

THE ADMIRALTY

In the fame Range of Buildings, ftood the *Admiralty* Office, built by the late King *William*; but tho' in itfelf a fpacious Building, is found fo much too Narrow now the Bufinefs is fo much increafed, and as there is a fufficient Piece of fpare Ground behind it, to inlarge the Building, we find a new and fpacious Office is now building in the fame Place, which fhall be fufficient to all the Ufes required.

Originally the ADMIRALTY was housed in a mansion which had belonged to Judge Jefferies, at the junction of Duke Street and Delahay Street, Westminster. This proving too small for its purpose the office was moved about the year 1695 to old Wallingford House, formerly the residence of George Villiers, Duke of Buckingham, as is shown by an extant grant, dated that year, of a portion of Spring Gardens for use in conjunction with the new headquarters. In course of time Wallingford House was also found to be too limited for the increasing activities of the

PLATE XL

THE ADMIRALTY OFFICE, WHITEHALL

Since " deservedly veiled," according to Horace Walpole, by Adam's " handsome screen."

From a print by T. Bowles, 1731

PLATE XLI

THE STATUE OF KING CHARLES I AT CHARING CROSS

From a print by Sutton Nicholls

Exceptional interest attaches to this particular view, looking from the Strand towards the Haymarket, as showing the statue surrounded by iron rails, the stand for sedan chairs around it, and on the right the old Royal mews, approximately where the Nelson monument now is

NORTHUMBERLAND HOUSE AND THE GOLDEN CROSS INN AT CHARING CROSS

From a print published by Sayers

Navy, and in 1722 Thomas Ripley, the architect with Colin Campbell, of Sir Robert Walpole's seat, Houghton Hall, was commissioned to draw out designs for a new building. This was duly begun in 1722 and finished towards the close of 1725, the French traveller, De Saussure, noting on December 16th of that year that it had then been ' recently completed.' At this time an unsightly wall enclosed the courtyard, and it was not till 1760 that Robert Adam was commissioned to erect his screen, as it is to-day, in its place—a screen which even Walpole, generally an unfriendly critic of this architect, allowed to be ' handsome.'

This Office is, perhaps, of the moſt Importance of any of the publick Parts of the Adminiſtration, the Royal Navy being the Sinews of our Strength, and the whole Direction of it being in the Hands of the Commiſſioners for executing this Office. The *Navy* and the *Victualling* Offices, are but Branches of this Adminiſtration, and receive their Orders from hence, as likewiſe the Docks and Yards receive their Orders from the Navy: The whole being carried on with the moſt exquiſite Order and Diſpatch. The *Admiralty* has been in Commiſſion ever ſince the Death of Prince *George*; the present Commiſſioners are, Right Honourable *James* Earl of *Berkeley;* Sir *John Jennings; John Cockburn*, Eſq; *William Chetwynd*, Eſq; Sir *John Norris;* Sir *Charles Wager; Daniel Pultney*, Eſq.

CHARING CROSS: ' A MIXTURE OF COURT AND CITY '

From this Part of the Town, we come into the publick Streets, where nothing is more remarkable than the Hurries of the People; *Charing-Croſs* is a mixture of Court and City; *Man*'s Coffee-houſe is the *Exchange-Alley* of this Part of the Town, and 'tis perpetually throng'd with Men of Buſineſs, as the others are with Men of Play and Pleaſure.

From hence advancing a little, we ſee the great Equeſtrian Statue of King *Charles* the Firſt in Braſs, a coſtly, but a curious Piece; however, it ſerves ſufficiently, to let us know who it is, and why erected there. The Circumſtances are Two, he faces the Place where his Enemies triumph'd over him, and triumphs, that is, tramples in the Place where his Murtherers were hang'd.

' THE KING'S STABLES CALLED THE MEUSE '

From this Place due *North*, are the King's Stables, called the *Meuſe*, where the King's Horſes, eſpecially his Coach-Horſes, are kept, and the Coaches of State are ſet up; it is a very large Place, and takes up a great deal of Ground, more than is made Uſe of: It contains Two large Squares, beſides an Out-let *Eaſt*, where is the Managerie for teaching young Gentlemen to Ride the great Saddle; in the middle of the firſt Court is a Smith or Farryer's Houſe and Shop, a Pump and Horſe-Pond, and I ſee little elſe remarkable, but old ſcatter'd Buildings; and, indeed, this Place ſtanding where a noble Square of good Buildings might be erected, I do not wonder that they talk of pulling it down, contracting the Stables into leſs Room, and building a Square of good Houſes there, which would, indeed, be a very great Improvement, and I doubt not will be done.

This passage is interesting: first, because it gives some details of the interior of the Royal Mews; and secondly, because Defoe here anticipates the Trafalgar Square about a century later. The ROYAL MEWS occupied the ground now partly covered by the National Gallery and the larger part of Trafalgar Square. Rocque's plan shows the two large squares here referred to by Defoe, the smaller of which was then called The Green Meuse. South of this and partly divided from it by the range of stables was the other large enclosed space known as the Royal Meuse, the gateway of which stood approximately where the Nelson statue now is, flanked by shops on each side, the whole forming a kind of convex frontage to the street, with King Charles's statue just in front of it. An excellent view of this portion of the Mews is obtained from the accompanying rare illustration, which, unlike the majority of views of this spot, shows it in its original state before Kent's reconstruction.

It is not to be supposed that the Meuse here described by Defoe resembled the building of which so many illustrations are to be met with in later Eighteenth century prints, representing the place as rebuilt by Kent in 1732. What Defoe here describes was essentially that which had been erected, in the reign of Edward VI, on the site of a still earlier one dating from the time of Richard II, when not horses but falcons (hence the supposed derivation of the name) were kept here while they *mewed* or moulted their feathers.

When the construction of Trafalgar Square and the National Gallery was decided on in 1829, thus fulfilling Defoe's prophetic suggestion, the Mews was of course taken down and the great square, as we know it, was finally completed in 1841.

NORTHUMBERLAND HOUSE

On the right Side of the Street, coming from *White-Hall*, is *Northumberland-Houfe*, fo called, becaufe belonging to the *Northumberland* Family for fome Ages; but defcending to the Duke of *Somerfet* in Right of Marriage, from the late Dutchefs, Heirefs of the Houfe of *Piercy*.

'Tis an Ancient, but a very good Houfe, the only Miffortune of its Situation is, its ftanding too near the Street; the back part of the Houfe is more Modern and beautiful than the Front, and when you enter the Firft Gate, you come into a noble fquare fronting the fine Lodgings: 'Tis a large and very well defign'd Building, and fit to receive a Retinue of One hundred in Family; nor does the Duke's Family come fo far fhort of the Number, as not very handfomely to fill the Houfe.

The prefent Duke having married the greateft Heirefs in *Britain*, and enjoy'd her and the Eftate for above Forty Years, and befides, having been Mafter of the Horfe many Years alfo, he is immenfely Rich, and very well merits the good Fortune he has met with.

NORTHUMBERLAND HOUSE, one of the finest and, historically and architecturally, most interesting of London's great private palaces, was erected by Henry, first Earl of Northampton, who had purchased the site once occupied by a cell and chapel called St. Mary Rouncivall. He is said by some to have been his own architect, but it is more likely that he employed Bernard Janson and Gerard Chrismas, with perhaps some assistance from a contemporary architect, Moses Glover, to design the house, which was completed in 1605. Lord Northampton bequeathed the place to his nephew, the first Earl of Suffolk, whose daughter was married here to Lord Broghill, an event which gave rise to Suckling's famous ' Ballad on a Wedding,' the first lines of which run:

> ' At Charing Cross, hard by the way
> Where we (thou know'st) do sell our hay,
> There is a house with stairs.'

Suckling describes the wedding as a country yokel might be supposed to do: hence the reference to the house having stairs, and to the neighbouring haymarket.

Lord Suffolk (who had added a river front to the mansion) died in 1626, and it was his granddaughter, married, as his second wife, to the 10th Earl of Northumberland, who brought the place into the possession of the Percy family. Eventually it descended to Lady Elizabeth Percy, daughter of the 10th Earl of Northumberland, who had as a child been married to the Earl of Ogle, son of the Duke of Newcastle. Lord Ogle, however, died before he and his wife had lived together; and Lady Ogle was then married to Thomas Thynne, 'Tom of Ten Thousand,' in 1681. These two also never lived together, and after Thynne's murder by Konigsmarck in the Haymarket in 1682, Lady Elizabeth Thynne became the wife of the 6th Duke of Somerset.

This Duke of Somerset thus obtained combined wealth and influence, in addition to his own, from the Percies and the Thynnes, and although Defoe here remarks that he merits his good fortune, other contemporary writers are not so lenient. He was known as ' The Proud Duke,' and extant anecdotes, as well as the record of Swift, confirm the fact that he was imperious to a remarkable degree even for those days. His Duchess died in 1722, he himself in 1748. His Mastership of the Horse lasted from 1702 to 1712.

Innumerable pictures and prints of this part of the city show Northumberland House, and those who remember it before its demolition in 1874 will realise the truth of Defoe's criticism that, as may be seen in the accompanying illustration, it stood far ' too near the street'; in fact, its long frontage immediately abutted on the pavement, and it had become stultified by shops of small character built cheek by jowl with it, among them being Coles's Truss warehouse, immortalised in *Friendship's Garland*, by Matthew Arnold, who makes ARMINIUS apostrophise ' a Coles's Truss Manufactory standing where it ought not, a glorious monument of individualism and industrialism, to adorn the " finest site in Europe." '

THE NEW HAYMARKET THEATRE

Advancing hence to the *Hay-Market*, we fee, Firſt, the great New Theatre, a very magnificent Building, and perfectly accommodated for the End for which it was built, tho' the Entertainment there of late, has been chiefly Operas and Balls.

Theſe Meetings are called BALLS, the Word *Maſquerade* not being ſo well reliſhed by the *Engliſh*, who, tho' at firſt fond of the Novelty, began to be ſick of the Thing on many Accounts; However, as I cannot in Juſtice ſay any thing to recommend them, and am by no means, to make this Work be a Satyr upon any Thing; I chooſe to ſay no more; but go on.

In Defoe's day the HAYMARKET had not become a misnomer perpetuating the memory of what had once been. It was an actual market for hay and such like commodities, dating from 1664, the year in which St. James's Fair, which was formally held here, was suppressed, and successive acts of William and Mary deal with it as such. Then there was a toll-gate at its upper end and the Phœnix Inn at the lower was a popular resort; while other hostelries in it during the eighteenth century were the Black Horse and the Blue Posts. But notable people also inhabited it including Dr. Garth and the Duke of Dorset (in whose house Lord George Sackville was born in 1716); and here Mrs. Nance Oldfield resided and Joseph Addison wrote his *Campaign*.

The theatre referred to was not that which had been opened in December 1721 just north of the present Haymarket Theatre and was called 'The Little Theatre,' but Vanbrugh's Opera House on the west side of the street.

Defoe is obviously restraining his inclination to introduce more scathing comments on the subject of Balls and Masquerades, feeling that they would be out of place in his topographical description, but his few caustic words leave no doubt in the reader's mind as to his attitude towards these entertainments which had recently become a Society vogue, conducing much to its immorality. They continued to flourish for many years under the special patronage of George II and the management of the notorious Heidegger in spite of Hogarth's satires, Church sermons, the Society for the Reformation of Manners—and even a Royal Proclamation. Heidegger was presented by the Grand Jury of Middlesex in 1729 as the ' principal promoter of vice and immorality.' The name Masquerade was once more changed, this time to Ridotto, and this appears to have been the sole result of the popular outcry.

From hence *Weſtward* and *Northward*, lie thoſe vaſtly extended Buildings, which add ſo exceedingly to the Magnitude of the whole Body, and of which I have already ſaid ſo much: It would be a Taſk too great for this Work, to enter into a Deſcription of all the fine Houſes, or rather Palaces of the Nobility in theſe Parts: To touch them ſuperficially, and by halves, is too much to imitate what I complain of in others, and as I deſign a particular Account of all the Houſes of the Nobility and Men of Quality in *London*,* and the Country Fifteen Miles round, in a Work by itſelf; I beſpeak my Readers Patience, and go on.

* There is no evidence that Defoe carried out this project.

The Hospitals and Charities of London

—————————✎—————————

The Hofpitals in and about the City of *London*, deferve a little further Obfervation, efpecially thofe more remarkable for their Magnitude, as,

I. BETHLEM OR BEDLAM*

This and *Bridewell*, indeed, go together, for though they are Two feveral Houfes, yet they are Incorporated together, and have the fame Governors; alfo the Prefident, Treafurer, Clerk, Phyfician and Apothecary are the fame; but the Stewards and the Revenue are different, and fo are the Benefactions; but to both very great.

The Orders for the Government of the Hofpital of *Bethlem* are exceeding Good, and a remarkable Inftance of the good Difpofition of the Gentlemen concerned in it, efpecially thefe that follow;

1. That no Perfon, except the proper Officers who tend them, be allowed to fee the Lunaticks of a *Sunday*.

2. That no Perfon be allowed to give the Lunaticks ftrong Drink, Wine, Tobacco or Spirits, or to fell any such thing in the Hofpital.

3. That no Servant of the Houfe fhall take any Money given to any of the Lunaticks to their own Ufe; but that it fhall be carefully kept for them till they are recovered, or laid out for them in fuch things as the Committee approves.

4. That no Officer or Servant fhall beat or abufe, or offer any Force to any Lunatick; but on abfolute Neceffity. The reft of the Orders are for the good Government of the Houfe.

This Hofpital was formerly in the Street now called *Old Bedlam*, and was very Ancient and Ruinous: The New Building was Erected at the Charge of the City in 1676, and is the moft beautiful Structure for fuch a Ufe that is in the World, and was finifhed from its Foundation in Fifteen Months; it was faid to be taken ill at the Court of *France*, that it was built after the Fafhion of one of the King of *France*'s Palaces.

The Number of People who are generally under Cure in this Hofpital, is from 130 to 150 at a Time.

There are great Additions now making to this Hofpital, particularly for the Relief and Subfiftence of Incurables, of which no full Account can be given, becaufe they are not yet finifhed, or the full Revenue afcertained: The firft Benefactor and Author of this Defign itfelf, was Sir *William Withers* late Alderman, and who had been Lord Mayor, who left 500*l.* to begin it with.

II. THE HOSPITAL OF BRIDEWELL

as it is an Hofpital, fo it is alfo a Houfe of Correction. The Houfe was formerly the King's City Palace; but granted to the City to be in the Nature of what is now called a Workhoufe, and has been fo employed, ever fince the Year 1555.

As Idle Perfons, Vagrants, &c, are committed to this Houfe for Correction, fo there are every Year, feveral poor Lads brought up to Handicraft Trades, as Apprentices, and of thefe the Care is in the Governors, who maintain them out of the ftanding Revenues of the Houfe.

There are two other *Bridewells*, properly fo called, that is to fay, Houfes of Correction; one at *Clarkenwell*, called *New Prifon*, being the particular *Bridewell* for the County of *Middlefex*, and another in *Tuttle-fields*, for the City of *Weftminfter*.

* An Annotation on Bedlam Hospital will be found on page 25.

PLATE XLII

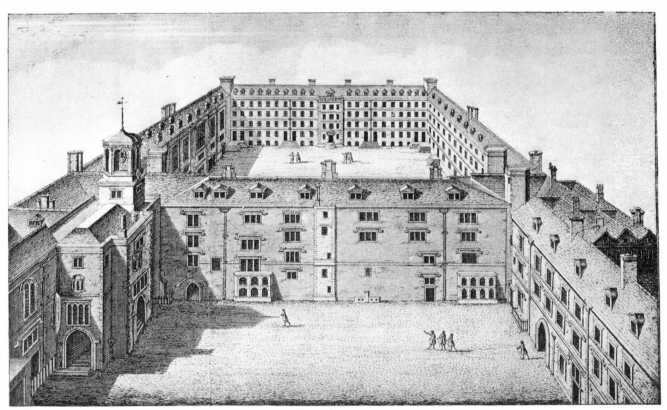

BRIDEWELL
From a print by J. Kip, 1720

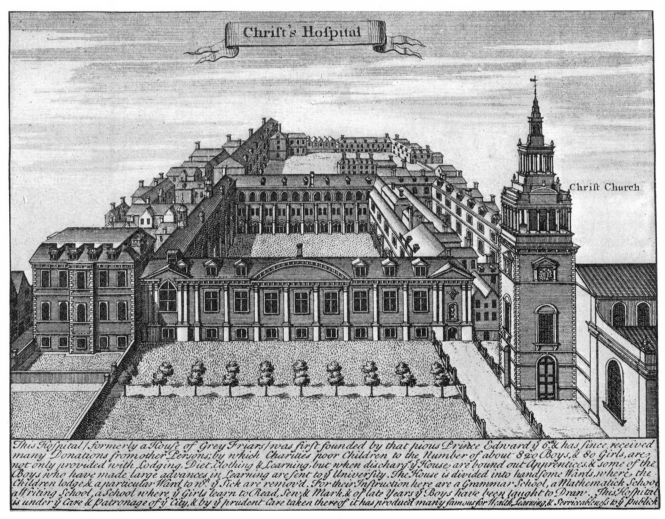

CHRIST'S HOSPITAL
From a print published by John Bowles, 1725

PLATE XLIII

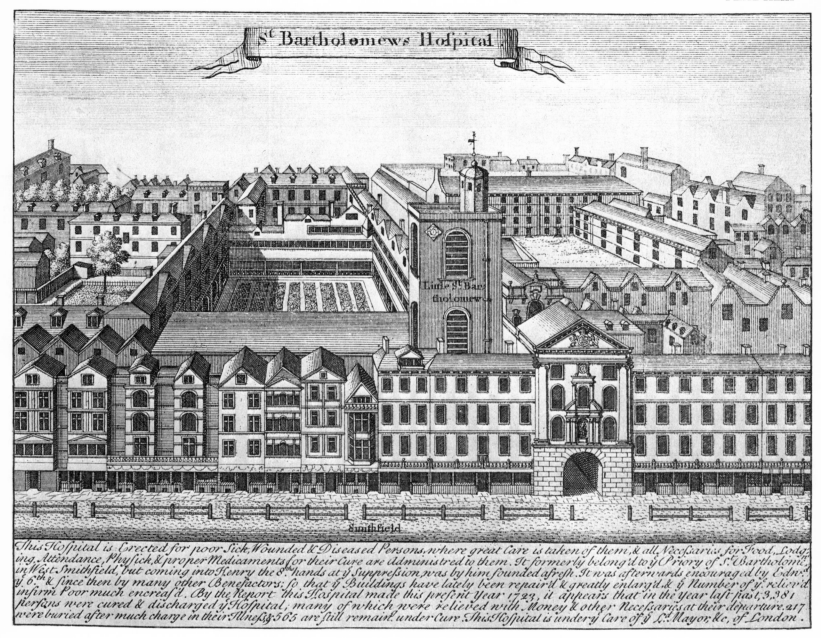

ST. BARTHOLOMEW'S HOSPITAL

From a print published by John Bowles, 1725

The Palace of BRIDEWELL, named after the old Holy Well of the adjoining Parish Church of St. Bride's in Fleet Street, was originally erected by Henry VIII in 1522, but the proximity of the then unsavoury Fleet River rendered it impossible as a royal dwelling and it was handed over by Edward VI to the City as a Poor House and a House of Correction in 1553, the confirmatory Charter only being signed ten days before the King's death. The aim of the City Fathers, urged on by Bishop Ridley, was the correction and reformation of the ' idle apprentices,' vagrants and immoral women of the day, something on the lines of our modern Borstal.

The place was destroyed in the Great Fire, but was rebuilt in 1668, and from then onwards became the chief centre where beggars and loose-women and such-like were confined; being later on united to Bethlehem Hospital and managed by a single board of Governors. Its history during the eighteenth century is a curious one, references to it being found, by and large, in the literature of the period, when it became notorious not only as a sort of prison, but as a show-place where the *haut ton* was frequently to be seen impelled there by curiosity and even less respectable motives. The place was cleared away in the 'sixties of the last century, but its name is perpetuated in Bridewell Place which runs through a portion of its site. The main part of that site is let off for business premises, but the Governors of Bridewell and Bethlehem still have their offices here, with a large Court Room hung with pictures including the famous contemporary painting of Edward VI granting the Royal Charter of Endowment to the Lord Mayor.

In course of time the term ' Bridewell ' came to be used more for what we should call a workhouse, the corrective and reformatory element of the original institution having no part in the newer one. Defoe mentions the other two existing in his day. That at Clerkenwell dated from 1615 when a House of Correction was built at the east end of Clerkenwell ' upon a large garden plot' purchased for the purpose, and it was a sort of overflow place for its earlier namesake. Here, says Hatton, writing in 1708, ' idle loose persons in the County are set to work, and those guilty of lewdness, night-walking, picking of pockets, etc., are corrected.' It possessed twelve separate wards, with a gallery for females, and a courtyard common to both sexes for daily exercise, as shown in the illustration. In 1804 it was removed, its site being occupied by what was called the New Prison which remained till 1877, having in the meanwhile become a House of Detention.

The second Bridewell was in Tothill Fields adjoining the Green Coat Hospital and was ' a place for the correction of such idle and loose livers as are taken up within this Liberty of Westminster, and thither sent by the Justices of the Peace for correction; which is whipping, and beating of hemp (a punishment very well suited to idleness); and are thence discharged by order of the Justices, as they in their wisdom may find occasion. The keeper of this Bridewell is Mr. Reading.' There was yet another Bridewell, which Defoe does not, by the way, mention; perhaps because it was more generally entitled White Lyon Prison. It occupied a site between Queen's Bench Prison and St. George's Church, in Southwark, and it was on a portion of its site that the later Marshalsea, associated by Dickens with the fortunes of the Dorrit family, was erected in 1811.

The other City Hoſpitals, are the *Blue-coat* Hoſpital for poor Freemen's Orphan Children, and the Two Hoſpitals for Sick and Maimed People, as St. *Bartholomew*'s and St. *Thomas*'s: Theſe Three are ſo well known by all People that have ſeen the City of *London*, and ſo univerſally mention'd by all who have written of it, that little can be needful to add; however, I ſhall ſay ſomething as an Abridgment.

III. CHRIST'S HOSPITAL

was originally conſtituted by King *Edward* VI. who has the Honour of being the Founder of it, as alſo of *Bridewell*; but the original Deſign was, and is owing to the Lord Mayor and Aldermen of *London*, and the Chriſtian Endeavours of that Glorious Martyr, Dr. *Ridley* then Biſhop of *London*, who never ceaſed moving his Charitable Maſter, the King, till he brought him to join in the Foundation. The Deſign is for entertaining, educating, nouriſhing and bringing up the poor Children of the Citizens, ſuch as, their Parents being dead, or Fathers, at leaſt, have no way to be ſupported, but are reduced to Poverty.

Of theſe, the Hoſpital is now ſo far increaſed in Subſtance, by the Benefaſtions of worthy Gentlemen Contributors, they now maintain near a Thouſand, who have Food, Cloathing and Inſtruſtion, uſeful and ſufficient Learning, and exceeding good Diſcipline; and at the proper Times they are put out to Trades, fuitable to their feveral Genius's and Capacities, and near Five thoufand Pounds a Year are expended on this Charity.

CHRIST'S HOSPITAL, or the Blue-Coat School, as it is more generally termed, was inftituted in 1553, at the same time as Bridewell, and both were largely due, as our author states, to the exertions of Bishop Ridley, which found fallow ground in the receptive and still active mind of the dying boy-King. But work on the old thirteenth-century Greyfriars premises had been begun to this end during the previous year, according to Stow, and from what he says, something like a systematized school must have been already set on foot, at least six months before the charter was actually signed. The original building suffered so considerably in the Great Fire that it was found necessary to rebuild it, and this was done by Sir John Frederick, at a cost to himself of more than £5,000, in 1680, probably more or less on the architectural lines of the earlier structure which Evelyn mentions in 1657 as ' a very goodly gothic building.' Another contemporary bene-factor, indeed a still larger one than Sir John Frederick, was Sir Robert Clayton whose gifts to the institution were recorded beneath the statue of Edward VI over the entrance. To-day Christ's Hospital has migrated (since 1902) to Horsham, and the site of the old school is absorbed in the new buildings of the General Post Office and St. Bartholomew's Hospital.

IV. ST. BARTHOLOMEW'S HOSPITAL

adjoyns to *Chrift* Church, and St. *Thomas*'s is in *Southwark*, both which, however, being the fame in kind, their Defcription may come under one Head, tho' they are, indeed, Two Foundations, and differently Incorporated: The firft Founder is efteem'd to be King *Henry* VIII. whofe Statue in Stone and very well done, is, for that very Reafon, lately erected in the new Front, over the Entrance to the *Cloyfter* in *Weft-Smithfield*: The King gave 500 Marks a Year, towards the Support of the Houfe, which was then founded for an Hundred poor Sick, and the City was obliged to add 500 Marks a Year more to it.

From this fmall Beginning, this Hofpital rofe to the Greatnefs we now fee it arrived at, of which take the following Account for One Year, *viz.* 1718;

Cur'd and difcharg'd, of Sick, Maimed and Wounded, from all Parts 3088
Buried at the Expence of the Houfe 198
Remaining under Cure 513

ST. BARTHOLOMEW'S was originally founded by Rahere in 1123, and was part and parcel of his splendid Priory, although it seems to have been in certain respects independent. After a number of revisions of the relations between the two foundations, the Hospital first became a distinctly separate institution when Henry VIII, in 1544, refounded it, confirming the charter he then gave by a new one in 1547. But it was in Defoe's own day—that period when scientific activity first began to make itself felt under the friendly ægis of a sovereign who showed a marked leaning for such investigations, a fact often overlooked in estimating the character of Charles II—that a more systematic attempt at improving the character of the hospital was set in hand. Then (1662) students attended anatomical classes and a library of medical books was first formed; while Defoe lived to see an Anatomical and Chirurgical Museum instituted in 1724, under the super-vision of John Freke at that time assistant-surgeon here.

V. ST. THOMAS'S HOSPITAL

in *Southwark*, has a different Foundation, but to the fame Purpofe; it is under the fame Government, *viz.* the Lord Mayor, Aldermen and Commonalty of the City of *London*, and had a Revenue of about 2000 *l. per Annum*, about 100 Years ago.

This Hofpital has received greater Benefactions than St. *Bartholomew*'s; but then 'tis alfo faid to have fuffered greater Loffes, efpecially by feveral great Fires in *Southwark* and elfewhere, as by the Neceffity of expenfive Buildings, which, notwithftanding the

PLATE XLIV

ST. THOMAS'S HOSPITAL

From a print published by Bowles in 1720

(The original site of this Hospital, in Southwark, is now occupied by the London Bridge Railway Station)

PLATE XLV

GUY'S HOSPITAL AS IT APPEARED WHEN OPENED IN 1725

From a contemporary print by John Bowles

charitable Gifts of divers great Benefactors, has coft the Hofpital great Sums. The State of this Hofpital is fo advanced at this Time, that in the fame Year as above, *viz.* 1718, the State of the Houfe was as follows;

Cur'd and difcharged of Sick, Wounded and Maimed, from all Parts 3608
Buried at the Expence of the Houfe 216
Remaining under Cure 566

The origin of ST. THOMAS'S HOSPITAL, in Southwark, is not so ancient as that of St. Bartholomew's, but it is sufficiently old, for it dates from 1213 as an almonry founded in connection with the great Priory of Bermondsey which then dominated this district of London. It was not until 1552 that it was actually formed into a hospital in the modern acceptation of the word, when, at the Dissolution, the London citizens purchased the place from the Royal Commissioners for that purpose. For a century and a half the Hospital continued its work in the old building in High Street, Southwark. It was rebuilt during the years 1701-6, one of the chief benefactors being Thomas Guy, who was a Governor of the Hospital. After another century and a half had elapsed the site was sold to the South Eastern Railway, the splendid range of buildings in which the Hospital is now housed being erected with the proceeds in 1868 and opened by Queen Victoria three years later.

VI. GUY'S HOSPITAL

Adjoining to this of St. *Thomas*'s, is lately laid a noble Foundation of a new Hofpital, by the charitable Gift and fingle Endowment of one Perfon, and, perhaps, the greateft of its kind, next to that of *Sutton*'s Hofpital, that ever was founded in this Nation by one Perfon, whether private or publick, not excepting the Kings themfelves.

This will, I fuppofe, be called *Guy*'s Hofpital, being to be Built and Endowed at the fole Charge of one Mr. *Thomas Guy*, formerly a Bookfeller in *Lombard ftreet*, who lived to fee the faid Hofpital not only defign'd, the Ground purchafed and cleared, but the Building begun, and a confiderable Progrefs made in it, and died while thefe Sheets were in the Prefs.

It was not till this Gentleman died, that the World were told it was to be a feparate Hofpital; but it was generally underftood to have been intended for a Ward, or an Addition to the old Hofpital of St. *Thomas*'s, for the Reception of fuch as were accounted Incurable.

But when Mr. *Guy* died, his Will being made publick, it appeared, that it was really a feparate, independent and diftinct Hofpital, under diftinct Governors, and for a feparate Purpofe, to wit, for receiving fuch poor Perfons as have been difmiffed from other Hofpitals as Incurable.

Nor are thefe reftrained to the Patients of the adjoining Hofpital of St. *Thomas* only; but they are allowed to receive fuch from St. *Bartholomew*'s alfo, and alfo from *Bethlehem*, only with this Reftriction as to the latter, That the Number of Incurable Lunaticks fhall never exceed Twenty at a Time.

This Hofpital is, by Mr. *Guy*'s Will, to confift of Two great Squares of Buildings, in which, befides the Offices and Accommodation for neceffary Servants and Overfeers, who muft be lodg'd in the Houfe, fuch as Stewards, Treafurer, Mafters, Matrons, Nurfes, &c. are to be Beds and Apartments furnifhed for Four hundred Patients, who are all to be fupplied with Lodging and Attendance, Food and Phyfick.

THOMAS GUY'S WEALTH AND CHARITIES

What the Revenue, when fettled, will be; what the Building will amount to when finifhed; what the Purchafe of the Land, and what the Expence of finifhing and furnifhing it, cannot be eftimated, 'till it be further look'd into; but we are told without Doors, that befides all the Expence of Purchafe, Building, Furnifhing and Finifhing as above; there will be left more than Two hundred Thoufand Pounds for Endowing the Hofpital with a fettled Revenue, for maintaining the faid Poor, and yet the charitable Founder was fo immenfely Rich, that befides leaving Four hundred Pounds a Year to the *Blue-coat* Hofpital of *London*, and befides Building an Hofpital for Fourteen poor People at *Tamworth* in *Staffordfhire*, where he was chofen Reprefentative; and befides feveral confiderable Charities which he had given in his Life-time; He alfo gave away, in Legacies, to his Relations and others, above a Hundred thoufand Pound more, among which 'tis obfervable, That there is a Thoufand Pounds a piece given to near Eighty feveral Perfons, moft of them of his own Relations; fo that he cannot, as has been faid by fome, be faid to give a great Charity to the Poor, and forget his own Family.

How Mr. *Guy* amafs'd all this Wealth, having been himfelf in no publick Employment or Office of Truft, or Profit, and only carrying on the Trade of a Bookfeller, till within a few Years of his Death, that is not the Bufinefs of this Book; 'tis enough to fay, he was a thriving, frugal Man, who God was pleafed exceedingly to Blefs, in whatever he fet his Hand to, knowing to what good Purpofes he laid up his Gains: He was never Married, and lived to be above Eighty Years old; fo that the natural Improvements of this Money, by common Intereft, after it was firft grown to a confiderable Bulk, greatly increafed the Sum.

This Hofpital is left to the immediate Direction of his Executors, and the Governors, named in his Will, who are at prefent moft of them, if not all, Governors of St. *Thomas*'s Hofpital, and he has appointed them to apply to his Majefty and the Parliament to have them Incorporated. The Executors are as follows:

Sir *Gregory Page*, Bart. appointed alfo to be firft Prefident of the Corporation, when obtained.
John Kenrick, Efq;
John Lade, Efq;
Dr. *Richard Mead*

Charles Joy, Efq; appointed alfo Treasurer of the Houfe.
William Clayton, Efq;
Mr. *Thomas Hollis* Sen.
Mofes Raper, Efq;
Mr. *John Sprint*.

Alfo he defires, That when the Corporation fhall be obtained as above, either by Letters Patent or Act of Parliament, all the Nine Perfons named as above, to be his Executors with the Fourteen following, may be the Firft Committee for managing the faid Charity, *viz.*

Mr. *Benj. Braine*, Sen.
Mr. *Thomas Clarke*
William Cole, Efq;
Dr. *William Crow*
Dr. *Francis Fanquier*
Dr. *Edward Hulfe*
Mr. *Jofhua Gee*

Mr. *Matthew Howard*
Mr. *Samuel Leffingham*
Mr. *Henry Lovell*
Mr. *Samuel Monk*
Mr. *Jofeph Price*
Mr. *Daniel Powell*
Mr. *Thomas Stiles*.

Defoe is here so particular in his description of GUY'S HOSPITAL that there is little to add to his remarks. It may be observed, however, that the exact date when this portion of Defoe's work was being printed, is settled by the author's remark that Guy died ' while these sheets were in the press,' the date of Guy's death, at the age of eighty, being December 27th, 1724. We might assume that at the time when Defoe was penning the words descriptive of Guy's great bene-faction the building of the new hospital had not been begun, from the way in which he phrases his remarks, but the fact is that building had been progressing for some years, that, indeed, the place was built and roofed in, and that it was actually opened within a fortnight of Guy's death, no fewer than sixty patients being admitted on January 6th, 1725. The whole accommodation was arranged to be for four hundred patients, and the building and endowment are stated to have cost just upon £240,000, a large sum in itself, and in those days an enormous one.

As to how Guy, a bookseller in Lombard Street, came to make so much money, it seems fairly certain that the bulk of his wealth accrued, not, as was stated by Nichols in his *Literary Anecdotes*, from the sale of books and discounting sailors' pay warrants, but by judicious manipulations in Government securities, and a prudent buying and selling of South Sea stock, as indicated by Maitland in his *History of London*.

THE CITY WORKHOUSE

Next to thefe Hofpitals, whofe Foundations are fo great and magnificent, is the Work-houfe, or City Work-houfe, properly so called, which being a late Foundation, and founded upon meer Charity, without any fettled Endowment, is the more remarkable, for here are a very great Number of poor Children taken in, and fupported and maintained, fed, cloath'd, taught, and put out to Trades, and that at an exceeding Expence, and all this without one Penny Revenue.

It is Eftablifh'd, or rather the Eftablifhment of it, is fupported by an old Act of Parliament, 13, 14. *Car.* II, impowering the Citizens to raife Contributions for the Charge of Employing the Poor, and fuppreffing Vagrants and Beggars, and it is now, by the voluntary Affiftance and Bounty of Benefactors, become fo confiderable, that in the Year 1715 they gave the following State of the Houfe, *viz.*

Vagabonds, Beggars, &c. taken into the Houfe, including Fifty-five which remained at the End of the preceding Year - - - - - - - 418
Difcharged, including fuch as were put out to Trades - - - - - 356
Remaining in the Houfe - - - - - - - - - - 62
Not One Buried that whole Year.

But the Supplies and Charities to this commendable Work, have not of late come in fo readily as they ufed to do, which has put the Governors to fome Difficulties; upon which, *Anno* 1714, the Common Council, by Virtue of the Powers above-mentioned, agreed to raife Five thoufand Pounds upon the whole City, for the Support of the Houfe; but we do not find that any New Demand has been made fince that.

What Defoe here remarks concerning the workhouse may be supplemented by a reference from Strype, who says: 'The Workhouse in Bishopsgate adjoining Sir Paul Pindar's house, though it hath not a Penny Revenue, yet is able to maintain several Hundreds of poor Children, besides great Numbers of idle Persons of both Sexes'; and he proceeds to allocate no fewer than six folio pages to an elaborate description of its internal economy and management. The workhouse was founded in 1704, under the provisions of Acts of 13 and 14, Charles II. 'For the better Relief of the Poor of this Kingdom.' A long list of the benefactors and their gifts and legacies, as well as an account of the work done, is given by Strype, who remarks that 'Some years ago the Governors built a very strong and useful Building, and of large Dimensions, containing (besides other Apartments) three long Rooms or Galleries, one over another, for Workhouses, which are all filled with Boys and Girls at Work,' and he adds that 'they intend (if they get the money) to pull down the rest of the old houses, where now also the Poor and the Vagrants are kept at their several works, and to build a fair Court answerable to the aforesaid New Building which is on the Southside thereof.'

WESTMINSTER CHARITIES

There are Three confiderable Charities given by private Perfons in the City of *Weft-minfter, viz.*

1. The *Gray-coat* Hofpital, Founded by a generous Subfcription or Contribution; but chiefly by the Charity of one —— *Sands*, Efq; It maintains 70 Boys and 40 Girls, cloathed, fed, and taught, and in fome meafure provided for, by being put out to Trades.

2. The *Green-coat* Hofpital, in the fame Fields, Founded by King *Charles* I. for poor Fatherlefs Children of St. *Margaret*'s Parifh; and next to this Hofpital is the Houfe of Correction, or the *Weftminfter Bridewell.*

3. The *Emanuel* Hofpital, Founded by the Lady *Ann Dacres*, for Ten poor Men, and Ten poor Women, in the Forty-third Year of Queen *Elizabeth*. Near this, are Seven feveral Setts of Alms-houfes; but not of any Magnitude to be called Hofpitals.

There has been, alfo, a very noble Hofpital erected by Contribution of the *French* Refugees, for the Maintenance of their Poor: It ftands near the *Peft-houfe*, in the Foot-way to *Iflington* in the Parifh of *Cripplegate*, and Two Ranges of new Alms-houfes in *Kingfland* Road beyond *Shoreditch* Church.

The three hospitals (not for bodily ailments) here mentioned by Defoe, were situated in that part of Westminster, then more or less open fields, which is now a thickly populated area. The GREY-COAT HOSPITAL, so called because the children were obliged to wear clothes of that colour, was in Tothill Fields, and was founded in 1698 for the maintenance and education of seventy boys and forty girls of the parish of St. Margaret's, Westminster. To this, nine years later, another foundation was added, increasing the number of those receiving the charity and including the neighbouring parish of St. John the Evangelist. Its beautiful old buildings are, happily, still intact and can be seen through the wrought-iron gate which gives on to Grey Coat Place; on the other side is a spacious garden, and inside is a fine pannelled hall in which hangs a portrait of Queen Anne.

The GREEN-COAT HOSPITAL was founded in 1633, by letters patent from Charles I, who contributed £50 a year towards its maintenance. It was intended for the educational assistance of fatherless children among the poor of St. Margaret's parish. It was situated in Dacre Street, and when it was rebuilt in 1700, the famous headmaster of Westminster School, Dr. Busby, was a generous benefactor to it.

The third foundation of the kind, mentioned by Defoe, was known as EMMANUEL HOSPITAL, and was instituted by that liberal Lady Bountiful of the neighbourhood, Lady Dacre (sister of Thomas Sackville, Earl of Dorset, the poet) after whom it was sometimes called, as is a street in the vicinity. Her will, dated December 20th, 1594, provided that it should be founded for ' the relief of aged people and the bringing up of children in virtue and good and laudable acts '; and the hospital was duly incorporated on these lines in 1600. Lady Dacre survived her husband, and incidentally the making of her will, but a few months, and she lies buried with him under the beautiful monument in Chelsea Church. Executors were left to carry out the provisions of her will and the conduct of the hospital, but the last of them dying in 1623, the trust devolved under the Charter to the Lord Mayor and Corporation. As in the case of the other charities here mentioned, Emmanuel Hospital passed under the jurisdiction of the Westminster United Charities in 1873. Lady Dacre's original bequest was for the maintenance of twenty-four old men and women, sixteen of whom were to be parishioners of St. Margaret's. In the reign of Queen Anne the building became ruinous and was rebuilt, a chapel being added during the time of George II. Unhappily the picturesque structure has been demolished; it stood a little to the east of the existing Blue Coat School, founded in 1688, and housed in 1709 in its charming Wren-like building, still to be seen at the spot where James Street joins Caxton Street.

An examination of Rocque's plan not only shows the various hospitals and schools referred to, but also the comparatively rural character of the neighbourhood as it was in Defoe's time, as well as those other ' setts of alms-houses,' as he terms them, which then congregated in this area.

In addition to these Westminster charitable institutions our author speaks of a hospital erected by the French refugees (those expelled from France on the Revocation of the Edict of Nantes) in Cripplegate, as well as of the almshouses in Kingsland. The former of these stood, we are told, near the Pest House, in a lane, later to become Bath Street, City Road. It was founded on the death of M. de Gastigny, who was a Master of the Buckhounds, in the reign of William III, and who, in 1708, bequeathed £1,000 for the purpose. The piece of ground on which it was erected had been purchased from the Ironmongers' Company. It was capable of accommodating 200 inmates, and in 1718 was incorporated by Charter. Its successor is now on a spot close to Victoria Park. The Pest House referred to is mentioned also in Defoe's *Journal of the Plague*, and subsequently Pest House Row perpetuated its name; the original lazaretto remaining *in situ* till 1737.

PLATE XLVI

THE CHARTER HOUSE, OR SUTTON'S HOSPITAL

From a print by Sutton Nicholls, dated 1720

PLATE XLVII

A PROSPECT OF THE HOSPITAL CALLED BEDLAM

From a print by R.White. 1690.

The 'two new almshouses' in the Kingsland Road which were open fields when Pepys records walking there in the May of 1667, presumably refer to those of the Drapers' Company (1703) and those of the Ironmongers', in whose beautiful eighteenth-century buildings the Geffrye Museum (so named after the donor) is now housed.

THE CHARTER HOUSE

The Hofpital call'd the *Charter Houfe*, or *Sutton*'s Hofpital, is not by this fuppofed to be forgot, or the Honour of it leffen'd. On the other hand, it muft be recorded for ever, to be the greateft and nobleft Gift that ever was given for Charity, by any one Man, publick or private, in this Nation, fince Hiftory gives us any Account of Things; even not the great Bifhop of *Norwich* excepted, who built the great Church of *Yarmouth*, the Cathedral at *Norwich*, and the Church of St. *Mary*'s at *Lynn*; The Revenue of Mr. *Sutton*'s Hofpital being, befides the Purchafe of the Place, and the Building of the Houfe, and other Expences little lefs than 6000 *l. per Annum* Revenue.

The Royal Hofpitals of *Greenwich* and *Chelfea*, are alfo not mentioned in this Account, as not being within the Reach of the moft extended Bounds of the City of *London*.

Thefe are the principal Hofpitals, the reft of fmaller Note are touch'd before; but it will not be a ufelefs Obfervation, nor altogether improper to take notice of it here, That this Age has produced fome of the moft eminent Acts of publick Charity, and of the greateft Value, I mean from private Perfons, that can be found in any Age within the reach of our *Englifh* Hiftory, excepting only that of *Sutton*'s Hofpital; and yet they tell us, that even that of Mr. *Sutton*'s is exceeded in this of Mr. *Guy*'s, confidering that this Gentleman gave a very Noble Gift to this fame Hofpital before; befides that as before, he has left an Hundred thoufand Pounds in private Gifts among his own Relations; as to Children he had none, for he never was Married.

The other Benefactions, I fpeak of which this Age has produced, are already touch'd at in this Work, and may be referred to in the reading, fuch as Dr. *Ratcliff*'s Gift, amounting to above Forty thoufand Pounds to the Univerfity of *Oxford*: The Gift of Ten thoufand Pounds to *Magdalen* College in the fame Univerfity,* by their late Reprefentative; the feveral Charities of Sir *Robert Clayton*, Alderman *Ask*, Sir *Stephen Fox*, Dr. *Busby*, Sir *John Morden* and others.

'THE CHARITIES OF THIS AGE'

Thefe, added to the innumerable Number of Alms-houfes which are to be feen in almoft every Part of the City, make it certain, that there is no City in the World can fhew the like Number of Charities from private Hands, there being, as I am told, not lefs than Twenty thoufand People maintained of Charity, befides the Charities of Schooling for Children, and befides the Collections yearly at the Annual Feafts of feveral Kinds, where Money is given for putting out Children Apprentices, *&c.* fo that the *Papifts* have no Reafon to boaft, that there were greater Benefactions and Acts of Charity to the Poor given in their Times, than in our Proteftant Times; and this is indeed, one of the principal Reafons for my making mention of it in this Place; for let any particular Age be fingled out, and let the Charities of this Age, that is to fay, for about Fifteen or Twenty Years paft, and the Sums of Money beftowed by Proteftants in this Nation on meer Acts of Charity to the Poor, not reckoning Gifts to the Church, be caft up, it will appear they are greater by far, than would be found in *England* in any the like Number of Years, take the Time when we will.

Nor do I conclude in this, the Money Collected by Briefs all over *England*, upon Casualties by Fire, though that is an eminent Act of Charity as any can be; nor the Money

* In reply to our inquiries in regard to this the Bursars, both of Magdalen College, Oxford, and Magdalene College, Cambridge, inform us that no such benefactions can be traced in their records, so that it would appear that Defoe was misinformed.

given either in publick or private, for Re-building St. *Paul's* and other Churches demolished by the Fire of *London*, or the Augmentation of Poor Benefices by the Bounty of Queen *Ann*, and many other such Gifts.

NEW BUILDINGS ERECTED OR ERECTING SINCE THE FOREGOING ACCOUNT

I come now to an Account of new Edifices and publick Buildings, erected or erecting in and about *London*, since the writing the foregoing Account; and with this I conclude.

1. The fine new Church of St. *Martin's* in the *Fields*, with a very fine Steeple, which they tell us is 215 Feet high, all wholly built by the Contribution of that great Parish, and finished with the utmost Expedition.

2. The new *Admiralty* Office near *White-hall*, being on the same Ground where the old Office stood; but much larger, being both longer in Front and deeper Backward, not yet finished.

3. Mr. *Guy's* new Hospital for Incurables, mentioned above, situated on Ground purchased for that Purpose, adjoyning to St. *Thomas's* Hospital in *Southwark*, being a most magnificent Building not yet quite finished.

4. Two large Wings to the Hospital of *Bedlam*, appointed also for Incurables; proposed first by the charitable Disposition of Sir *William Withers* deceased; this also not yet finished.

5. A large new Meeting-house in *Spittle-fields*, for the Sect of Dissenters, call'd *Baptists*, or *Antepædo Baptists*.

6. The *South-Sea* House in *Threadneedle-street*, the old House being intirely pulled down, and several other Houses adjoyning being purchased, the whole Building will be new from the Foundation; this not finished.

7. Several very fine new Churches, being Part of the Fifty Churches appointed by Act of Parliament, *viz.* One in *Spittle-fields*, one in *Radcliff-High-way*, one in *Old-street*, one at *Limehouse*, with a very beautiful Tower, and one in *Bloomsbury*, and Five more not finished.

8. The Parish Church of St. *Botolph* without *Bishopsgate*, pulled down and Re-building, by the Contribution of the Inhabitants, not as one of the Fifty Churches.

N.B. *In removing the Corpses buried in this Church, they found the Body of Sir* Paul Pindar, *buried there about Eighty Year before, which was taken up and deposited again; and we are told, a new Monument will be set up for him by the Parish, to which he was a good Benefactor.*

9. The *Custom-house*, which since the late Fire in *Thames-street*, is ordered to be inlarged but is not yet finished.

All these Buildings are yet in building, and will all, in their several Places, be very great Ornaments to the City.

10. A new Street or Range of Houses taken out of the *South* Side of the *Artillery Ground* near *Morefields*, also an Enlargement to the new Burying Ground as it was formerly called, on the *North* Side of the same Ground.

11. The Iron Balustrade, or as others call it, Balcony, on the Lanthorn upon the Cupolo of St. *Paul's* Church, gilded. It was done at the Cost and as the Gift of an *Irish* Nobleman, who scarce lived to see it finished.

12. A new *Bear-Garden*, called *Figg's Theater*, being a Stage for the Gladiators or Prize-Fighters, and is built on the *Tyburn* Road.

N.B. *The Gentlemen of the Science, taking Offence at its being called* Tyburn *Road, though it really is so, will have it called the* Oxford *Road; this publick Edifice is fully finished, and in Use.*

Anyone writing an account of London to-day would have to add at the close of the volume additional information in order to bring the work up to date. For every day sees new buildings erected and old ones demolished. This was the case, although on a smaller scale, in Defoe's time; and so we here find him completing his perambulation of the City by references to ' new Edifices and publick Buildings erected or erecting in and about the City, since the writing of the foregoing Account.'

1. The first of these is ST. MARTIN'S IN THE FIELDS. The old church with which Defoe had been all his life familiar was a small structure built by Henry VIII, who is said to have had the church erected in order to obviate the necessity of funerals passing Whitehall on their way to St. Margaret's, Westminster. In 1607 the chancel was added by Henry, Prince of Wales. But the increasing parish found this still inadequate, and the existing church was decided upon, and begun, by James Gibbs, in 1721. It was completed in 1726, at a cost of about £37,000; a sum which included £1,500 for the organ.

2. The new ADMIRALTY was that reconstruction of old Wallingford House to which we have already referred on page 64, and which resulted in the Whitehall frontage with its Ionic portico and projecting wings as seen in our illustration. Among the severe criticisms passed on the new edifice was the remark that 'The Portico, which was intended as an ornament, rather disgusts than pleases by the immoderate heights and ill shape of the columns.'

3. GUY'S HOSPITAL, to which reference has already been made, was first opened in January 1725, a week after Guy's death. It originally consisted of the street frontage with two wings enclosing two large quadrangles, and was capable of holding four hundred patients. By subsequent additions it has become as we know it to-day. The bronze statue of the founder in the first quadrangle was executed by Scheemakers, and was set up on February 11th, 1734. The illustration here given shows the Hospital as it was in Defoe's day.

4. BETHLEHEM HOSPITAL, then in Bishopsgate Without, fronting London Wall, was begun in 1675 and completed in the following year, from the designs of Robert Hooke. Its appearance about this time can be seen from the accompanying illustration, which shows that the two wings here spoken of by Defoe were at the extreme ends of the building and at right angles with the frontage, running back, as it were, from the two corners, in London Wall, towards Moorfields behind.

5. The ' large new MEETING HOUSE in *Spittle-Fields* ' here mentioned can be identified on Rocque's plan, where it is seen standing in the large, tree-studded open space, being approached from the west by Mason's Court, with its avenue of trees, from Brick Lane. The fact that Defoe specifically refers to it as among the new buildings then recently put up seems to indicate that it was of some architectural importance.

6. The old SOUTH SEA HOUSE faced Broad Street, and was entered by a passage from that thoroughfare which communicated with a small courtyard. The new one stood immediately south of this, and had its long façade in Threadneedle Street at the point where that street joins Bishopsgate Street. Defoe here speaks of the old house being entirely pulled down, but this hardly coincides with Rocque, who shows it still standing in 1746, as does Strype in the sectional map of this district depicting the block of South Sea *Houses*. Noorthouck's account (1773) of the place runs thus: ' At the north east extremity of Threadneedle Street, where it enters Bishopsgate Street, is situated the South Sea House. This house stands upon a large extent of ground, running back as far as Old Broad Street facing St. Peter le Poor. The back front was formerly the Excise Office; then the South Sea Company's office; and hence is distinguished by the name of the Old South Sea House. As to the new building in which the Company's affairs are now transacted, it is a magnificent structure.'

The illustration of the later headquarters here given bears out what Noorthouck says. Through the entrance can be seen the large quadrangle, the building in the distance being the back of the old South Sea House.

7. Of the churches here spoken of as being in course of erection as a result of the Act (1708) for the Building of Fifty new Churches in London, that in Spital Fields is CHRIST CHURCH designed by Hawksmoor and completed in 1729. It is probably the best and, architecturally, most notable of this architect's contribution to the fifty churches.

The church in Ratcliffe Highway is ST. GEORGE'S IN THE EAST, which had been begun in 1715 and occupied fourteen years in building. It was another of Hawksmoor's designs, and has some resemblance to an earlier effort of his—St. Anne's, Limehouse. The original estimate for it was £13,500, but it eventually cost nearly another £5,000.

The OLD STREET CHURCH is St. Luke's which was not completed and consecrated till many years later, to be precise in 1733.

ST. ANNE'S, LIMEHOUSE, was one of the first Hawksmoor designed in London, having been commenced in 1712 and finished eight years later, just ten years before St. George's, Bloomsbury, was completed by the same industrious architect. This latter church is interesting from the fact that it is said to have been the first furnished with a portico—a feature which for a time at least played an important part in ecclesiastical architecture—and also for the fact that it is the only church the steeple of which is surmounted by a royal statue, that of George I.

It is a little difficult to say which were the other five churches indicated by Defoe as ' not finished,' in view of his statement regarding St. Luke's. But probably St. Leonard's, Shoreditch, which was completed in 1739; St. Giles's in the Fields, designed by Flitcroft and first used for service in 1734; and St. Olave's, Tooley Street, completed in 1739, were among them.

8. The foundation stone of ST. BOTOLPH, BISHOPSGATE WITHOUT, was laid in April 1725, and the building completed in 1728. On a print of it published in 1802, the name of ' G. Dance 1727 ' appears as its architect. But it seems probable that Giles Dance, and not his better-known son, George, to whom it has also been ascribed, was its designer.

The monument to SIR PAUL PINDAR (who died in 1650) was duly erected, and may be seen on the north wall of the church. Sir Paul Pindar, a noted merchant of the time, spent nine years as Ambassador to the Porte. He accumulated great wealth, much of which he lost through loans to Charles I. His picturesque house was in Bishopsgate Street, on part of the site now occupied by Liverpool Street Station, and, when it was demolished, its frontage was preserved and is now to be seen in the Victoria and Albert Museum.

9. Although Defoe tells us that the Custom House was not ' yet finished ' when he came to this part of his work (which from other evidence appears to have been about the year 1724), we know that Ripley was commissioned to design it soon after the destruction of Wren's earlier one in 1715; and in Strype (1720) is a large plate of it showing it in its completed form. There may have been subsidiary portions of Ripley's reconstruction still unfinished, and Defoe probably refers to these.

10. By a comparative reference to Ogilby and Morgan's 1682 plan and that of Rocque of 1746, we can at once see ' the new Street or Range of Houses taken out of the *South* side of the *Artillery Ground.*' For in the former, the area extends, and is open, to Chiswell Street; whereas in the latter, the whole frontage on this side of the ground is covered with houses, between which two alleys, Artillery Court and Pied House Yard, give access to the open space from the street. Houses also appear along its west frontage, which before was open to Bunn Hill.

In the same way the space on the north side of the Artillery Ground which is shown, in 1682, as a bare field, with some Dog-Houses at its north-east corner, and a pathway across it diagonally from the south-east to the north-west corner, is, later, indicated with its upper portion cut off and divided between ' The Burying Ground ' and ' Tindal's Burying Ground,' the former occupying a strip of ground marked ' The City Churchyard ' in 1682.

11. The inclusion of so relatively insignificant a matter as the gilding of the balustrade round the cupola of St. Paul's, among the references to the new edifices which arose or were arising when Defoe come to this part of his work, might seem curious did we not remember the importance attached to such things by no less a reader of character than Napoleon I who, on a famous occasion, being told that the Parisians were growing restless, replied, ' Gild the dome of the Invalides. It will give them something to think about.' Wren himself wished the dome of St. Paul's to be gilded; although he was never in favour of the stone balustrade which crowns the upper cornices of the whole structure, which was forced on him by the Commissioners. ' I never,' he said on one occasion, ' designed a balustrade, but ladies think nothing well without an edging.' The Irish peer who is here said to have paid for the gilding of the balustrade was the Earl of LANESBOROUGH.

12. This was the ' BOARDED HOUSE ' in Marylebone, off the Oxford Road, which was erected by James Figg, or Fig as the name is sometimes spelt, who was financed by the Earl of Peterborough. It had for its sign ' The City of Oxford.' The place and its owner have been perpetuated in the verse of Pope, Bramston, and Soame Jenyns; and in the *Weekly Journal* for March 10th, 1720, is the following advertisement of one of the contests here:

' At the Boarded House in Marybone Fields, on Wednesday next, March 16th, will be performed a Trial of skill between John Parkes from Coventry and James Figg from Thame in Oxfordshire, master of the whole science of defence, at the usual weapons fought on the stage.'

PLATE XLVIII

The South Sea House, in Bishopsgate Street

THE SOUTH SEA HOUSE, AS RECONSTRUCTED IN DEFOE'S DAY

From a print by Bowles

Figg was the first of the heavy-weight champions of England, acquiring the title in 1719, and holding it till his death in 1734. He is said to have invented the roped-in square ring, first introducing it at his headquarters in Marylebone in 1720. A portrait of him appears among the crowd attending the morning levee of the hero in ' The Rake's Progress ' and Hogarth again introduces him in his ' Southwark Fair.'

The famous John Broughton succeeded Figg, but had his later premises built in 1742-3 behind those of his predecessor, near the ' Adam and Eve ' Tea Gardens, at the top of the Tottenham Court Road. In Figg's day it was, of course, isolated among fields. Defoe probably calls the place a Bear Garden, because it was, no doubt, a circular building shaped on the lines of those old Bear Gardens popular in the days of the Tudors and Stuarts, and bear-baiting may have taken place here occasionally, although this brutal pastime was at this time slowly dying out.

CONCLUSION AND ESTIMATE OF PRESENT POPULATION

I conclude this Account of *London*, with mentioning fomething of the Account of Mortality, that is to fay, the Births and Burials, from whence Sir *William Petty* thought he might make fome Calculations of the Numbers of the Inhabitants, and I fhall only take Notice, that whereas, the general Number of the Burials in the Year 1666, and farther back, were from 17000 to 19000 in a Year, the laft yearly Bill for the Year 1723, amounted as follows,

Chriftenings 19203. Burials 29197.

Here is to be obferved, that the Number of Burials exceeding fo much the Number of Births, is, becaufe as it is not the Number Born, but the Number Chriftened that are fet down, which is taken from the Parifh Regifter; fo all the Children of Diffenters of every Sort, *Proteftant, Popifh* and *Jewifh* are omitted, alfo all the Children of Foreigners, *French, Dutch, &c.* which are Baptized in their own Churches, and all the Children of thofe who are fo poor, that they cannot get them Regiftred: So that if a due Eftimate be made, the Births may be very well fuppofed to exceed the Burials one Year with another by many Thoufands.

It is not that I have no more to fay of *London*, that I break off here; but that I have no Room to fay it, and tho' fome Things may be taken Notice of by others, which I have pafs'd over; yet I have alfo taken Notice of fo many Things which others have omitted, that I claim the Ballance in my Favour.

I am, S I R,
Yours, &c.

The END *of the* FIFTH LETTER.

PLATE XLIX

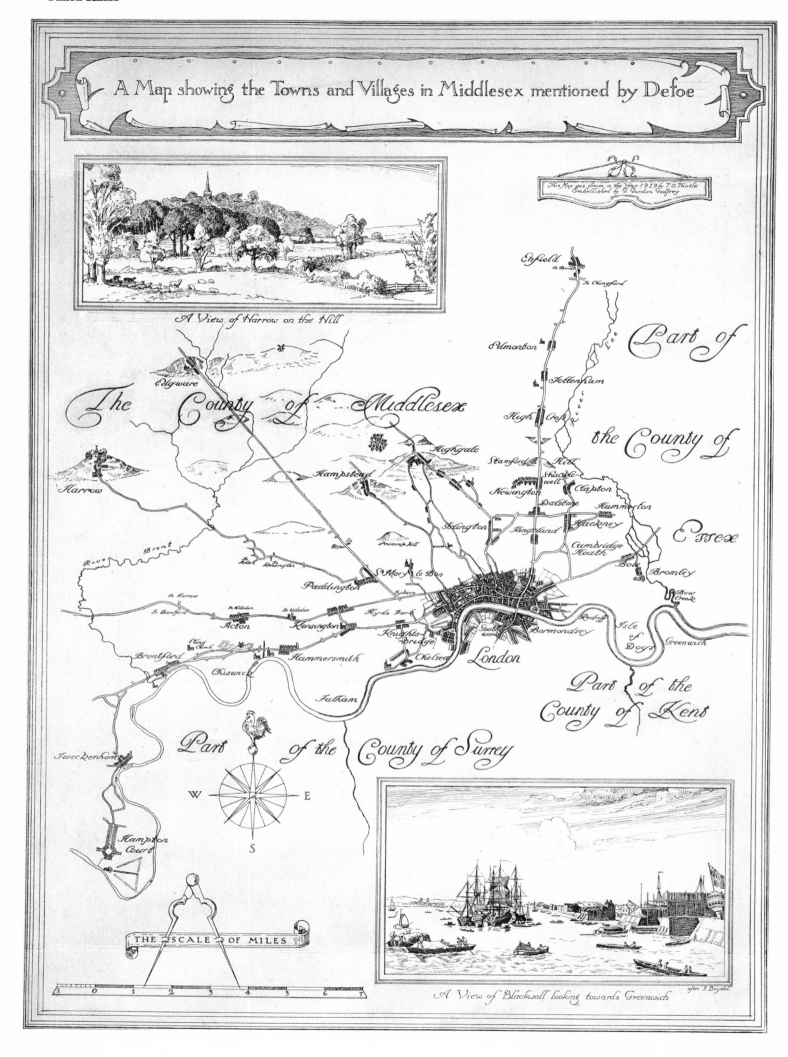

A Map showing the Towns and Villages in Middlesex mentioned by Defoe

This Map was drawn in the Year 1929 by T.O.Thirtle Embellished by S. Gordon Godfrey

A View of Harrow on the Hill

The County of Middlesex

Part of the County of

Essex

Part of the County of Kent

Part of the County of Surrey

W E
S

THE SCALE OF MILES

A View of Blackwall looking towards Greenwich

after J. Boydel.

EXTRACTS FROM LETTER VI.

Containing some description of the VILLAGES ROUND LONDON, in the County of Middlesex.

———————✂———————

I HAVE fpent fo much Time, and taken up fo much room in my Defcription of *London*, and the adjacent Parts, that I muft be the more cautious, *at leaft*, as to needlefs Excurfions in the Country near it.

The Villages round *London* partake of the Influence of *London*, fo much, that it is obferv'd as *London* is Encreafed, fo they are all Encreafed alfo, and from the fame Caufes.

I have taken notice of this in my firft fetting out, and particularly in the Counties of *Effex*, *Kent*, and *Surrey*; and as the fame appears to an extreme in *Middlefex*: I fhall only give fome Difcriptions, and fay the lefs of the reafon of it.

> Only those sections of Letter VI. are reproduced which refer to the 'Villages round London' in Middlesex which, as Defoe expresses it, 'though nowhere joining to London' . . . 'partake of the influence of London.' Suburban Middlesex developed for obvious geographical reasons before suburban Surrey, Kent and Essex, and many of these 'villages,' if not yet ' a part of the Great Mass,' can certainly be regarded in modern parlance as a part of the 'Greater London' of his day. Starting with Hackney, Defoe claims that this 'whole town' may '*in some respects* be called a part of London,' but we must not forget to underline his qualification. Nearly a century was to pass before Hackney became completely absorbed, and the same slow rate of absorption holds good in the case of many of these Middlesex villages. Not till the first decade of the nineteenth century do we find from one of Mogg's plans that the road called Cambridge Heath, with its northern continuation as Mare Street and Church Street, is beginning to be built over. Grove Street was still a small hamlet, and Newington had the same relation to London as Edmonton has now. Even in Greenwood's immense and detailed plan, based on a survey made during 1824-6, these places are, although increased in size, shown still entirely separate from the City itself, and it is only in Stanford's equally elaborate plan of 1862 that they appear as actual portions of London.

Hackney and *Bromley* are the firft Villages which begin the County of *Middlefex*, Eaft; for *Bow* as reckon'd to *Stepney*, is a Part of the Great Mafs. This Town of *Hackney* is of a great Extent, containing no lefs than 12 Hamlets of feparate Villages, tho' fome of them now join, *viz.*

> *Church-ftreet, Hummerton, Wyck-Houfe, Grove-ftreet, Clapton, Mare-ftreet, Well-ftreet, Cambridge-Heath, Shacklewell, Dalftone, Kingfland, Newington.*

All thefe, tho' fome of them are very large Villages, make up but one Parifh (*viz.*) of *Hackney*.

All thefe, except the *Wyck-houfe*, are within a few Years fo encreas'd in Buildings, and fo fully inhabited, that there is no Comparifon to be made between their prefent and paft State: Every feparate Hamlet is Encreas'd, and fome of them more than Treble as big as formerly; Indeed as this whole Town is included in the Bills of Mortality, tho' no where joining to *London*, it is in fome refpects to be call'd a part of it.

This Town is fo remarkable for the retreat of Wealthy Citizens, that there is at this time near a Hundred Coaches kept in it; tho' I will not join with a certain Satyrical Author* who faid of *Hackney*, that there were *more Coaches than Chriftians in it.*

* Probably Tom Brown (1663-1704) in punning allusion to the dual meaning of the word Hackney.

Newington, Tottenham, Edmonton, and *Enfield* ſtand all in a Line N. from the City; the encreaſe of Buildings is ſo great in them all, that they ſeem to a Traveller to be one continu'd Street; eſpecially *Tottenham* and *Edmonton*, and in them all, the new Buildings ſo far exceed the Old, eſpecially in the value of them, and figure of the Inhabitants, that the faſhion of the Towns are quite altered.

'MANY IMMENSELY RICH' IN TOTTENHAM HIGH CROSS

At *Tottenham* we ſee the remains of an Antient Building called the *Croſs*, from which the Town takes the name of *High-Croſs*. There is a long account of the Antiquities of this Place lately Publiſhed, to which I referr, Antiquities as I have obſerved, not being my Province in this Work, but a Deſcription of things in their preſent State.

Here is at this Town a ſmall but pleaſant Seat of the Earl of *Colerain*, in *Ireland*; his Lordſhip is now on his Travels, but has a very good Eſtate here extending from the Town to *Muzzle-hill*, and almoſt to *High-gate*.

The firſt thing we ſee in *Tottenham* is a ſmall but Beautiful Houſe, built by one Mr. *Wanly*, formerly a *Goldſmith*, near *Temple Bar*; it is a ſmall Houſe, but for the Beauty of the Building and the Gardens, it is not outdone by any of the Houſes on this ſide the Country.

There is not any thing more fine in their Degree, than moſt of the Buildings this way; only with this Obſervation, that they are generally belonging to the middle ſort of Mankind, grown Wealthy by Trade, and who ſtill taſte of *London*; ſome of them live both in the City, and in the Country at the ſame time: yet many of theſe are immenſly rich.

HIGH-GATE—'PARTICULARLY FIXED ON BY THE JEWS'

High-gate and *Hampſtead* are next on the North-ſide; At the firſt is a very beautiful Houſe built by the late Sir *William Aſhurſt*, on the very ſummit of the Hill, and with a view from the very loweſt Windows over the whole Vale, to the City: And that ſo eminently, that they ſee the very Ships paſſing up and down the River for 12 or 15 Miles below *London*. The *Jews* have particularly fixt upon this Town for their Country Retreats, and ſome of them are very Wealthy; they live there in good Figure, and have ſeveral Trades particularly depending upon them, and eſpecially, Butchers of their own to ſupply them with Proviſions kill'd their own way; alſo, I am told, they have a private Synagogue here.

This Sir William Ashurst was M.P. for the City in 1700; he became Lord Mayor in 1694. The house he built possessed a chesnut staircase designed by Inigo Jones, and the carvings of the over-doors and the tapestried chambers are said to have been specially admirable. The grounds, which were laid out with great taste, now form part of Highgate Cemetery. The mansion itself was later occupied by Sir Alan Chambre, one of the Justices of the Common Pleas. It was demolished in 1830, and St. Michael's Church erected on its site, two years later.

With regard to the Jews Synagogue, no other record seems to be extant; but when Howitt was writing his *Northern Heights of London*, he refers to a Synagogue in connection with a school conducted there by a Mr. Hyman Hurwitz; and this may possibly have been a relic of the one in Defoe's time.

* * * * * * * * *

HAMPSTEAD—'GROWN SUDDENLY POPULOUS'

Hampſtead indeed is riſen from a little Country Village, to a City, not upon the Credit only of the Waters, tho' 'tis apparent, its growing Greatneſs began there; but Company increaſing gradually, and the People liking both the Place and the Diverſions together; it grew ſuddenly Populous, and the Concourſe of People was Incredible. This conſequently raiſed the Rate of Lodgings, and that encreaſed Buildings, till the Town grew up

PLATE L

The North West View of Newington.

Chatelain delin. J. Roberts Sculp.

Publish'd according to Act of Parliament

The South East View of Brook House

Chatelain delin. J. Roberts Sculp.

Publish'd according to Act of Parliament

The South East View of Cambray House

Chatelain delin. J. Roberts Sculp.

Publish'd according to Act of Parliament

PLATE LI

Her Majestie's Royal Palace at Kensington

To Her most Serene and most Sacred Majesty. Kt Evelyn: By Grace of God QUEEN of Great Britain France & Ireland &c

From a print by J.Kip.1724.

from a little Village, to a Magnitude equal to fome Cities; nor could the uneven Surface, inconvenient for Building, uncompact, and unpleafant, check the humour of the Town, for even on the very fteep of the Hill, where there's no walking Twenty Yards together, without Tugging up a Hill, or Stradling down a Hill, yet 'tis all one, the Buildings encreafed to that degree, that the Town almoft fpreads the whole fide of the Hill.

HAMPSTEAD HEATH—'SO NEAR HEAVEN'

On the Top of the Hill indeed, there is a very pleafant Plain, called the Heath, which on the very Summit, is a Plain of about a Mile every way; and in good Weather 'tis pleafant Airing upon it, and fome of the Streets are extended fo far, as that they begin to build, even on the higheft Part of the Hill. But it muft be confeft, 'tis fo near Heaven, that I dare not fay it can be a proper Situation, for any but a race of Mountaineers, whofe Lungs have been ufed to a rarify'd Air, nearer the fecond Region, than any Ground for 30 Miles round it.

It is true, this Place may be faid to be prepared for a Summer Dwelling, for in Winter nothing that I know can recommend it: 'Tis true, a warm Houfe, and good Company, both which are to be had here, go a great way to make amends for Storms, and feverity of Cold.

Here is a moft beautiful Profpect indeed, for we fee here *Hanflop Steeple* one way, which is within eight Miles of *Northampton*, N.W. to *Landown-Hill* in *Effex* another way, Eaft at leaft 66 Miles from one another; the profpect to *London*, and beyond it to *Banfted Downs*, South; *Shooters-Hill*, S.E. *Red-Hill*, S.W. and *Windfor-Caftle*, W. is alfo uninterrupted: Indeed due North, we fee no farther than to *Barnet*, which is not above fix Miles; but the reft is fufficient.

BELLSIZE—'A TRUE HOUSE OF PLEASURE'

At the Foot of this Hill is an old Seat of the Earls of *Chefterfields*, called *Bellfize*; which for many Years had been neglected, and as it were forgotten: But being taken lately by a certain *Projector* to get a Penny, and who knew by what Handle to take the gay Part of the World, he has made it a true Houfe of Pleafure; Here, in the Gardens he Entertained the Company with all kind of Sport, and in the Houfe with all kinds of Game, to fay no more of it: This brought a wonderful Concourfe of People to the Place, for they were fo effectually gratified in all forts of Diverfion, that the Wicked part at length broke in, till it alarm'd the Magiftrates, and I am told it has been now in a manner fupprefs'd by the hand of Juftice.

'SOMETIMES MORE GALLANTRY THAN MODESTY'

Here was a great Room fitted up with abundance of Dexterity for their Balls, and had it gone on to a degree of Mafquerading as I hear was actually begun, it would have bid fair to have had half the Town run to it: One faw Pictures and Furniture there beyond what was to have been expected in a meer Publick Houfe; and 'tis hardly credible how it drew Company to it; But it could not be, no Britifh Government could be fuppofed to bear long with the Liberties taken on fuch Publick Occafions: So as I have faid, they are reduc'd, at leaft reftrain'd from Liberties which they could not preferve by their Prudence.

Yet *Hampftead* is not much the lefs frequented for this. But as there is (efpecially at the Wells) a Conflux of all Sorts of Company, even *Hampftead* itfelf has fuffered in its good Name; and you fee fometimes more Gallantry than Modefty: So that the Ladies who value their Reputation, have of late more avoided the Wells and Walks at *Hampftead*, than they had formerly done.

*   *   *   *   *   *   *   *   *

Without going deeply into the history of BELSIZE, which will be found described by Park in his *History of Hampstead*, Howitt, and others, we may say that this property at the Dissolution came into the hands of the Wadd or Wade family. From Lady Wade, in 1667, it passed to her son who had been created Lord Wotton. Pepys speaks of seeing the house and garden; 'wonderful fine' he calls the latter, 'too good for the house,' in 1668. On Lord Wotton's death the property went to his half-brother, Philip, second Earl of Chesterfield, a writer of *Letters*, although not so well known in that capacity as was the 'great' 4th Earl. Povey, of the Sun Fire Office, appears to have been a tenant in 1718, but two years later the place became a fashionable centre of amusement under the direction of one Howell. The Prince and Princess of Wales dined here in July 1721; hundreds of important people attended a deer hunt organised here in the following year; and gambling drew hither a still vaster crowd. Races were also an attraction which Howell, the Welsh Ambassador, as he was called, organised; and foot-races and such-like sports went on till 1745, the year that saw the closing of the house, which became subsequently ruinous and was pulled down and replaced by a less pretentious structure (*circa* 1798), this in turn being demolished in 1854 when the Belsize Estate was laid out. The 'certain Projector' of Defoe's text was, of course, Howell, who was not a particularly reputable person.

It was Dr. Gibbons, who figures in Garth's 'Dispensary,' as 'Mirmillo,' who was the first to advertise the medicinal qualities of the HAMPSTEAD SPRINGS at the beginning of the eighteenth century, and Hampstead Wells, on the north side of the present Well Walk, soon became famous as being as efficacious as Tunbridge Wells and, of course, for the Londoner, far easier of access. As a result places of entertainment were very soon inaugurated around them, and there arose a tavern, a bowling-green, what were called raffling shops, and even a chapel. The news sheets of the day, the *Postman* and *The Tatler*, etc., are full of advertisements of the Wells and the attendant amusements, and from *Read's Weekly Journal* for September 8th, 1716, we learn that Sion Chapel, as the place of worship was called, was chosen by persons of the best fashion wherein to be married. It would seem, however, that these unions were rather in the nature of the later Fleet and Keith's Mayfair Chapel weddings. Fairs and races were also held on the Heath, but the latter were abolished on account of the rowdiness attending them. It was here, too, that the Middlesex elections were decided before their *venue* was changed to Brentford in 1701.

In course of time, however, the popularity of the place so far as a medical resort was concerned, and even as one of amusement, began to wane. A Dr. John Soame, who resided here, endeavoured to revive its fame by the publication of his *Hampstead Wells; or Directions for Drinking the Waters;* but fashion went elsewhere, although it left as a residuum an ever-increasing permanent population. In the latter respect Hampstead has never looked back, and might be said to deserve to-day the somewhat flamboyant description of its 'magnitude' which Defoe gives us in his picture of the new suburb.

'WEST FROM LONDON' AND 'WHAT THE COUNTRY AFFORDS THAT WAY'

But I muſt travel no farther this Way, till I have taken a Journey Weſt from *London*, and ſeen what the Country affords that Way; the next Towns adjacent to *London*, are, *Kenſington, Chelſea, Hammerſmith, Fulham, Twickenham*, &c. all of them near, or adjoyning to the River of *Thames*, and which, by the Beauty of their Buildings, make good the North Shore of the River, anſwerable, to what I have already deſcrib'd.

KENSINGTON AND THE KING'S PALACE THERE

Kenſington cannot be nam'd without mentioning the King's Palace there; a Building which may now be call'd entirely New, tho' it was Originally an old Houſe of the Earl of *Nottingham's* of whom the late King *William* bought it, and then enlarg'd it as we ſee; ſome of the old Building ſtill remaining in the Center of the Houſe.

The Houſe it ſelf fronts to the Garden three ways, the Gardens being now made exceeding Fine, and enlarged to ſuch a Degree, as to reach quite from the great Road to *Kenſington* Town, to the *Acton* Road North, more than a Mile.

The firſt laying out of theſe Gardens was the Deſign of the late Queen *Mary*, who finding the Air agreed with, and was neceſſary to the Health of the King, reſolved to make it agreeable to her felf too, and gave the firft Orders for enlarging the Gardens: the Author of this Account, having had the Honour to attend Her Majefty, when fhe firft viewed the Ground, and directed the doing it, fpeaks this with the more Satisfaction.

The late Queen *Anne* compleated what Queen *Mary* began, and delighted very much in the Place; and often was pleafed to make the Green Houfe which is very Beautiful, her Summer Supper Houfe.

DESERTED BY GEORGE I. FOR HAMPTON COURT—

But this Houfe has loft much of its Pleafantnefs on one Account, namely, that all the Princes that ever might be faid to fingle it out for their Delight, had the Fate to dye in it; namely, King *William*, Prince *George* of *Denmark*, and laftly, Queen *Anne* her felf; fince which it has not been fo much in requeft, King *George* having generally kept his Summer, when in *England*, at *Hampton Court*.

As this Palace opens to the Weft, there are two great Wings Built, for Lodgings for fuch as neceffarily attend the Court, and a large Port Cocher at the Entrance, with a Poftern and a Stone Gallery on the South fide of the Court which leads to the great Stair-Cafe.

This South Wing was burnt down by Accident, the King and Queen being both there, the Queen was a little furprized at firft, apprehending fome Treafon, but King *William* a Stranger to Fears fmil'd at the Suggeftion, chear'd Her Majefty up, and being foon drefs'd, they both walked out into the Garden, and ftood there fome Hours till they perceived the Fire by the help that came in, and by the Diligence of the Foot Guards, was gotten under Foot.

KENSINGTON PALACE originally belonged to Heneage Finch, second Earl of Nottingham, who died in 1689, and whose successor sold it soon afterwards to William III. At one time Holland House had nearly been selected as the King's residence, but it was, on trial (for William stayed there a week or two), found unsuitable, and Nottingham House was decided on. The sum paid for it was £18,900 and Wren was immediately called in to enlarge and reconstruct the mansion. The original building and the great architect's additions can be plainly seen to-day; while the further additions made by Kent in George II's reign are equally apparent. The Orangery, which Defoe calls here the Green House, was designed by Wren in 1706. It may be noted that besides the sovereigns mentioned by Defoe as having died in Kensington Palace, George II expired there suddenly on October 25th, 1760, while, as everyone knows, both Queen Victoria and Queen Mary were born there.

The notice of the fire refers to the outbreak recorded by Evelyn in November, 1691, when the diarist states that ' part of the King's house at Kensington was burnt.' The damage was not, however, very considerable and was immediately repaired.

When William III purchased Nottingham House, which then became known as Kensington Palace, there were only twenty-six acres of ground attached to the mansion, and these were laid out, ' according to the royal taste, being entirely military, with cut yew and variegated holly hedges, under the auspices of London and Wise, the royal gardeners, to imitate the lines, angles, bastions, scarps and counter-scarps of regular fortifications.' In 1705, Queen Anne much improved the gardens, so that Bowack, writing his *Antiquities of Middlesex* in that year, can remark that ' there is a whole collection of foreign plants, and some neat greens, which makes it pleasant all the year, and the contrivance, variety and disposition of the whole is extremely pleasing, and so frugal have they been of the room they had, that there is not an inch but what is well improved.' But it was under Queen Caroline, the wife of George II, that the chief improvements were undertaken. They comprised the enlargement of the gardens (200 acres being taken from Hyde Park) and their laying out under the ægis of Bridgeman and Kent, and the damming and deepening of the old course of the Westbourne Brook, then little more than a string of ponds, in order to form the Serpentine, at a cost of £6,000.

—AND THE GROWTH OF KENSINGTON CONSEQUENTLY ARRESTED

It is no wonder if the Court being fo much at *Kenfington*, that Town has encreafed in Buildings, fo I do not place that to the fame Account as of the reft; On the South Side of the Street over againſt the Palace, is a fair New large Street, and a little way down a noble Square full of very good Houſes, but ſince the Court has ſo much declin'd the Palace, the Buildings have not much encreaſed.

The ' fair NEW LARGE STREET ' here referred to by Defoe, was not, of course, what we know as the Kensington Road and Knightsbridge, but a new thoroughfare which William III had constructed, and, to the wonder of all, lighted the whole way with lamps. It stretched from the Palace to Hyde Park Corner Turnpike and is to-day represented by the roadway from Kensington Gardens eastward, in the Park, past the Barracks.

KENSINGTON SQUARE, 'the noble Square full of good Houses' of Defoe's phrase, was begun in the reign of James II, and according to Faulkner there was at one time to be seen a tablet at the north-east corner indicating the year of its completion, 1698. It was originally intended to be called King's Square, for there is a record of a plot of ground being sold in 1687 to Thomas Young (from whom the adjoining Young Street takes its name) being ' neere King's Square in ye Parish of Kensington.' In the following year this same Young, a well-known local builder, had erected at least three houses on the ' Easte Row ' of the Square. For years the ground around was open fields; indeed, it was not till the 'forties of the last century, when the ' New Town ' of Kensington was begun, that the land on the north and west of the square began to be covered; while the later development of 1860, helped to hedge it round on the other sides with streets and houses. The heyday of the square's fashion was in the reign of Queen Anne, and again in that of George II when ' upwards of forty carriages were kept in and about the neighbourhood,' and so crowded was it that ' an Ambassador, a Bishop and a Physician all occupied apartments in the same house.' The Duchesse de Mazarin was living here as early as 1692, being visited almost daily by St. Evremond; others were the Earl of Gainsborough in 1697; Mr. Pitt, an ancestor of Earl Rivers, in 1693; Sir Hele Hook, and the Duke of Shrewsbury in 1699; Joseph Addison, before he went to Holland House, with whom Swift used to come to sup, as recorded in the Journal to Stella, in 1710. Steele was also here in 1708; and the Marquess of Montgomery in 1721, to mention but a tithe of the notable residents in Defoe's time.

CHELSEA—' A TOWN OF PALACES '

South of this Town ſtands *Chelſea*, a Town of Palaces, and which by its New extended Buildings ſeems to promiſe itſelf to be made one time or other a Part of *London*, I mean *London* in its new extended Capacity, which if it ſhould once happen, what a Monſter muſt *London* be, extending (*to take it in a Line*) from the farther End of *Chelſea*, Weſt, to *Deptford-Bridge* Eaſt, which I venture to ſay, is at leaſt Eleven Miles.

There is no occasion here to delve deeply into the origin and early history of the Manor of CHELSEA before the time of Defoe. Charles, Viscount Cheyne, sold it to Sir Hans Sloane, in 1712, through whose daughter, married to Charles, second Baron Cadogan, it passed into the family which still owns the larger portion of it, the remainder belonging to the Sloane-Stanleys. Its right to be called, as L'Estrange was the first to call it, a ' Village of Palaces,' is obvious when we remember the number of great mansions which once studded it: Beaufort House, Lindsay House, Danvers House, Cremorne House, Monmouth House, and the rest. The tale of its famous residents is a long and distinguished one, and the ghosts of many of the illustrious of three centuries must foregather in its still picturesque streets and byways. One of these was Sir Robert Walpole, who purchased Heer Van Halse's house here for £1,100 in 1722, a house afterwards occupied by that incompetent Statesman, but clever party politician, the Duke of Newcastle, some twenty odd years later. Here Swift lodged in a house in Church Lane close to Dr. Atterbury's, and thither he used to walk from Mrs. Vanhomrigh's, in Suffolk Street, or from his London abode in Bury Street, St. James's. Here too might have been met Dr. Arbuthnot who removed hither in 1714, Sir Isaac Newton who was living here from 1709 to 1710, or Mr. Joseph Addison, who in the latter year came to a house near Sir Richard Steele's abode (from 1714-15) by the river.

In those days, Chelsea, which was to London something like Richmond was to be a century later, but which is now completely absorbed in the ' Wen,' as Cobbett called it, was a self-contained village sought for on account of its rurality and quiet and because of the excellence of the soil and the relative purity of the air. The earlier London cartographers disregarded it,

PLATE LII

Chelsea.

Publish'd According to Act of Parliament September y.ᵉ 25 1738.

Sold by T. Preist near the Ferry at Chelsey, & to be had of
W. H. Toms Engraver in Union Court Near Hatton Garden Holborn

Chiswick

These scarce and interesting views of Chelsea and Chiswick were drawn and etched by Thomas Preist in
1738, and represent the crude beginnings of pictorial topography dealing with the 'outparts of London.'
Both these and the drawings by Chatelain (shown in Plate L) of some of the 'villages' in Middlesex
mentioned by Defoe, are of a slightly later date than that of the publication of the *Tour*. It would
appear that the suburbs had as yet failed to attract the real artists who confined their attention to the
outstanding features of the metropolis itself

PLATE LIII

THE ROYALL HOSPITALL AT CHELSEY

To the Right Hon.ble Sr. Stephen Fox Kn.t &c.ry Employ'd by King Charke the Second to take Care and build the Royal Hospital at Chelsea for ye Superannuated and Indigent Officers & Soldiers ... which he then Conveiied and Carryed on the Work with Constant Consultations ... which he gave the Ground and a third part of his Office of paymaster to the Army ... towards which, he gave the ground and a third part of his Office of paymaster to the Army ... with Constant Consultations.

From a print by J. Kip. 1724.

as it was too far west to come into their purview of the metropolis, and even Rocque shows us little beyond the splendid ground plan of Chelsea Hospital, Ranelagh House with its ample gardens, and some rows of lesser dwellings along what was known as Turks Row, Wilderness Row, Jews Row, and a little to their north the street known as Strumbelo.

In our reproduction of Kniff's picture we see Lindsay House facing the river, the same yet not quite the same as the divided Lindsay House of to-day, and just to its east, but lying further back, Beaufort House, where Sir Thomas More once abode to be followed by Villiers, Duke of Buckingham and his profligate son, the first two Dukes of Beaufort, and Sir Hans Sloane. It stands with its vast grounds stretching to the north and east and its formal garden front reaching to the river edge. Along that riverside, between the grounds of Beaufort House and the Thames, there is a long row of small but picturesque dwellings; and in the distance can be seen Kensington House (Palace), Campden House, and Holland House. Here and there in Chelsea beautiful examples of the brickwork of Defoe's day are still to be met with, but much has gone, amongst it that lovely little collocation of houses known as Paradise Row where the Duchesse de Mazarin and Mrs. Mary Astell, Charles Duke of St. Albans with his mother, Eleanor Gwynn, and Dr. Richard Mead, *inter multos alios*, lived at one time or another in the time of Defoe.

'THE BEST FOUNDATION OF ITS KIND IN THE WORLD'

Here is the Nobleſt Building, and the beſt Foundation of its kind in the World, *viz.* for the Entertainment of Maimed and Old Soldiers. If we muſt except the Hoſpital call'd *des Invalids* at *Paris*, it muſt be only that the Number is Greater there, but I pretend to ſay that the OEconomy of the Invalids there, is not to compare with this at *Chelſea*; and as for the Proviſions, the Lodging, and Attendance given, *Chelſea* infinitely exceeds that at *Paris*. Here the Poor Men are lodg'd, well cloathed, well furniſh'd, and well fed, and I may ſay there are Thouſands of poor Families in *England* who are ſaid to live well too, and do not feed as the Soldiers there are fed; and as for *France*, I may add, they know nothing there what it is to live ſo. The like may be ſaid of the Invalid Sea Men at the Hoſpital of *Greenwich*.

THE 'PARADISE OF RANELAGH'

Near this Hoſpital or College, is a little Palace, I had almoſt call'd it a *Paradiſe*, of the late Earl of *Ranelagh*. It is true that his Lordſhip was envied for the Work, but had it been only for the Beauties of the Building, and ſuch things as theſe, I ſhould have been hardly able to cenſure it, the Temptation wou'd have been ſo much; In a Word, the Situation, the Houſe, the Gardens, the Pictures, the Proſpect, and the Lady, all is ſuch a Charm; who could refrain from coveting his Neighbours . . . *&c.*

CHELSEA HOSPITAL is one of Wren's enduring monuments and is certainly Chelsea's chief ornament. Gone is Ranelagh; gone Don Saltero's with his amazing collection of curiosities; gone the famous Chelsea Bun Shop where Swift not only bought the delicacies at a penny each, but carefully records the fact for Stella's benefit; gone, too, with one exception, are all the noble houses with their historic associations. But Chelsea Hospital remains, a monument to the wisdom of Sir Stephen Fox (owing, perhaps, also something to the generous heart of Nell Gwynn and the easy acquiescence of her royal lover), but above all, in its outward form at least, to the genius of our greatest architect.

It was erected on the spot where Chelsea College (founded in James I's time by Dr. Matthew Sutcliffe) had stood, and was begun in 1682, in the March of which year Charles II laid the first stone. The place was ready for use in 1702, by which time just on £150,000 had been expended on the actual structure. The work is thus shown to have covered a long period, and no doubt this was due to the habitual lack of money in those days for anything which did not minister to the pleasures of the Court. It is known that in November, 1684, the King asked the Archbishop of Canterbury (Sancroft), in a published letter, for assistance in money from the clergy and philanthropic people generally, and that Sancroft himself contributed £1,000 to the fund.

The 'LITTLE PALACE,' as Defoe calls it, was the residence which the Earl of Ranelagh, then only a Viscount and Paymaster-General of the Forces, had built, it is said from his own designs, on the east side of the Hospital, in or about the year 1690. Gibson, in his *Views of the Gardens near London*, published in 1691, describes it then as ' very fine within, all the rooms being wainscotted with Norway oak, and the garden plats and walks curiously kept and elegantly designed '; while Bowack, writing fourteen years later, states that the gardens were ' esteemed to be the best in England, the size considered.' The ground occupied by the house and gardens had been granted to Lord Ranelagh (who, by the way, figures as Jones in De Grammont's memoirs) by William III, on March 12th, 1690, for a term of sixty-one years.

What happened to the place after Lord Ranelagh's death in 1712 is a little obscure, but as in the plan of the Parish of St. George's, Hanover Square, published in 1724, it is shown marked with the name of Lady Catherine Jones, an unmarried daughter of Lord Ranelagh, it was probably on her death that it was sold (in 1733) to Lacy, of Drury Lane Theatre. Nine years later it was opened as the famous Ranelagh which bulks so insistently in the annals of social life in London during the remainder of the century. Lord Ranelagh's house remained in existence as part of the place of entertainment till its close in 1805, when it was demolished. Those who sit listening to the band at the Chelsea Flower Shows are on the exact site of Ranelagh Gardens. The great Rotunda, familiar in pictures by Canaletto and other contemporary artists, occupied the centre of these grounds, and was designed by William Jones, the East India Company's official architect.

It is impoffible to give an account of all the reft of *England* in this one Volume, while *London* and its Adjacent Parts, take up one half of it: I muft be allowed therefore to abate the Defcription of Private Houfes and Gardens, in which (this part efpecially) fo abounds, that it would take up two or three Volumes equal to this, to defcribe the County of *Middlefex* only.

'THREE THOUSAND FINE HOUSES BUILT SINCE THE YEAR 1666'

Let it fuffice to tell you that there's an incredible Number of fine Houfes built in all thefe Towns, within thefe few Years, and that *England* never had fuch a glorious Show to make in the World before; In a Word, being Curious in this part of my Enquiry, I find Two Thoufand Houfes which in other Places wou'd pafs for Palaces, and moft, if not all the Poffeffors whereof, keep Coaches in the little Towns or Villages of the County of *Middlefex*, Weft of *London* only; and not reckoning any of the Towns within three Miles of *London*; fo that I exclude *Chelfea, Kenfington, Knights-Bridge, Marybon,* and *Paddington*; as for *Hampftead*, that lying North of *London*, is not concerned in the Reckoning, for I reckon'd near a Thoufand more fuch in the Towns North of *London*, within the County of *Middlefex*, and exclufive of *Hackney*, for *Hackney* I efteem as Part of *London* itfelf as before: among all thefe three Thoufand Houfes I reckon none but fuch, as are Built fince the Year 1666, and moft of them fince the Revolution.

Among thefe, that is to fay, among the firft two Thoufand new Foundations, there are very many Houfes belonging to the Nobility, and to Perfons of Quality, (fome of whom) have been in the Miniftry; which excel all the reft. Such as the Lord *Peterborough's* at *Parfons Green*; Lord *Hallifax* at *Bufhy* Park, near *Hampton Court*; the late Earl of *Marr*, Earl of *Bradford*, Earl of *Strafford*, Earl of *Shrewsbury*, Earl of *Burlington*, Earl of *Falconberg*, Lady *Falkland*, Lord *Brook*, Lord *Dunbarr*, *Mofes Hart*, Mr. *Barker*, Sir *Stephen Fox*, Sir *Thomas Frankland*, General *Whettham*, Sir *Godfrey Kneller*, Secretary *Johnfon's*, and others.

MR. SECRETARY JOHNSON'S 'DELIGHTFUL PLACE'

This laft is a Seat fo exquifitely finifh'd, that His Majefty was pleafed to dine there, to view the delightful Place, and Honour it with his Prefence, that very Day, that I was writing this Account of it. The King was pleafed to dine in the Green Houfe, or rather in a pleafant Room which Mr. *Johnfon* built, joyning to the Green Houfe; from whence is a Profpect every way into the moft delicious Gardens; which indeed for the Bignefs of them are not out-done in any Part of the World.

'A COMPLEAT VINEYARD'

Here is a compleat Vineyard, and Mr. *Johnfon* who is a Mafter of Gardening, perhaps the greateft Mafter now in *England*, has given a Teftimony that *England* notwithftanding the changeable Air and uncertain Climate, will produce moft excellent Wines, if due Care be taken in the Gardening or Cultivating, as alfo in the curing and managing Part; and without due Care in thefe, not *France* it felf will do it.

The Mr. Secretary *Johnson* here referred to by Defoe, was James Johnstone, Secretary of State for Scotland. In 1702 he obtained a lease of a property at Twickenham, afterwards to become known as Orleans House. He demolished the old building and erected on its site the present house, modelled, it is said, from the country seats of Lombardy. The large octagon room was built by him for the reception of Queen Caroline who used to visit him and his wife Lady Catherine here. Macky, in his *Tour through England* (1720), says that Secretary Johnstone had the best collection of fruit of most gentlemen in England; that he had slopes for his vines from which he made some hogs-heads of wine a year; and that Dr. Bradley, in his *Treatise on Gardening*, ranked him among the first gardeners in the kingdom.

After Johnstone's death, his property at Twickenham was purchased by George Morton Pitt, once Governor of Fort St. George. From him it passed to his son-in-law, Lord Brownlow Bertie, brother of the Duke of Ancaster. Later it was bought by Sir George Pococke, who had married one of Pitt's grand-daughters, and his son, George, succeeded him here. Louis Philippe, as Duke of Orleans, on his return from America in 1800, rented the place from Pococke. Hence its present name. Later owners were R. Burnett, Esq., Alexander Murray, Esq., and the Earl of Kilmorey, from the last of whom it was bought by the Duc d'Aumale, and still later, under the ægis of Sir John Astley, it became the Orleans Club.

'THE FLOWER OF ALL PRIVATE GENTLEMEN'S PALACES'

Sir *Stephen Fox's* Houfe at *Chifwick* is the Flower of all the private Gentlemens Palaces in *England*. Here when the late King William, *who was an allowed Judge of fine Buildings, and of Gardening alfo*, had feen the Houfe and Garden, he ftood ftill on the Terras for near half a quarter of an Hour without fpeaking one Word, when turning at laft to the Earl of *Portland*, the King faid, *This place is perfectly fine, I could live here five Days.**

IN HAMMERSMITH 'A WOOD OF GREAT HOUSES' AND 'A NOBLE SQUARE'

In the Village of *Hammerfmith*, which was formerly a long fcattering Place, full of Gardeners Grounds, with here and there an old Houfe of fome Bulk: I fay, in this Village we fee now not only a Wood of great Houfes and Palaces, but a noble Square built as it were in the middle of feveral handfome Streets, as if the Village feem'd enclin'd to grow up into a City.

Here we are told they defign to obtain the Grant of a Market, tho' it be fo near to *London*, and fome talk alfo of building a fine Stone Bridge over the *Thames*; but thefe Things are yet but in Embryo, tho' it is not unlikely but they may be both accomplifhed in Time, and alfo *Hammerfmith* and *Chifwick* joyning thus, would in Time be a City indeed.

One of Hammersmith's most notable residents had been Queen Catherine of Braganza who, as the widow of Charles II, prior to her final departure from England in 1692, came to live on Upper Mall in what Faulkner calls a house of 'large but humble exterior.' It occupied the site where Riverscourt Road joins the Mall, between Kelmscott House and River Court; and it was

* N.B. *This was an expression the King used on no Occasion, but such, as where the Places were exquisitely Fine, and particularly pleased him: and it was not observ'd that ever his Majesty said it of any Place in* England, *but of this, and of* Burleigh-House *by* Stamford *in* Lincolnshire, *the Seat of the Earl of* Exeter. [NOTE BY DEFOE.]

during the Queen's residence here that the front of the Mall was curved out into the river, with bastions, in order apparently to allow of coaches turning at this otherwise narrow spot. This house was afterwards occupied by the famous Dr. Radcliffe.

The 'noble square' referred to by Defoe, was probably the large space now known as The Broadway, as there was no residential square here in those times, and only one, St. Peter's Square, at a considerably later period. Neither Bowack nor Faulkner, by the way, mention a square here at all; but the former tells us that 'Hammersmith was inhabited (1705) by gentry and persons of quality, and for above a hundred years past has been a summer retreat for the nobility and wealthy citizens.'

With regard to the bridge which Defoe, speaks of being under consideration, nothing seems to have been done until almost exactly a century later, when the Hammersmith Suspension Bridge was erected (1824–27). Once more a century passes and we are demanding again to-day not less than two additional bridges for the Western Exits across the Thames.

THE 'BORDERS OF MIDDLESEX' OUTSIDE THE LONDON AREA

I have now ranged the beſt part of *Middleſex*, a County made *Rich*, *Pleaſant*, and *Populous* by the Neighbourhood of *London*: The Borders of the County indeed have three Market Towns; which I ſhall but juſt mention, *Stanes*, *Colebrook*, and *Uxbridge*; This laſt, a Pleaſant large Market Town, famous in particular, for having abundance of Noble Seats of Gentlemen and Perſons of Quality in the Neighbourhood: But I can not deſcribe all the fine Houſes, it would be endleſs. This Town is alſo famous in Story, for being the Town where an attempt was in vain made in the late War, to ſettle the Peace of theſe Nations, by a Treaty; Some ſay both Sides were ſincerely inclin'd to Peace; ſome ſay neither Side; all I can ſay of it is, in the Words of Bleſſed St. *Paul, Sathan Hindred*. There are but three more Market Towns in the County, viz. *Brentford, Edgworth* and *Enfield*.

THE 'VISIBLE CHURCH' OF HARROW

On the right Hand as we ride from *London* to *Uxbridge*, or to *Colebrook*, we ſee *Harrow*, a little Town on a very high Hill, and is therefore call'd *Harrow on the Hill*: The Church of this Town ſtanding upon the Summit of the Hill, and having a very handſome and high Spire, they tell us, King *Charles* II. ridiculing the warm Diſputes among ſome Critical Scripturalliſts of thoſe times, concerning the viſible Church of Chriſt upon Earth; us'd to ſay of it, that if there was e'er a viſible Church upon Earth, he believ'd this was one.

APPENDIX A

'A Scheme for a Royal Palace
in the Place of Whitehall'

T H E following detailed description of this scheme, originally embodied in the text of the *Tour*, is here printed as an appendix, in order that the continuity of Defoe's narrative should not be interrupted, and requires a few words of explanatory introduction.

Beginning with the construction of the Banqueting House by Inigo Jones, for James I, in 1619, to replace the one destroyed by fire in the previous year, the idea of building a new Royal Palace, of which this beautiful structure was to form a small section of the Whitehall front, constantly engaged the attention of successive sovereigns. Various plans were, from time to time, submitted to Charles I, Charles II, and William III, and were originally identified with the name of Inigo Jones until Mr. GOTCH's recent researches have shown that they are more probably to be credited, in their completed form, to WEBB, the great architect's able assistant and son-in-law; although doubtless portions of them were at least adumbrated by Inigo Jones.

Exactly what relation the scheme here referred to by Defoe, which, by the way, includes not only the construction of a Palace and a range of government offices, but also a park, a zoo, botanical gardens, etc., bears to the plans published by Kent and Colin Campbell soon after the publication of Defoe's *Tour*, it is difficult to say. The extract from STRYPE, given in our annotations, mentions a Mr. WEEDON as having made a model which appears to have been submitted to William III, and Defoe may conceivably be referring to him. In any case, it is perhaps safe to assume that in Mr. Weedon's scheme there is some lineal succession of architectural ideas back through Webb to the original conception of Inigo Jones. Be this as it may, however (and for a careful study of the whole somewhat complicated subject we would refer our readers to Mr. Gotch's elaborate monograph as well as to his remarks in his admirable volume entitled *The English Home*), this idea of a Palace which never materialised forms one of the fascinating 'might-have-beens' of London topography, analogous to Wren and Evelyn's well-known plans for the reconstruction of the City, on geometrical lines, after the Great Fire.

Fortunately there exists an imaginary sketch, drawn by Thomas Sandby, the famous topographical artist, which shows the proposed new Palace, based on the Inigo Jones-Webb designs, as it would have appeared to anyone looking across the bend of the Thames from the gardens of old Somerset House towards Westminster. Our readers will note in our reproduction of this that the new Westminster Bridge is in existence as is the old Somerset House, so that the date of the sketch is thus fixed as being between 1750, when the former was completed, and 1775 when the latter was destroyed to make way for the existing Somerset House.

This sketch has here been supplemented by the plan, which has been carefully redrawn to show the outlines of the Palace itself plotted out according to the detailed description and measurements given by Defoe, and also those of the Palace grounds and precincts which were to extend east and west from the river to Buckingham House, and north and south from Charing Cross almost to Tothill Street.

Both sketch and plan indicate how vast would have been the change in the development and present appearance of Westminster and Whitehall and St. James's Park had this splendid scheme, outlined by a century of architects and toyed with by a century of sovereigns, materialised. Whitehall Palace would have emerged more imposing than the Louvre and vaster than the Escorial.

'First, it was Propofed, That the whole Building fhould be of *Portland* Stone, and all the Front be exactly after the Model of the *Banquetting* Houfe, with fuch Alterations only, as the Length and Height of the Building made neceffary.

'That the Firft Floor of the Building fhould be raifed from the prefent Surface, at leaft Eight Feet, as the prefent Building of the *Banquetting* Houfe now is.

'That the whole Building fhould make Four Fronts, one to the Water-fide and one to the *Canal* in the *Park*, a Third to the *North* facing *Charing-Crofs*, and the Fourth to the *South* facing *King-ftreet* in *Weftminfter*.

' That every Front fhould contain 400 Yards, or 1200 Feet, in length; that there fhould be Four Areas or Squares in the Infide of the Building, the Firft from the *North* Entrance to be Oblong, taking up the whole Length of the Building from *Eaft* to *Weft*, and that then a long Building fhould crofs the whole Work, Eighty Feet broad, and from the *Eaft* Range One thoufand Feet broad to the *Weft*; and in the middle of which, fhould be a great Arch or Gate looking to the *South* Gate of the Palace: That the other Side of the Palace be divided into Three Squares, having Two Ranges of Buildings to run crofs them from *South* to *North*, and each Range to joyn the great Range of Building which runs from *Eaft* to *Weft*.

' That the whole Building be withdrawn from the River fo far, at leaft, as where the Statue of King *James* II. now ftands, and a fpacious Terras to be carried on into the *Thames* Twelve Feet beyond Low-water-Mark, and over the River a handfome Foot-Bridge of Twelve great Arches only, with a Caufeway at the End over St. *George*'s Fields; That the Terras and Space between the Palace and the Water, be made into a fine Garden, with an Orangery on the *North* Side, reaching to the Edge of the Terras fo effectually, as it may cover the Garden from the View of any of the Buildings on the *Strand* Side, and a Royal *Bagnio* at the other End likewife, to cover the neceffary Buildings for the Kitchins which are behind it.

' For the Extent *North*, 'tis propofed, That all the Buildings be taken down to the Wall of *Northumberland* Houfe, on that Side; and to the *North* Side of the *Spring Garden*, oppofite to *Suffolk-ftreet* and the *Hay-Market* on the other Side; fo the Front of the Building that Way, will extend from the hither part of *Scotland-yard-Gate*, to Prince *Rupert*'s Garden, and the Gate of the Palace being in the Center of the Building, will open in that which is now called the *Spring Garden*.

' One Gate of the Palace opening thus *North*, a Balluftrade of Iron, like that which furrounds St. *Paul*'s Church, fhould take in a large Parade, reaching to the *Meuse*-Gate, a Space for the Street only excepted, and in proportion the other way towards *Pall-Mall*; and here on the *Eaft* Side, and on the *Weft* Side, Two large Guard-houfes fhould be erected, fitted, the one for the Horfe Guards, and the other for the Foot, both within the Balluftrade, but without the Palace, and Two fmaller Guard-houfes for Detachments of both, be likewife placed on the *South* Side, all at a proper Diftance from the main Building, and all low built.

' The *Canal* in the Park would be neceffarily filled up for about a Hundred Yards, for the Extent of the Building that Way; the Street that now is, muft, at the fame Time, be turned, and a large Street for Communication with *Weftminfter*, be allowed to crofs the Park from the *Pall-Mall South*, towards *Weftminfter*, to come out at the New Iron Gate, now leading to *Queen's-Square* and *Tottil-ftreet*; but no Houfes to be built in it, and Four Gates in the faid Street, to lead over the Street, from the Firft Floor of the Palace, by Galleries into the Park; All Buildings adjoining to the Park to be taken down, nor any private Doors or Keys to be allowed; a Stone Wall of Twenty Feet high and Eight Feet thick, to be built round the Park, and the Park to be extended *Weft*, by taking in *Buckingham* Houfe, with its Gardens.

' In this Building, the Propofer's Scheme was, To have all the Offices of the King's *Exchequer*, the Revenue, the Council, the Secretaries of State, the Admiralty, the Courts of Juftice, and both Houfes of Parliament, contain'd within the Palace, as was the Ufage in former Times.

' To this purpofe, the crofs Range of Buildings, going from *Eaft* to *Weft*, through the Center of the Palace, and looking into the great oblong Court, which would contain a Thoufand Feet, exclufive of the *Eaft* and *Weft* Fronts, and of the great Arch or Gate in the Center, fhould be divided thus; That Part on the *Eaft* Side of the Gate to contain Two fpacious Rooms, one for the Houfe of Peers, the other for the Houfe of Commons, with fufficient Offices, Galleries of Communication, Rooms of Conference for Committees, a Court of *Requefts*, &c. for the Ufe of the Members, and Rooms for all other Occafions of Parliament Bufinefs.

' The *Weft* Part of this great Range of Building to contain a Hall, as *Weftminfter-Hall* now is, with proper feparated Courts for the *King's Bench*, *Chancery*, *Common-Pleas*, and *Exchequer-Bars*, and a diftinct Court fix'd, and fuitably prepared, for Tryals of Peers or others, by the Houfe of Lords, notwithftanding which, this Court would be fufficiently large to celebrate the Coronation Feaft, with all its Ceremonies, the Building being from the middle Arch to the *Weft* Range of Buildings, Five hundred Feet long at leaft, and One hundred Feet broad.

' Thus the King's Court of Juftice, his High Court of Parliament, and all the Affairs of the Adminiftration, would be managed within his own Houfe, as it anciently was; and as the Two crofs Ranges of Buildings, which form'd the Three Courts on the *South* Side of the Parliament Houfe and Hall of Juftice, would be very large, they would afford Room for the Lord *Chamberlain*'s Office, the *Admiralty*, the *War* Office, the *Green-Cloth*, the *Wardrobe* Office, and all the other Family Offices, too many to name here.

VIEW OF WHITEHALL PALACE AS IT WOULD HAVE APPEARED IF COMPLETED

From an unfinished water colour by Thomas Sandby, R.A.

PLATE LIV*

PROSPECT OF THAMES-SIDE FROM SOMERSET HOUSE GARDENS

From a wash drawing by Canaletto

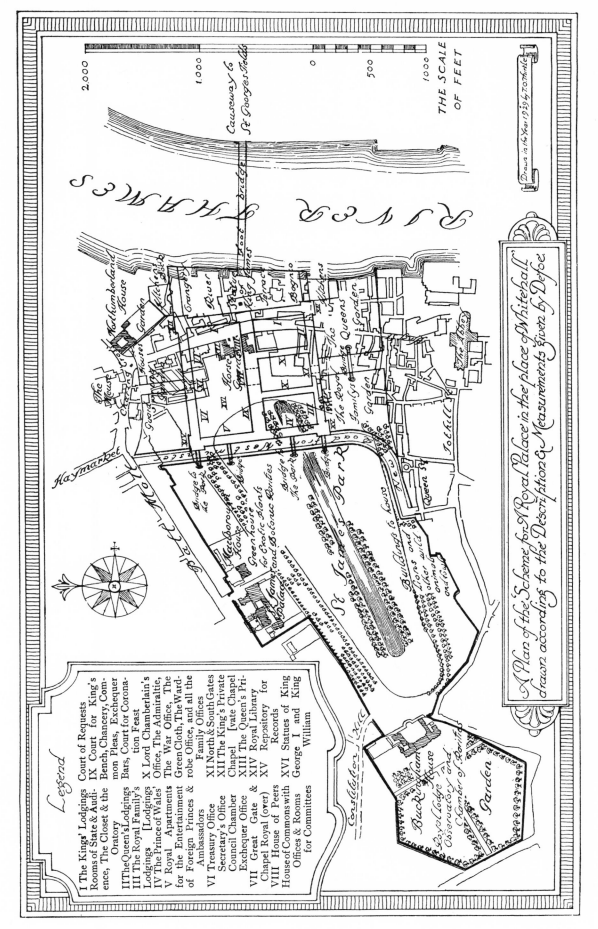

Legend

I The Kings' Lodgings Rooms of State & Audience, The Closet & the Oratory
II The Queen's Lodgings
III The Royal Family's Lodgings
IV The Prince of Wales'
V Royal Apartments for the Entertainment of Foreign Princes & Ambassadors
VI Treasury Office Secretary's Office Council Chamber Exchequer Office
VII Great Gate & Chapel Royal (over)
VIII House of Peers House of Commons with Offices & Rooms for Committees

Court of Requests
IX Court for King's Bench, Chancery, Common Pleas, Exchequer Bars, Court for Coronation Feast
X Lord Chamberlain's Office, The Admiraltie, The War Office, The Green Cloth, The Wardrobe Office, and all the Family Offices
XI North & South Gates
XII The King's Private Chapel [vate Chapel
XIII The Queen's Private Chapel
XIV Royal Library
XV Repository for Records
XVI Statues of King George I and King William

THE SCALE OF FEET

Drawn in the Year 1929 by T.M.Vardle

A Plan of the 'Scheme for A Royal Palace in the place of Whitehall' drawn according to the Description & Measurements given by Defoe.

NOTE.—The green overlay represents the outlines of the proposed palace and its precincts super-imposed on a plan of the district prepared from contemporary sources.

93

PLATE LV

RIVER FRONT OF THE PROJECTED PALACE OF WHITEHALL

From an engraving by A. Benoist, E. Rooker, Canot, and D. M. Müller, Jun.

' Then the main Range of Building on the *North* Side of the Palace, fhould contain (becaufe neareft the City) the *Treasury* Office, the *Secretary*'s Offices, the Council Chambers, and the *Exchequer* Offices.

' The Apartments of the other Three Ranges to be wholly taken up with the King's Houfhold: for Example;

' 1. For the Royal Apartments, being the King's Lodgings, Rooms of State and Audience,theClofet, the Oratory, and all the Rooms belonging to the Apartment of a King; this to take up the *Eaft* Range, fronting the Terras Garden and the *Thames*, and looking directly towards the City.

' 2. The Queen's Lodgings to be in the *Eaft* End of the *South* Range, fronting the City of *Weft-minfter*; but between the faid City and the Lodgings, the Queen's Garden to be extended from the Terras Garden mentioned before, to a Wall joining a Paffage from *Weftminfter* to the *South* Gate, which Wall begins at the Iron Balluftrade and Gate of the great Parade before the *South* Entrance of the Palace, and ends at the outer Stone Wall, which furrounds the Garden and Park. The Family for the Royal Children, to take up the *Weft* End of the faid *South* Range of Buildings, with the like Garden alfo, and a Gate joyning the Two Walls in the middle of the Paffage, leading to the *South* Gate of the Palace, by which, with as eafy Afcent of Steps, a Communication fhould be made between the faid Two Gardens.

' The *Weft* Range of Buildings fronting the Park, fhould be divided alfo into Two Parts, the firft being the *North* End, to confift of Royal Apartments for the Entertainment of Foreign Princes and Foreign Ambaffadors, at the Pleafure of the King, and the other Half, or *South* End to be called the Prince's Lodgings, and to be for the Prince of *Wales* for the Time being, and his Family.

' The great Arch in the Center of the whole, and in the middle of the long Range of Buildings, to support a large Church or Chapel Royal, for the Service of all the Houfhold, and for Preaching before the Houfes of Parliament on publick days, as is now at St. *Margaret*'s and at the *Abbey*: over this Church a large Dome or Cupola of Stone, covered with Copper and double gilded.

' At the Two Angles of the Buildings, fronting the River, Two private Chapels, the one for the Queen and her Houfhold, and the other for the King and his Houfhold, and either of thefe to fupport a Dome covered with Copper and gilded, as before, tho' fmaller than the other, with a large Lanthorn on the Top, and a fmall Spire, all of Stone.

' The Fronts to have Pavilions and Pediments in their proper Places; the whole Work to be built with the utmoft Regularity, in the *Corinthian* Order of Building, and with all poffible Beauty and Ornament.

' The Galleries of the Royal Chapel to be fupported with Pillars of Marble, of the fineft and moft beautiful Workmanfhip alfo, the *E.* End of the Building, the Altar and Baluftrade of the same, alfo Niches, with their Columns, and Pediments of the fame, and Two Pillars of the fineft Marble, Eighteen Feet high, ftanding fingle, one on each Side the Steps to the Communion Table, and on them Two Statues of the Apoftles St. *Paul* and St. *Peter*, or as the King fhall direct, the Statues to be large as the Life, the Capitals of the Columns gilded.

' All the Carv'd Work in the Walls, and round the Cornifh, and Architrave within and without, double gilded; the Ceiling of the Chapel to contain one great Oval, the Rim of it of Stone, carved as at St. *Paul*'s, and gilded, and the Middle painted by the beft Mafters, with either a Figure of the Afcention or the Refurrection, the Device to be new.

' All the Carved Work in Wood, and Mouldings, and Cornifh in the Quire and over the Stalls, to be double gilded, as likewife of the Organ and Organ Loft.

' All the Gates and Door Cafes in the Out-fides of the Work, with all the Columns and Carv'd Work belonging to them, efpecially the *North* and *South* Gates, and the Two Fronts of the great Arch in the middle, to be of the fineft Marble.

' All the Chimneys and foot Paces before them, to be of Marble of divers Colours, as well *Englifh* as Foreign: The Steps, alfo, of the King and Queen's great Stair-Cafes to be of Marble, all the other Stair-Cafes to be of the fineft Free-Stone, fetch'd from *Stamford* in *Lincolnfhire*, where is the whiteft Stone in *England*, and to be built as the Stair-Cafe in that called the *Queen*'s Houfe at *Greenwich*; no Wood to be allowed in any of the Stair-Cafes, except for Wainfcotting up the Side.

' All the great Stair-Cafes to be painted in the moft curious Manner poffible, as alfo the Ceilings of all the Royal Apartments, as well the Queen's as the King's.

' An Equeftrian Statue of the King in the Center of one Half of the firft great Court, and the like of the late King *William*, in the other Half.

' Large Fountains to be kept conftantly playing in the fmaller Courts, and in the Terras Garden.

' *Buckingham-Houfe* to be bought, and taken in, to be made a Royal Lodge for the Park, with an Obfervatory, and a Chamber of Rarities: And *Marlborough Houfe* to be bought, and to be made a

Green-houfe for *Exotick* Plants, and all *Botannick* Rarities, and the old Royal Garden to be again reftored, laid open to the Park, and be a planted Orangery; all the Orange and Lemon Trees to be planted in the Earth, fo as not to be removed in the Winter, but covered and secured feparately, as at *Beddington* in *Surrey*.

' A large Building to be added under the Wall in the Park, next to *Tottil-ftreet*, *Weftminfter*, with feparate Wards for keeping the *Lyons* and other the ftrange and foreign bred Brutes, which are now kept in the *Tower*, and Care to be taken to furnifh it with all the Rarities of that Kind that the World can procure, with Fowls, alfo, of the like foreign Kinds.

' A Royal Bagnio annexed to the Green-Houfe in the Terras Garden, like that for the Ladies in the Queen's Garden; but both diftant from the Palace.

' A large Alottment from the Lodgings at the Two Ends of the *N.* and *E.* Ranges, for the King's Kitchens, which fhould have alfo an additional Range of low Buildings, feparate from the Palace, and running down to the Water-fide; this Building would ftand juft between the Terras Garden Wall, which fhould hide it, and the Wall of *Northumberland Houfe*: And here (a Dock being made for that purpofe) all heavy Things, needful for the Kitchens, and for the whole Palace, fhould be brought in by Water; as Coals, and Wood, and Beer, and Wine, &c. at the *Eaft* End, and the Prince's at the *Weft* End; the Kitchens for the Queen and the younger Princes or Childrens Apartments, to be at the other Extremes of their refpective Appartments.

' Every range of Building to have double Rows of Rooms on the fame Floor; but the Royal Apartments to have alfo a long Gallery behind them, reaching the whole Length, the one End to joyn to the *Treafury* Office and Council Chamber in the *North* Range, and the other End to reach to the Queen's Royal Lodgings at the *South* Range; on the *Eaft* Side of this Gallery and in the Peers, between the Windows on the *Weft* Side, fhould be placed, all the fine Paintings that the Court are poffefs'd of, or that can be procur'd.

' In the *North Weft* Angle of the Building, a large Room or Rooms for the Royal Library, with Apartments for the Library Keeper; Galleries in the great Room to come at the Books, and a Cupola upon the Top.

' In the *South Weft* Angle, a like Repofitory for the Records, as well of the *Exchequer* as of Parliament, with Apartments for the Record-keeper, or Regifter, and a Dome over it as at the other Angle.

' The *North* and *South* Gates of the Palace to be Embellifhed in the moft exquifite Manner poffible, and the Statues of the King and Prince over the Arch wrought in Marble, in the fineft Manner poffible; the Gates to rife Twenty Five Feet above the Building, with an Attick, and fuch other Work as fhall be contriv'd for the utmoft Beauty and Ornament.

' The great Stair-Cafes to be in the Angles of the Building, built projecting into the Squares, that of the King's Apartment, to open into the firft Court, and into the Garden alfo, and in the like Manner the Queen's Stair-Cafe, at the other Side, to open into the little Square and into the Privy Gardens.

' The Stair-Cafes to land upon the Galleries, before they enter the Apartments, and for that Reafon, to be in the Infide of the Building, and to be diftinct from it, to prevent taking up any of the Apartments of the Angles, which are appointed for other purpofes; in the Middle of the King's great Gallery, Doors should be made, leading into the great middle Range of Buildings; by one of which, His Majefty may enter a Gallery leading to the Houfe of Lords, and by the other, enter thro' another Gallery to the Chapel Royal: In the great Gallery and in the Hall, Sixteen large Bouffetts or Cupboards of Gold and Gilt Plate of all kinds, to be fet open on publick Days.

' Likewife by thefe Doors, the King will have ready Accefs to all the Offices, to all the Lodgings, and through the Gates formerly mention'd, croffing the great New Street, which have Steps to pafs over their Arches, and defcend into the Park.'

APPENDIX B

Perambulations and Meditations in Westminster, Etc.

T H E two following ' newspaper articles ' (as we should term them to-day) which were written by Defoe for *Applebee's Journal* in the same year as the second volume of his *Tour*, which includes his chapter on London, are reprinted here primarily because they help to fill in the gaps in his topographical account of the ' Court-End ' of the town in the main text. They serve admirably also to illustrate Defoe's characteristic qualities of style as satirist and moralist and the peculiarly ' modern touch' which distinguishes his writings on matters of topical interest of the day from those of all his great contemporaries, qualities which have earned for him his title as the father of modern journalism. These particular articles deal with a matter which seriously affected the interests of the business community of the West End, and they reflect the feeling of what we now call the man in the street, with regard to those frequent and long absences from England with which George I tried to solace himself for what was practically an exile, although no doubt a glorious one, from his own long accustomed environment in Hanover. The general stagnation due to the King's Continental excursions is well indicated in Defoe's lucubrations, which show us a West End denuded of its fashionable inhabitants following the royal example of absenteeism. Another point to be noted in these extracts is the *cacoëthes ædificandi* which appears then to have overtaken London, as it is doing to-day. Indeed but few alterations would be needed to some of the following paragraphs to bring them actually up to date.

EVILS OF THE KING'S LONG ABSENCE.
PERAMBULATION OF WESTMINSTER

(*From Applebee's Journal, Sept. 4, 1725*)

Sir, In this State of Emptiness which, as by your last Papers, all our Journals suffer the Affliction of, I took a walk the other Day out of the City to the Court; or, as the Citizens vulgarly call it, the *'tother End of the Town.* I did it indeed in Charity to your Paper, thinking to pick up something at that Part of the Town for your Service; that being the usual Place for Intelligence, where the greatest People and the greatest Number of People resort.

But 'tis impossible for me to express my Surprize to you, when I came thither and found that Part of the World all as it were in Desolation; indeed I may liken it to Hell in one respect, for I think there was *Weeping and Wailing and Gnashing of Teeth.* In one Thing indeed it was unlike, and that was in the fewness of the Inhabitants.

The Weeping in the first Place I found among the Principal House-Keepers, most of whose Houses had Bills upon the Doors of Rooms to be Let, and they made a great Moan that they could not let their Lodgings; that the usual Income, or Rent of Apartments let out for Lodgings, was the Means by which, at least, they paid their Rent, and sometimes maintained their Families; and that this Year they saw nothing before them but Ruin, for that they not only had no Lodgers now, but were like to have none a great while; and as for the return of the Court, they had no Account when that would be, and if it was late in the Winter, or towards Spring, as some People made them Fear, they should be undone.

Sick with these Complaints, and being able to give the poor People no Comfort, I left them, and went away towards *Hyde Park;* being told of a fine new Avenue made to the East side of the Park, fine Gates, and a large *Visa*, or Opening, from the new Squares called *Hanover Square*, &c.

In this Tour I passed an amazing Scene of new Foundations, not of Houses only, but as I might say of new Cities. New Towns, new Squares, and fine Buildings, the like of which no City, no Town, nay, no Place in the World can shew; nor is it possible to judge where or when, they will make an end or stop of Building.

Before I came into this new World of Brick and Tile, I saw abundance of empty Houses, as well as empty Lodgings, and Bills upon the Doors, even in some of the principal Squares and Streets of that part of the Town, such as Streets about *Covent-Garden, St. Martin's,* nay even in *Leicester-Fields* itself.

This was the most incongruous thing of its Kind imaginable to me, when I considered the Addition of Houses and Streets in one Part, and the spare Houses in the other; especially when I reflected that many of those Houses with Bills upon the Doors, wanting Tenants, were some of the most considerable Houses in the Place. Certainly then, said I, the City does not increase, but only the Situation of it is a going to be removed, and the Inhabitants are quitting the old Noble Streets and Squares where they used to live, and are removing into the Fields for fear of Infection; so that, as the People are run away into the Country, the Houses seem to be running away too.

All the Way through this new Scene I saw the World full of Bricklayers and Labourers; who seem to have little else to do, but like Gardeners, to dig a Hole, put in a few Bricks, and presently there grows up a House. The Streets are at present Peopled with only such as these; and with Carpenters, Joiners, and other Workmen, and Alehouse Keepers to receive the Money they spend. When, and from whence Inhabitants are to come to fill up the void Spaces, is as mysterious as a double Tongued Oracle; for while they build Streets, as if they intended to make the Town, *Nineveh like, by Three Days Journey long*, we see the rest of the Town empty and abandoned, weeping for want of Inhabitants, and looking like the Picture of Desolation.

Coming back from this Prospect, I went to *Charing Cross*, among some Shop-keepers who owed me some Money, thinking to receive a good Sum to pay Bills of Exchange with; but if they were *Weeping* before, they were *Wailing* here. Money they gave me none, they rather upraided my Unreasonableness for expecting it when every Body was out of Town; Court, Term, Parliament, all in Recess. ' Money,' said one of my Customers, ' How should Shop-Keepers have Money without Trade? How Trade without People? Why,' says he, 'Don't you see every Body is gone? We'll pay you some Money when His Majesty &c. comes home again, but you must stay till then.' However, they said nothing undutiful of his Majesty, only lamented the Case of poor Tradesmen, with an absent Court and an empty Town.

MEDITATIONS IN PALACE YARD, WESTMINSTER HALL, THE ABBEY AND THE PARK

(*From Applebee's Journal, Sept.* 11, 1725)

Sir, History has recorded, and it is still more authentically attested, by the living Testimony of many People of venerable Antiquity,—especially of the Female Sex—that in the Time of the late Visitation, (so we, of the precise Speakers, politely express the Plague Year 1665,) the Town was so empty of People, and those that were left went so little Abroad that the Grass grew in the Streets; nay, I won't be positive that they did not say the *Royal Exchange* wanted Mowing, only that no Body could be found to make the Hay.

Be that as it will, I could not forbear calling the Memoirs of those evil Days to mind,—when the other Day I had Occasion to cross over the Street from *Channel Row* to *Westminster Hall*,—all that unfrequented Vacancy called *Palace Yard*, once so thronged with Coaches, seem'd to me to be a Void in Creation; a useless Spot of Ground, like a barren Common in the Country, laying open to the Road, neglected and Waste, as neither fit for the Plough nor the Hoof, neither for Corn nor Cattle.

While I stood staring about me, and wondering a little,—at least diverting my Thoughts with the Difference of the Face of Things,—I saw a Man walking across the Yard, out of the ordinary Path, in a direct Line, and taking large Strides, as if he was measuring the Ground by Paces. As I found by his stepping he would come near the Place where I stood, I waited till he came close up to me, when, on a sudden, he stopped;—' a Hundred! ' says he aloud, and then cut a Notch in a Stick, with his Knife, which he held ready for that purpose.

' What are you doing Sir,' *said I to him*, ' are you measuring the Ground? ' 'Yes Sir,' says he very courteously, and seeming, as I thought, a very civil Fellow, and willing enough to talk, I ask'd him if I might be so free with him as to inquire into the meaning of it. ' Yes Sir,' *says he,* ' with all my Heart. I had heard, the other Day,' *says he,* ' that this Piece of Vacant Ground was to be let to build on, and as I am a Projector ' *says he,* ' I have been measuring it out, and I think it will make a very handsome Square this Way; ' and with that he points it out with his Finger; ' or that Way, Sir,' *says he* 'it will make two very fine Streets.'

I smiled, but perceived he was not pleas'd at it. ' I find Sir,' *says he,* ' you seem to laugh at my Design, I presume you do not understand those Things so well as I. 'Tis my Business, Sir, I laid out the Plan of all the ancient fine Buildings in the Town, I built *Dunkirk House,* and *St. James's Square;* I laid out all the fine Streets in *Hatton Garden* and the Noble Pile of Buildings call'd *Portugal Row* in *Lincoln's Inn Fields ;* all your new contracted Squares of *Soho, Golden Square, Red Lion Square,* ay, and your *Hanover Square* too, are Fools to them.'

' Pray Sir,' *said I, and made him a Leg,*—' do not mistake me; I did not laugh at you, but smiled to see how our Thoughts agreed, for I was just musing upon the same Thing, namely, the Uselessness of this Piece of Ground, only that I was laying it out for other Business, for I am no *Builder.* But Sir,' *said I,* ' In your Design, what Care have you taken to keep a Way open to the Great Hall there, for that you know is a place of Business? ' ' O dear! ' *says he,* ' that's true, indeed I had forgot that. Why, will the Lawyers come to it again? ' ' Yes, Yes,' *says I,* ' 'tis very likely they may.' ' Well, Well,' *says he,* ' 'tis but giving a new Turn to my Design, and I shall make a Passage, broad enough for all honest Men I warrant you.' ' Hum! ' *Says I,* ' for honest Men? But you must allow Room for the rest too,' says I, ' or it won't do.' That troubled him a little but I perceived he went to take a new Survey of the Ground, and so I left him, after we had, upon this short Acquaintance, appointed where to meet in the Evening to finish our Conference.

I went on then to the Hall, where I found the Doors open indeed, and the Spider-left Ceiling preserved the ancient dull Lustre of *Irish Oak.* The Trophies of *Blenheim* seemed to be following the Memory of the Great Duke of *Marlborough,* and indeed of Mankind, for they hung in Rags and began to rot; so certain is it, that Fame, like the Bones of Men, must return to its first Nothing; and, that *Immortal Memory, is Nonsense in terminis.* Neither Marble nor Brass, no, nor Tombs of Adamant, can prevent the sinking of every Thing into Nothing; but that by the Way. In a Word,—there was the venerable Old Pile, the vacant Throne of Justice stood at the upper End, and the Ruins of the most eminent Shops for Trade remained; but for all other Things, all was silent, empty, and void, and put me in mind of the Ruins of the Old World after the Deluge. So I resolved to do as the rest of Mankind seem'd to have done, (viz.) abandon it; as they tell us the Inhabitants of *Arch-Angle* do, who leave the Country during the vacancy of Commerce, and return again at the proper Season. From Hence, I went to the *Abbey,* and there, indeed, I found the Royal Tombs, and the Monuments of the dead, remaining and encreased; but the Gazers, the Readers of Epitaphs, and the Country Ladies to see the Tombs, were strangely decreased in Number. Nay, the Appearance of the Choir was diminished; for setting aside the Families of the Clergy resident, and a very few more, the Place was forsaken.

' Well,' *said I,* ' then a Man may be Devout with the less *Disturbance ;* ' so I went in, said my Prayers, and then took a Walk in the *Park.*

Both sides of the *Park* look'd Gay and Green, but *alas!* all the fine Company was gone, the benches were vacant, the Beauties were absent, I miss'd the noble Train of Ladies, the Glory of *Britain,* that used to shine there; all the Gentry I could find were some few Officers of the Guards, whose Companies I suppose were upon Duty,—now and then a Barber, going with his Instruments to Shave,—some Footmen going of Errands, and here and there a fallen Woman; for the rest, the Parade was quite empty, the Mall wanted weeding, the very Ducks in the Canal miss'd their ancient Benefactors the Nurses and Nursery Maids with the Children, to give their Breakfast to the Wild Fowl. The Houses round, whose Windows enjoy'd the pleasant Prospect of the *Park,* look'd all heavy, the Window-Shutters fast closed, and not a Face to be seen. Upon this melancholy Day I took up a sudden Resolution, that since all the World was gone Abroad, I would go and look for them; for why should I live alone when the Company was perhaps as Merry as ever, if I could but find them out? Accordingly I took my Horse for *Tunbridge,* and there I found them, to my inexpressible Satisfaction, as you shall hear in its Place.

Your Humble Servant.

APPENDIX C

Some Contemporary Descriptions of London

T H E Title-pages here reproduced in exact facsimile are those of such smaller works on London (in a sense the forerunners of the later guide-books) as appeared during Defoe's lifetime, and are interesting as representing the earliest attempts to describe the city, after the far earlier *Surveys* of John Stow, 1598 and 1603, and Howell, whose *Londinopolis* appeared in 1657. *No.* 1 is the well-known work in two volumes compiled by E. HATTON, remarkable for its mass of detailed information, as is indicated by its title-page. *No.* 2 is the work of JOHN MACKY, who wrote *inter alia* a *History of the Secret Service*, and gives us a valuable picture of London on its social side from the point of view of a peripatetic visitor. It has sometimes been confounded with Defoe's *Tour* itself. *No.* 3 is the later edition of THOMAS DELAUNE's little book which first appeared in 1681, to both editions of which frequent references are made in our text and appendices. *No.* 4 is the far less ambitious work, indeed essentially a pocket-companion, compiled by one N. BAILEY, who is otherwise unknown. *No.* 5 is also a small, but more comprehensive work, issued by W. STOW (not to be confounded with his sixteenth-century namesake, John Stow), and is typographically interesting as having been printed on old London Bridge. What, if any, connection there was between the father of London topography and the author of this rare and interesting little work is unknown, and it may be that the name was merely used as an appropriate pseudonym.

(1)

A

New View of *LONDON*;

OR, AN

Ample Account of that C I T Y,

In Two Volumes, or Eight Sections.

Being a more particular Defcription thereof than has hi-
) therto been known to be publifhed of any City in the World.

I. Containing the Names of the *Streets, Squares, Lanes, Markets, Courts, Alleys, Rows, Rents, Yards* and *Inns* in London, *Weftminfter* and *Southwark* ; fhewing the Derivations thereof ; Quality of Building and Inhabitants ; Dimenfions, Bearing and Diftance from *Charing Crofs*, St. *Paul's* Cathedral, or the *Tower* of *London*.

II. Of the *Churches* ; Their Names, Foundation, Order of Building, Ornament, Dimenfions, Altitude of Steeples, and Number of Bells therein ; Benefactors ; Monuments, Tombs, Cenotaphs, &c. defcribed ; with their Epitaphs, Infcriptions, Motto's, Arms, &c. The Nature and Value of Livings and Tythes, what each are Rated in the Queen's Books, and the Names of the Patrons, Impropriators, Rectors, Vicars, Lecturers ; the Hours of Prayer, Organs, &c.. Alfo the Number of Ward and Parifh Officers, the Contents or Bounds of every Parifh and Number of Houfes therein.

III. Of the feveral *Companies*, their Nature, Halls, Armorial Enfigns Blazoned, &c. *Guild-Hall, Exchanges, Eaft India, African, Trinity*, &c. Houfes and Fraternities, an Account of the *Cuftom-Houfe, Leaden-Hall, Bank of England*, &c.

IV. Of the *Queen's Palaces*, Eminent Houfes, &c. of the Nobility, Houfes of Lords and Commons. *Tower* of *London* and things remarkable therein : *Weftminfter-Hall, Hicks's-Hall, Juftice-Hall*, &c.

V. *Colleges*, Libraries, Mufæums, Repofitories of Rarities, Free-Schools, Inns of Serjeants, Court, and Chancery, Courts of Judicature from the higheft to the loweft ; Offices of Law, and others, fhewing their Bufinefs, Situation, &c.

VI. The *Hofpitals, Prifons*, Work-Houfes, Houfes of Correction, Alms-Houfes and Charity-Schools ; their Foundation, Prefent State, &c.

VII. Of Fountains, Bridges , Conduits, Ferries, Docks, Keys, Wharfs, Plying-places for Boats and their Diftances from *London Bridge* : Waters and Lights ufed by the City ; Infurances of all kinds, Bagnio's, Baths, Hot and Cold.

VIII. An Account of about 90 publick Statues, their Situations, Defcriptions, &c. The Matter in each *Section* being in Alphabetical Order, and including all things worthy of Note in *London, Weftminfter* and *Southwark*.

To which is added,
An Explanation of the Terms of Art ufed in this Treatife ; alfo a *Supplement*.
And to the whole is prefixed,
An Introduction concerning *London* in General ; its Antiquity, Magnitude, Walls and Gates, Number of Houfes, Inhabitants, Males, Females, Fighting Men ; its Riches, Strength, Franchifes, Government, Civil, Ecclefiaftical and Military, &c.
Illuftrated with 2 Plans, *viz.* 1. Of *London*, as in Q. *Eliz.* Time. 2. As it is at prefent ;
Alfo the Arms of all the City Companies, and other Copper Plates.
A Book ufeful not only for Strangers, but the Inhabitants, and for all Lovers of Antiquity, Hiftory, Poefie, Statuary, Painting, Sculpture, Mathematicks, Architecture and Heraldry.

V O L U M E   I.

L O N D O N, Printed for R. *Chifwell*, *A.* and *J. Churchill*, T. *Horne*, *J. Nicholfon*, and R. *Knaplock*, 1708.

2

A
JOURNEY
THROUGH
ENGLAND.
IN
Familiar Letters
FROM
A GENTLEMAN Here,
TO
His FRIEND Abroad.

―――― *In Junonis Honorem,*
Aptum dicit equis Argos, *diteiſq;* Mycœnas.
Me nec tam patiens Lacedæmon,
Nec tam Lariſſæ *percuſſit campus opimæ*
Quam domus Albaniæ *reſonantis.* Hor.

LONDON:
Printed for JOHN HOOKE, at the*Flower-*
de-Luce, and T. CALDECOTT, at
the *Sun*, both againſt St. *Dunſtan*'s Church
in *Fleetſtreet.* 1714.

3

ANGLIÆ METROPOLIS:
OR
The Preſent State
OF
LONDON:
WITH
𝕸emo𝖗ials
COMPREHENDING
A Full and Succinct Account
OF
The Ancient and Modern
State thereof.
Its Original, Government, Rights, Liber-
ties, Charters, Trade, Cuſtoms, Privi-
ledges, and other Remarkables,*&c.*

Firſt Written by the late Ingenious *THO. DELAUNE*
Gent. and Continu'd to this preſent Year by a careful hand.

Civitates ab initio Utilitatis Cauſa Conſtitutæ
ſunt, Ariſtot. Polit .1.

LONDON:
Printed by 𝔊. 𝕃. for 𝕵ohn 𝕳arri𝔰 at the *Hor*
row in the *Poultrey*, and 𝕿homa𝔰 𝕳awkin
in *George Yard* in *Lumbard-Street.* MDCXC.

4

THE
ANTIQUITIES
OF
LONDON
AND
WESTMINSTER.
BEING
An Account of whatſoever is Ancient, Curi-
ous or Remarkable, as to Palaces, Towers,
Caſtles, Walls, Gates, Bridges, Monaſteries,
Priories, Sanctuaries, Nunneries, Religious
Houſes, Cathedrals, Churches, Chapels,
Colleges, Inns of Court, Hoſpitals, Schools
and other Magnificent Buildings ; as Ex-
changes, Halls, Croſſes, Markets, Goals ;
and all Publick Edifices ; Alſo Rivers,
Brooks, Bourns, Springs, *&c.* and many
other curious Matters in Antiquity, where-
by will plainly appear the Difference between the Ancient and Preſent State of
theſe two Famous Cities.

By N. B.

LONDON:
Printed for *H. Tracy*, at the *Three Bibles* on
London-Bridge. 1722.

5

REMARKS
ON
LONDON:
BEING AN
Exact SURVEY
OF THE
CITIES of *London* and *Weſtminſter*, Borough
of *Southwark*, and the Suburbs and Liberties contiguous
to them, by ſhewing where every Street, Lane, Court,
Alley, Green, Yard, Cloſe, Square, or any other Place,
by what Name ſoever called, is ſituated in the moſt
Famous Metropolis ; ſo that Letters from the General
and Penny-Poſt Offices cannot Miſcarry for the future.
An Hiſtorical Account of all the Cathedrals, Collegiate
and Parochial Churches, Chapels, and Tabernacles,
within the Bill of Mortality : Shewing therein the ſett
Time of publick Prayer, Celebrating the Sacraments,
Morning and Evening Lectures, and Preaching Sermons,
both Ordinary and Extraordinary ; with many curious
Obſervations. Places to which Penny-poſt Letters and
Parcels are carried, with Liſts of Fairs and Markets.
What places ſends Members to Parliament. To what
Inns Flying-Coaches, Stage-Coaches, Waggons and
Carriers come, and the Days they go out ; lately col-
lected. Keys, Wharfs and Plying-places on the River
of *Thames*. Inſtructions about the General Poſt-Office.
Deſcription of the great and croſs Roads from one City
and eminent Town to another, in *England* and *Wales*. A
perpetual Almanack. The Rates of Coachmen, Chair-
men, Carmen, and Watermen. A perpetual Tide-Table ;
and ſeveral other neceſſary Tables, adapted to Trade
and other Buſineſs.
All Alphabetically digeſted ; and very uſeful for all
Gentlemen, Ladies, Merchants, Tradeſmen, both in City
and Country. The like never before extant.

By *W. STOW.*

LONDON : Printed for *T. Norris* at the *Looking-glaſs*,
and *H. Tracy* at the *Three Bibles*, on *London-Bridge.* 1722.

APPENDIX D

An Account of the General Post Office and the Inauguration of the Penny Post in the Reign of Charles II

T H E reference in Defoe's text to the large increase of the business carried on by the General Post Office is confirmed by the account of its labours during our author's early years, given in Delaune's *Present State of London*, 1681, which also affords an interesting and instructive picture of its methods of operation and the scale of its activity during that period. The section headed 'Of the Penny Post' is of particular value as tracing the inauguration of that department by private enterprise and the difficulties it encountered between the anvil of the monopoly claims of the Duke of York (as grantee of the Government) on the one hand, and the hammer of Labour, as represented by what Delaune calls 'some sort of Porters,' on the other—the latter resenting what they not unnaturally regarded as an encroachment on one of the chief perquisites of their calling.

When Defoe wrote his short notice of the Post Office, that institution, together with the 'Penny Post,' had definitely become a Government Department, and he only incidentally alludes to the period when, as he says, 'it was subject to Miscarriages and Mistakes,' a period which is fully explored by Delaune in his comprehensive survey and which deals with it some forty odd years earlier than when Defoe wrote his *Tour*.

OF THE POST OFFICE

This Office is now kept in Lumbard-street, formerly in Bishops-gate-street, the Profits of it are by Act of Parliament settled on his Royal Highness the Duke of York. But the King by Letters Patents, under the great Seal of England, constitutes the Post-Master-General.

From this General Office, Letters and Packets are dispatched,

On Mondays

To France, Spain, Italy, Germany, Flanders, Sweedland, Denmark, Kent and the Downs.

On Tuesdays

To Holland, Germany, Sweedland, Denmark, Ireland, Scotland, and all parts of England and Wales.

On Wednesdays

To all parts of Kent and the Downs.

On Thursdays

To France, Spain, Italy, and all parts of England and Scotland.

On Frydays

To Flanders, Germany, Italy, Sweedland, Denmark, Holland, Kent, and the Downs.

On Saturdays

All parts of England, Wales, Scotland, and Ireland.

Letters are returned from all parts of England and Scotland, certainly every Monday, Wednesday and Friday; from Wales every Monday and Fryday; and from Kent and the Downs every day: But from other parts more uncertainly, in regard of the Sea.

A Letter containing a whole sheet of paper is conveyed 80 Miles for 2d. two sheets for 4d. and an Ounce of Letters for 8d. and so proportionably; a Letter containing a sheet is conveyed above 80 Miles for 3d two sheets for 6d and every Ounce of Letters for 12d. A sheet is conveyed to Dublin for 6d. two for a shilling and an Ounce of Letters for 12d.

This Conveyance by Post is done in so short a time, by night as well as by day, that every 24 hours, the Post goes 120 Miles, and in five days, an answer of a Letter may be had from a Place 300 Miles distant from the Writer.

Moreover, if any Gentleman desire to ride Post, to any Principal Town of England, Post-horses are always in readiness, (taking no Horse without the consent of his owner) which in other Kings Reigns was not duly observed; and only 3d is demanded for every English Mile, and for every Stage to the Post-boy, 4d. For conducting.

Besides this Excellent convenience of conveying Letters, and Men on Horse-back, there is of late such an admirable commodiousness, both for Men and Women of better rank, to travel from London, and to almost all the Villages near this great City, that the like hath not been known in the World, and that is by Stage-Coaches, wherein one may be transported to any place, sheltred from foul weather, and foul ways, free from endamaging ones Health or Body by hard jogging, or over violent motion; and this not only at a low price, as about a shilling for every five miles, but with such velocity and speed, as that the Posts in some Foreign Countries, make not more Miles in a day; for the Stage-Coaches, called Flying-Coaches, make forty or fifty Miles in a day, as from London to Oxford or Cambridge, and that in the space of twelve hours, not counting the time for Dining, setting forth not too early, nor coming in too late.

The several Rates that now are and have been taken for the Carriage of Letters, Packquets, and Parcels, to or from any of His Majesties Dominions, to or from any other parts or places beyond the Seas, are as followeth, that is to say,

		s.	d.
Morlaix, St. Maloes, Caen, Newhaven, and places of like distance, Carriage paid	(Single	o	6
to Rouen	(Double	1	o
	(Treble	1	6
	(Ounce	1	6

(Here follows a list of the postal charges to all the chief towns in Europe and also Turkey)

* * * * * * * *

All Merchants Accounts, not exceeding a Sheet, Bills of Exchange, Invoices, Bills of Lading, shall be allowed without rate in the price of the Letters, and also the Covers of the Letters not exceeding a Sheet to Marseilles, Venice, or Legorn, towards Turkie.

The said Office is managed by a Deputy, and other Officers, to the number of seventy seven persons; who give their actual attendance respectively, in the dispatch of the business.

Upon this Grand Office, depends one hundred and eighty two Deputy-Post-Masters in England and Scotland; most of which keep Regular Offices in their Stages, and Sub-Post-Masters in their Branches; and also in Ireland, another General Office for that Kingdom, which is kept in Dublin, consisting of Eighteen like Officers, and Forty-five Deputy Post-Masters.

The Present Post-Master-General, keeps constantly, for the transport of the said Letters and Pacquets;

Between England and - - - - - (France, two Pacquet-Boats
(Flanders, two Pacquet-Boats
(Holland, three Pacquet-Boats
(Ireland, three Pacquet-Boats

And at Deal, two Pacquet-Boats for the Downs.

All which Officers, Post-Masters, Pacquet-Boats, are maintained at his own proper Charge.

And as the Master-piece of all those good regulations, established by the present Post-Master-General, for the better Government of the said Office, he hath annexed and appropriated the Market-Towns of England so well to their Respective Post-Stages, that there is no considerable Market-Town but hath an easy and certain Conveyance for the letters thereof, to and from the said Grand Office, in the due course of the Males every Post.

Though the Number of Letters Missive in England, were not at all considerable in our Ancestors days, yet it is now so prodigiously great (since the meanest People have Generally learnt to write) that this Office is Farmed for above 40, rather 50000*l.* a Year.

OF THE PENNY-POST

This Ingenious Undertaking being so extraordinary useful in the facilitating of Commerce and mutual Correspondence, and consequently very serviceable to Traders &c. shall be briefly handled; and, I hope, that what proceeds from me, will be resented Candidly, and Examined, as to the Argumentative part, according to the Solidity and Strength of the Reasons produced.

I have heard this Undertaking disparaged by some Censorious Persons, and have examined the Reasons, with the quality of the Objectors, and have found it all along opposed by none but the Ignorant, or such as preferred some particular Ends, before Publick Utility. To my knowledge I never saw nor corresponded directly nor indirectly with any of the Undertakers, till being very desirous to insert this Affair of the Penny-Post in this Book for the Publick Information, I made an Address to one of the Gentlemen concern'd who Courteously supply'd me with some particular Informations which I wanted, and for which I am beholding to him. This I speak, to satisfy the Objectors that I do voluntarily, and not by an inducement of theirs mention this Affair, which, in my opinion, is so far from being a prejudice, that the City, as well as the whole Nation, is beholding to them for their Ingenious Contrivance, and their Constancy and Generosity in minding the Publick Good so much as they have done; for 'tis certain that they have been at very great Expence to hold it up, under the Discouragements that some Persons have thrown upon them, and the necessary Charge to support it is yet very considerable. But to be more particular:

1. I will give some Hints of what this Undertaking is in Point of Practice.
2. Its general and particular Usefulness.
3. I will consider an Objection or two.

1. What I can say of this Undertaking in Point of Practice, is briefly what follows, only I would premise a few words as my own opinion, and the opinion of impartial Persons of my acquaintance, as to the thing in general.

This useful Invention is little more than a year old, being begun in April 1680. The chief Undertaker that introduc'd it into practice, is one Mr. William Dockwra, Merchant, a Native and Citizen of London, formerly one of his Majesties Sub-Searchers in the Custom-House of London, as in the List of those Officers appears. A person, whose approved Reputation for Industry and Fidelity was well known to all for above ten years in that Office: And to whom the Publick is obliged, he having, with his Partners, spent much time, and a great sum of money, to bring this Undertaking on foot, wherein they encountered no small Difficulties, not only by Affronts and Indignities from the Vulgar sort, who seldom weigh any Publick or Generous Designs, but as the Beam of Little, Selfish, By-Ends, but also by more dangerous Attaques; for there have been Attempts made, by some Persons, to persuade his Royal Highness the Duke of York, that it intrench'd upon the General Post-Office, and damnifi'd it; whereupon many Actions were brought, and a chargeable Suit of Law follow'd: But, questionless, the Duke is better inform'd now; for it is most certain that this does much further the Revenue of the Grand Post-Office and is an universal Benefit to all the Inhabitants of these Parts: so that whoever goes about to deprive the City of so useful a thing, deserves no thanks from the Duke, nor any Body else, but to be noted as an Enemy to Public and Ingenious Inventions.

It is with all Humility submitted to the Consideration of all worthy Citizens that happen to peruse this finall Tract, that it becomes not the Honour of the City to suffer any of its Ingenious Natives, especially Persons who have lived and do live in Good Fashion and Repute, to sink under the carrying on of an Undertaking so advantageous not only to the Publick, but also to private Persons, since their industrious Service to their Generation deserves encouragement from their Fellow-Citizens, and all others, viz.

(1) To discountenance petty Persons that would, for the profit of running of Errands, rob the Community (if they could) of this more than ordinary convenience for safe, cheap, and necessary Dispatches.

(2) To reject any INTRUDER that may attempt to set up another Penny-Post; because if the thing be hereafter profitable all the Reason and Equity in the world will plead for the Inventors, viz. that they ought to reap the Benefit. And it is a Note of Consideration, That Mr. Dockwra has a numerous Family of eight young Children; who being forsaken for some others soon after it began, and left to shift for himself, carried on this Undertaking singly, for above half a year at his own proper charge and hazard, against all the Difficulties, Oppositions and Discouragements that attended it, though now he hath several Citizens in partnership with him. But I am truly informed, that the Income does not yet amount to three fourths of the necessary Charge to support it; therefore I am persuaded that this Honourable City will employ the Inventers, rather than an Invader, if ever any such should be; And that 'tis much below such a Prince as His Royal Highness is, to desire the Ruine of such a Family.

I am the more large upon this particular, because it would be a general Discouragement to the Contrivers of useful and profitable Inventions, if others should be encouraged to reap the Crop of what they with so much charge and labor have sown.

This Penny-Post is thus managed.

The Principal Office to which all Accompts &c. are daily transmitted, is in Lyme-Street, at the Dwelling-house of the said Mr. Dockwra, formerly the Mansion-house of Sir Robert Abdy Knt.

There are seven Sorting-Houses, proper to the seven precincts, into which the Undertakers have divided London, Westminster and the Suburbs, situated at equal distances, for the better maintenance of mutual Correspondence.

There are 4 or 500 Receiving-houses, to take in Letters, where the Messengers call every hour, and convey them as directed; as also Post-Letters, the writing of which are much increased by this Accomodation, being carefully convey'd by them to the General Post-Office in Lombard-street.

There are a great number of Clerks and poor Citizens daily employed, as Messengers, to Collect,

Sort, Enter, Stamp and Deliver all Letters, every Person entertained giving Fifty pounds security, by Bond, for his Fidelity; and is to be subject to the Rules and Orders, from time to time, given by the Undertakers, who oblige themselves to make good anything delivered to their Messengers under the value of Ten pounds, if Sealed up, and the Contents Endorsed; And these Messengers have their Wages duly paid them every Saturday night.

By these are convey'd Letters and Parcels, not exceeding One Pound Weight, nor Ten Pound in Value, to and from all parts, at seasonable times, viz. of the Cities of London and Westminster, Southwark, Redriff, Wapping, Ratcliff, Lyme-house, Stepney, Poplar, and Blackwall, and all other places within the weekly Bills of Mortality, as also to the four Towns of Hackney, Islington, South-Newington-Butts, and Lambeth, but to no other Towns, and the Letters to be left only at the Receiving-houses of those four Towns, for the said four Towns; but if brought home to their Houses, a Penny more in those Towns; nor any letter to be deliver'd to them in the Street, but at the Receiving-houses.

They now do use Stamps to mark the hour of the Day on all Letters when sent out from their Office to be deliver'd, by which all Persons are to expect their Letters within one hour (little more or less, from the time marked thereon, excepting such Letters as are to be convey'd to the Out-Towns and Remotest Parts, which will be longer) by which the cause of delay of Letters may be easily discern'd, viz. whether it be really in the Office, or their Own Servants, (or others) with whom Letters are left.

The Marks they make use of for this purpose, are these:

Of which the First, signifies Eight in the Morning, the Last Four in the Afternoon, and the Middle-most, is the Letter of the chief Office in Lyme-Street, each Office having its proper Letter, and an Acknowledgement that the Penny-Post is paid, to prevent the giving of anything at the Delivery.

All persons are desired not to leave any Town-Letters after six of the clock in the Winter, and Seven in the Summer on Saturday Nights, because the poor Men employ'd may have a little time to provide for their Families against the Lords-day, having no leisure all the week besides.

Upon three days at Christmas, two days in Easter and Whitsuntide, and upon the 30 of January,* the Penny-Post does not go.

To the most remote places Letters go four or five times of the day, to other places six or eight times of the day. To Inns of Court, and places of business in Town, especially in Term of Parliament time, 10 or 12 times of the day. For better Information of People where the Receiving-houses are there are great Numbers of Printed Tickets dispersed from time to time amongst the Neighbourhood, and Advertisements in the Publick Intelligences, which all concern'd may take notice of, so that any body may be by the Neighbourhood immediately inform'd where a Receiving-house is. Carriers and Stage-Coach Letters are to have Two-pence inclosed to each Carrier or Coachman, because they often reject them for want of money; Hundreds of such being return'd, which any Inquirer may have again upon notice, for they lie Alphabetically disposed of in the chief Office for that end.

On all Post-Nights due Care is taken to call for and convey to the General Post-house in Lombard-street all Post-Letters whether Foreign or Inland, left in any of the Penny-Post Receiving-houses, at or before Nine of the Clock at Night. And I could wish, for Encouragement of the Undertakers, that all Persons would so far contribute to the continuance of this useful Design, as to send their Post-Letters by this Conveyance to the Post-Office in Lombard-street, which they do not Convey by themselves, or Servants.

If any Post-letters be left without Money that should pay beforehand, they will be returned to the Office, therefore such as send Money, are to endorse the Postage-money upon their Letters.

Such as inclose Money in Town-Letters, are to Indorse the true Sum on the outside, and to tye fast and seal up, under a plain Impression, all Parcels, which may be one way to prevent Disputes, in case anything be lost. The Undertakers will not answer for any contents unseen, unless sealed fast, and the Value Indorsed plain to be Read.

2. Some brief Hints of the Usefulness of this Office.

1. In and near this great and famous Emporium, is the usual Residence of our Kings, the High Court of Parliament, the fixed Seats of all the Courts of Judicature, and in it is managed a vast Trade, as was shew'd in the Chapter that treats of it; now a cheap, frequent, and safe way of Correspondence, is very advantageous for all that are concerned in Commerce, or Business.

* The anniversary of the execution of Charles I then kept as a Fast-day.

The principal Trade of London depends upon Navigation, and therefore the City and Suburbs are situate along the River of Thames, extending in length, as was shew'd, pag. 5. from the Lyme-house, to the end of Tattle-street, 7500 Geometrical Paces, that is seven miles and a half; and from the end of Blackman-street, to the end of St. Leonard Shoreditch, 2500 Paces in breadth, that is two miles; and the whole Circumference (as by Demonstration can be made apparent) is above 20 Miles taking in all the Contiguous Suburbs and Westminster, so that it is the longest, if not the greatest and most populous City in Christendom. This extraordinary Length, though it adds to its Splendor and Beauty, yet it renders speedy Communication and Intercourse in Business very uneasie, and much more troublesome than in such great Cities as Paris, which is almost of an orbicular Form. Now to keep up a necessary Correspondence, the way formerly used, was to hire Porters at excessive Rates to go on Errands, and to send Servants or Apprentices, who, in the meanwhile, lost that time that should be spent to learn their Trades, and benefit their Masters, and would often loyter, and get vicious habits, and evil company, &c. (when they need not) to their own and Masters hurt; or else as such as could not spare the Porter so much money, nor kept Servants, (as some poor Artificers and Labourers) have been forced to sweat and toil, and leave their work, for, it may be, half the day, to do that which now they may perform at the easie Rate of a Penny.

But now all these Inconveniences are remedied by the Penny-Post with great Safety and Celerity, for which the Contrivers really deserve the Thanks of all who reap benefit by it; and I may be bold to say, that all the Inhabitants in general, and their Fellow-Citizens in particular, are already very sensible of the great convenience thereof: for among the innumerable benefits of this Penny-Post, which, for brevity we omit, Friends may converse with Friends, at any distance; Merchants, Shop-keepers and Tradesmen with their Customers, or such as deal with them; Clients may consult with Lawyers; Patients with Doctors; poor Prisoners with Creditors, or Benefactors; and all Bills dispersed for Publication of any Concern; all Summons or Tickets conveyed; all Entries of Brewers to the Excise Office; and many more for one Penny.

3. The Objections I have heard of, are,

1. From some sort of Porters, viz that it hinders their Livelihood.

Answ. (1) 'Tis certain that this is a mistake, for their Livelihood never depended upon going on Errands, their Business being other laborious work, and carrying of Burdens, &c. But some of the Free-Porters are now in the Service of the Undertaking.

(2) Most Business dispatcht by this Undertaking, was formerly either not done at all, or performed by other hands, to save Charges, (Porters Rates being so dear) and Persons themselves, or their Servants, went on their own Errands.

(3) If the Porters, who are an inconsiderable number, in respect of the whole Inhabitants of this great City should suffer some small loss of Petty Employ by it, yet vast Numbers of Poor People, and others, are exceedingly eased and benefitted thereby, which deserve as much or more pity than the Porters: And a general and useful Undertaking, should not in Equity and Prudence be discountenanced, for the peculiar advantage of some few, any more than all the Pipes and Water-Conduits of the City should be destroyed, meerly for the Accomodation of Tankard-Bearers; Printing suppressed, to accomodate Writing Clerks; Guns for Fletchers; Navigable Rivers for Carriers; and the Trade of Jack-smiths, for Turn-spits &c. Nor have Porters any Authority to monopolize to themselves the Delivery of Letters, it being by Law free for any Person to use what Conveyance they think good for their Letters, within or without the Freedom. And Coach-men, Car-men, Water-men, &c. may as well be put out of their Callings, as the Undertakers disturbed in this Concern, because then the Porters may have more burdens to carry. Neither is any prohibited or restrained by this Undertaking, but they may still employ a Porter if they please, so that this Objection is causeless, and is levelled against the whole Body of Inhabitants, as well as the Undertakers in particular.

2. Others alledge, That their Letters are not speedily answered, and therefore say they miscarry.

Answ. That may be, because the Party is not at home, and his Servants do not produce his Letter as he ought, though punctually left by the Penny-Post Messenger (this I have very often known to be my own Case, and some of my Friends). Or the Party may not be at leisure, or not willing to write, or removed, or would pretend that he received it not, when Dun'd for money, which he cannot, or will not pay. And indeed I am also inform'd, that abundance of Letters are so ill superscribed, or uncertainly directed, when frequently the particular Trade of the Party, the Sign, or what noted Place is near, are omitted, that it is impossible to deliver such, which is the fault of the senders, and not of the Office.

To conclude this Subject. The Reader may expect hereafter a small Tract by itself, Printed for the Undertakers of the Penny-Post. What I have here inserted being briefly remarked as my own Notions, concerning so laudable a Design, by way of Specimen, and as a thing suitable to my present Work.

APPENDIX E

A Note on the Plans and Views of Old London

T H E earliest surviving representation of London is the famous Panorama of ' London, Westminster and Southwark,' by Anthony Van den Wyngaerde, *circa* 1550, the original drawing of which is preserved in the Bodleian Library. Extraordinarily valuable as this is, it is rather a picture of the general appearance of many of the architectural details of the London of Tudor days than a plan, and it was Ralph Agas with his bird's-eye map of London, *circa* 1560-70, who first gave us a clear idea of the outlines of the city and the alignment of its streets as they were in those times. Contemporary with Agas was Hoefnagel, whose beautiful plan of London, dated roughly about 1560, was reproduced in Braun and Hogenberg's *Civitates Orbis Terrarum*, published in 1572. As a work of art this is an exquisite production, but it is on too relatively small a scale to permit of our gaining from it more than a general idea of the chief streets and general demarcation of the city; the main arteries are however clearly shown, and its special value consists in the fact that it exhibits the vast structure of old St. Paul's, with its immense spire, as well as the bull- and bear-baiting yards on the Southwark bank. A few years later another plan—in this case divided into two, one showing London, and the other Westminster—was published by John Norden, in his *Speculum Britanniæ* of 1593. These two plans are also on a small scale, but have particular interest as bearing on the life of Shakespeare and the London in which he lived, particularly as in the London portion the Rose Theatre, erected in 1594, is clearly marked.

Coming to the seventeenth century, the first picture of London, for it is rather a Prospect of the city taken from the south bank than a plan, is that issued by Visscher in 1616, and so rare is it that the copy in the British Museum is supposed to be unique. Twenty-two years later Matthew Merlan produced a view of London, which is obviously a copy, although on a small scale, of Visscher's. In 1647 Hollar began his remarkable contributions to London cartography with his *View of London*, which on the whole gives us the best impression of what the city looked like in a general way before the Great Fire. But a far more elaborate addition to such pictorial topography was to come some ten years later, when William Faithorne, in collaboration with Newcourt, produced the quite remarkable bird's-eye view of London, dated 1658. If Hollar's large plan shows us the city as it appeared to anyone approaching it from the south, that of Faithorne and Newcourt enables us to walk about its streets and clearly to distinguish its outstanding buildings and monuments, two of which, St. Paul's and Westminster Abbey, are beautifully delineated in the margin, in which are, also, a number of descriptive notes. What Horwood did for the London of the end of the eighteenth century, and Rocque for the middle of that period, was done by Faithorne and Newcourt for the London of the Stuarts. After this, Porter's map, issued about two years later, is almost negligible, for it is small, and although interesting, as anything dealing with pre-Fire London cannot fail to be, it is not specially notable, except in so far as it may illustrate the slight development that took place after the greater plan had been issued. Before noticing the plans which appeared after the Great Fire, there is one which deserves to be particularly mentioned—we mean that of West Central London which Hollar executed about the year 1648. This is a bird's-eye view, and although only dealing with a certain portion of the Metropolis, roughly from St. Giles's to Lincoln's Inn Fields, and from the river to Holborn, it is a beautiful work of art and shows us this area as we might to-day see it (but how changed!) from an aeroplane.

Just twenty years later Hollar was again to make a bird's-eye view of the London whose heart had been eaten away by the flames. The value of this plan, which is reproduced in our end papers, hardly needs insisting on, for with the care for which in such matters this famous draughtsman was noted, he has here given us the exact delimitations of the Great Fire, showing us at a glance its extent and the chief buildings destroyed in its progress; while at the top of the plan is a beautiful picture of what the city must have appeared like while the conflagration was raging. A plan by Jonas Moore, dated 1662, is on a very small scale, but it gives in addition to a charming view of London, which heads it, and one of Greenwich Reach below, a good idea of the suburbs as far as Charlton in Kent.

We now come to one of the most important plans of London ever issued, namely that based on the survey made by John Ogilby and William Morgan, which was originally published in 1682, and was reissued by Morden and Lea in 1732 with additions bringing it up to date. A plan of the ' City ' only, based on this survey, had been published by Morgan in 1677. It was practically the first plan of the whole of London (Westminster and Southwark) to be executed on scientific lines, and as such formed the basis on which the series of Parish and Ward plans, published in Strype's revised editions of Stow's *Survey of London* (1720 and 1754-5), were made by Richard Blome. Those who wish for an elaborate and detailed account of this invaluable record of Caroline London should consult the article on it by the late Mr. Walter Spiers, which appeared in Vol. V of the London Topographical Society's Record. After Ogilby's plan such others as were issued during the latter days of the seventeenth century come as something of an anti-climax.

With the opening of the following century we have the remarkable bird's-eye view produced by John Kip in 1710-20. This view is taken from Buckingham House (now Buckingham Palace), and so far as the West End is concerned is particularly valuable; but necessarily the eastern portion of the city dwindles away into perspective, and besides, much of the area of the map, or rather bird's-eye view, is taken up by an enlarged picture of St. James's Park (then immediately underneath the artist's eye). The costumes and equipages of the period are shown with interesting particularity and constitute an attractive and artistic adjunct as valuable as the more purely topographical portion.

From this time onward the business of map-making and map-publishing developed rapidly in England, based largely on the example of Holland, and many plans of London appeared, but none of outstanding importance until we come to Rocque's great and famous plan of 1746. This, which in its re-issued form, extends to no fewer than forty-five oblong folio sheets, was begun in 1738, and was originally published eight years later ' by John Pine, at the Golden Head, against Burlington House, Piccadilly, and John Tinney, at the Golden Lion, Fleet Street.' Its scale is nine inches to the mile. With it were issued an Index Plan and a Book of Reference to the various streets and alleys. It was destined to remain the most elaborate example of London cartography until Horwood, in 1794, published his vast map in which every house in the Metropolis is shown and numbered.

Although, as the date of its commencement indicates, Rocque's plan is slightly later than the period during which Defoe wrote his *Tour*, and in the ten or twelve years that intervened a considerable amount of new building development occurred, we can, making allowance for these changes, construct from it a very clear picture of what the city was like during our author's time.

Rocque initiated a far higher standard of accuracy in his cartography than that of any of his predecessors, and on his large plan one may follow almost exactly the detailed description of Defoe's Circuit of the Suburbs, and this plan has been of great assistance in the preparation of the Map which has been specially drawn to illustrate his ' Line of Measurement round the Continued Buildings of the City.' In addition to this and the other maps specially drawn, we have reproduced two contemporary maps of the London of our period on the front and end papers of this volume. That on the front is reproduced from Strype's 1720 revised edition of Stow's *Survey*. It bears neither date nor the name of the cartographer or engraver, but, having been issued with a volume dated 1720, some years before Defoe's *Tour*, cannot be considered a reliable guide in regard to the *suburban* extensions to which Defoe pays so much attention. It is a typical example of the maps produced in the first quarter of the eighteenth century. They had lost much of the artistic charm of those of the seventeenth century and, while showing some improvement in the technique of map-making, lacked the accuracy which marks the work of Rocque and his successors. This difference is well exemplified in our reproduction on the back end-papers referred to above of the well-known plan of the city engraved by Hollar from a survey made by John Leake and others in 1676 to the order of the Corporation showing the ' ruines ' of the area devastated by the Great Fire of the preceding year. This represents the city as Defoe knew it as a child and combines the old and new methods of map-making, the streets in the burnt-out areas being indicated by lines only, while those in the unburnt areas are shown with their buildings and gardens drawn in a sort of perspective ' View ' or ' Prospect.'

Just as to-day the traveller by road out of London would consult a Dunlop or Michelin guide, as his grandfather did a Paterson's Road Book, so in Defoe's time those passing through the immediate environs of the city into the further country would have referred to Ogilby's *Britannia Depicta* which, originally issued in 1680, was brought down to date by subsequent editions as required. The map of the country round London showing the Towns and Villages of Middlesex, which we have had prepared, and which faces page 81, is largely based on Ogilby's sequence of these ' ribbon ' maps, and includes all the ' Towns and Villages in Middlesex ' mentioned by our Author in Letter 6 of his Tour. The inset vignettes of Harrow-on-the-Hill and Blackwall represent the two geographical limits of the outskirts of Greater London specially explored by Defoe in this section of his Tour.

APPENDIX F

The Water Works at Old London Bridge

T H E following description and diagram of the famous wheels and waterworks at London Bridge should appeal to those of our readers who have an interest in mechanics, as well as to those lovers of London prints in which these waterworks figure prominently in the pictures of old London Bridge in the arches at the City end. It has been copied from a book entitled *Hydraulia—or an historical and descriptive account of the Water-works of London*, written by William Matthews and published in 1835:

'For a very minute account of the once greatly admired London-bridge waterworks, the public are indebted to Mr. Beighton, an engineer, who carefully described them, and accompanied his detail with an engraving, which had proper references for its elucidation. It appeared in the Philosophical Transactions for the year 1731; but whether at that time all the works were precisely the same in

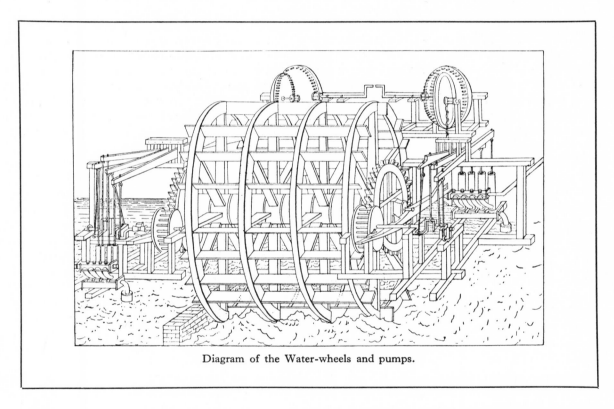

Diagram of the Water-wheels and pumps.

form and action as those first constructed, or any improvement had occasionally been introduced, is not stated. The following summary contains the purport of Mr. Beighton's description; and it may be right to premise that the water wheels and machinery, being fixed in strong frames of oak, they gradually rose and fell with the tides.

'When Mr. Beighton wrote his description of the machinery at London-Bridge, there were three water-wheels of the respective diameters of nineteen and twenty feet, having axles of three feet diameter, and twenty-six float boards, fourteen feet long by eighteen inches wide. The pumps employed had cylinders, with a length of four feet nine inches, and an interior diameter of seven inches above, and nine inches below the valve. The cylinders of the pumps were fixed to the top of an inclosed square iron cistern, which had appropriate apertures with valves, just below the places where they were attached. To one end of the cistern was also attached a pipe, having a grating at the end, to prevent weeds and other things from entering it; and it extended into the bed of the river, for the purpose of supplying water to the pumps,—these being worked by cranks, which the revolving of the water-wheels kept in constant motion, whenever the tides were flowing either up or down the river. One wheel communicated motion to sixteen pumps, and their cranks were arranged for four of them to work alternately, so that each set might draw its supply of water from the cistern in succession. Thus a comparatively small quantity of water only was conveyed into another inclosed square cistern, placed above the valves, and nearly parallel with the tops of the cylinders, and likewise connected with the pumps by bent pipes, having flanches; therefore, whenever the pistons of the pumps ascended, the water was forced along the bent pipes into the upper cistern, from which a large pipe conducted it to supply the houses. The latter pipe had an horizontal direction for some length, and then another was fixed to it, having a slight ascent, so as to form a very small angle; and these were fitted with valves to prevent the return of the water. One turn of all the wheels occasioned the whole of the pumps to make 114 strokes, and when the tide flowed quickly, it produced six revolutions in one minute, thus the total number of strokes in that short time amounted to 684, which raised 1954 hogsheads of water in one hour. Mr. Beighton suggested some improvements, and stated that such was the power of the machinery that it would enable an ordinary man to raise fifty tons weight.'

* * * * * * * * *

In the same book the following reference is made also to the ' York Buildings ' Waterworks, which figure even more prominently in the old London prints of Thames-side. The conical tower which was their distinguishing feature is shown in our reproduction of Thomas Sandby's sketch of the proposed new Whitehall Palace.

'In the year 1691, waterworks were constructed for supplying a part of Westminster; and the persons who engaged in this undertaking obtained an Act of Parliament for incorporating them by the designation of "The Governor and Company of Undertakers for raising Thames' water in York Buildings." The establishment was situate on the bank of the river, contiguous to the Strand, at the bottom of Villiers-street, under which their principal cistern or reservoir extended. These works conveyed water as far as Piccadilly, Whitehall, and Covent Garden, with the intervening streets; but the greatest number of houses that at any time received a supply from this concern was about 2700.'

INDEX

INDEX

INDEX

INDEX

INDEX

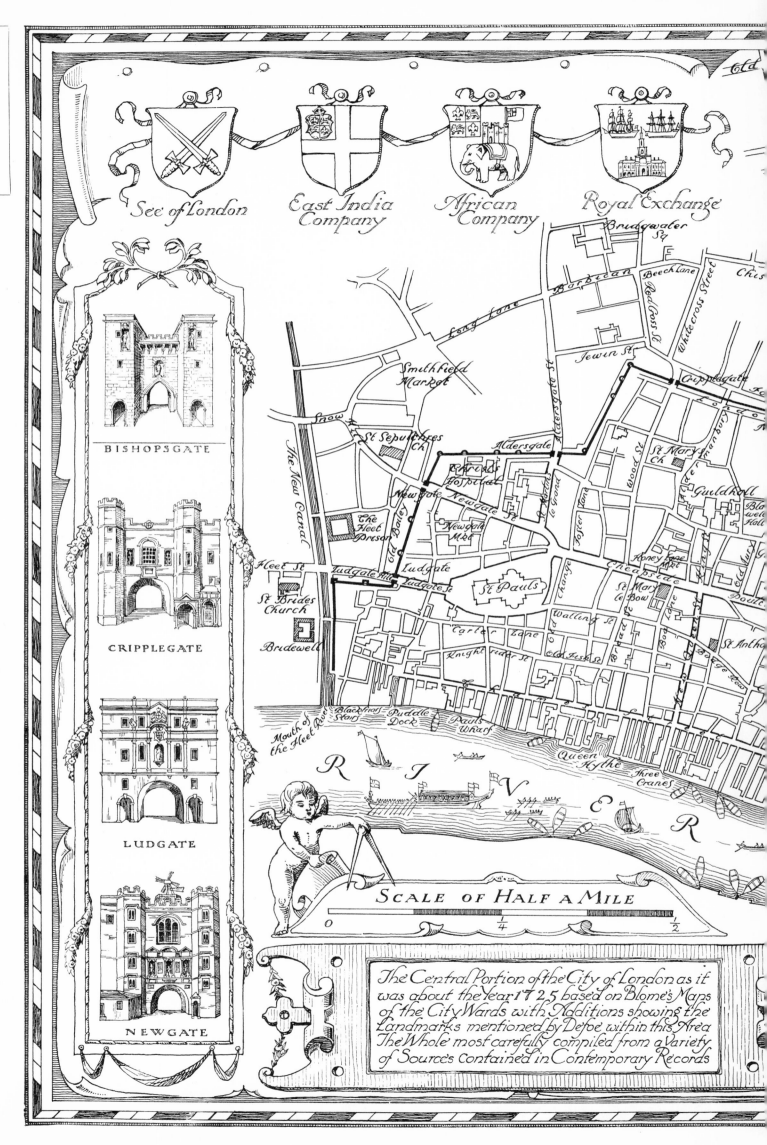

PLATE LVI

MAP OF THE CENTRAL
PORTION OF THE CITY
OF LONDON AS IT WAS
ABOUT THE YEAR 1725
SHOWING THE LAND-
MARKS MENTIONED
BY DEFOE

See of London

East India Company

African Company

Royal Exchange

BISHOPSGATE

CRIPPLEGATE

LUDGATE

NEWGATE

SCALE OF HALF A MILE

0   ¼   ½

The Central Portion of the City of London as it was about the Year 1725 based on Blome's Maps of the City Wards with Additions showing the Landmarks mentioned by Defoe within this Area The Whole most carefully compiled from a Variety of Sources contained in Contemporary Records

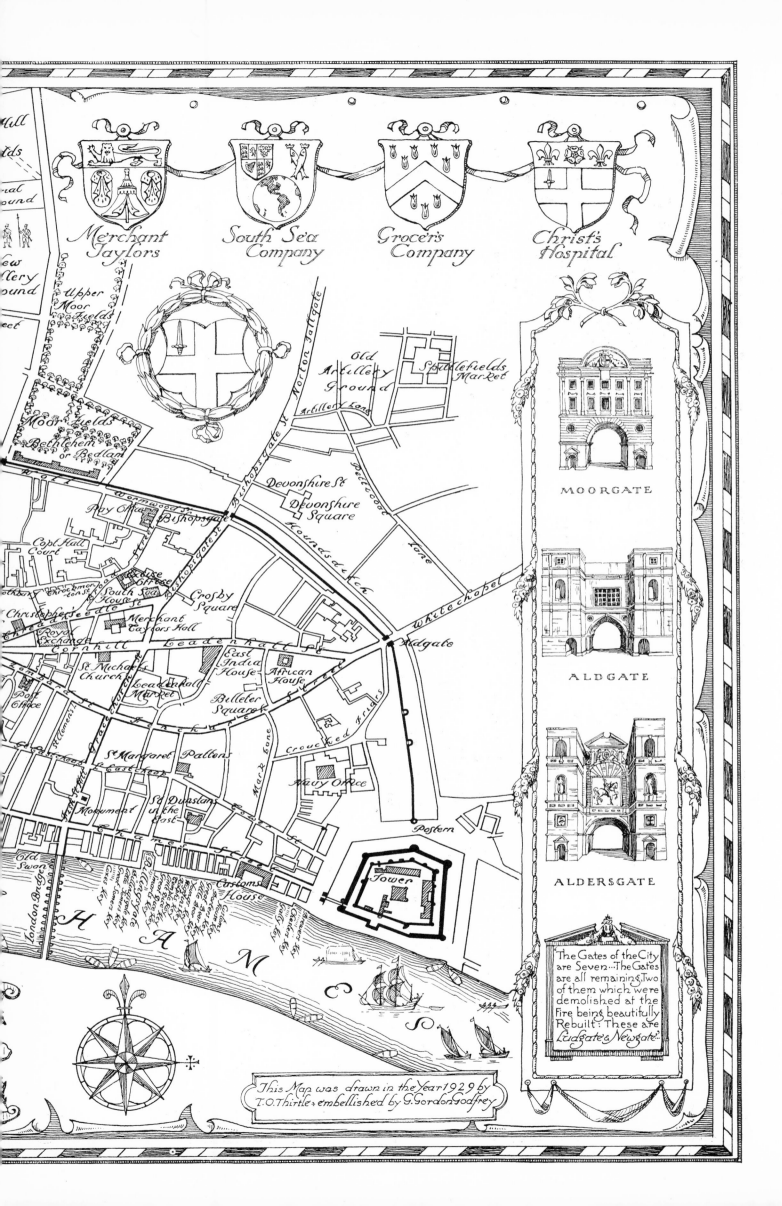

Merchant Taylors

South Sea Company

Grocer's Company

Christ's Hospital

MOORGATE

ALDGATE

ALDERSGATE

The Gates of the City are Seven···The Gates are all remaining, Two of them which were demolished at the Fire being beautifully Rebuilt: These are Ludgate & Newgate·

This Map was drawn in the Year 1929 by T.O.Thirtle & embellished by G.Gordon Godfrey

Upper Moor Fields

Moorfields

Bethlehem or Bedlam

Wormwood St

Bishopsgate

Devonshire St

Devonshire Square

Old Artillery Ground

Spitalfields Market

Artillery Lane

Norton Falgate

Bishopsgate St

Hounsditch

Petticoat Lane

Whitechapel

Aldgate

Postern

Copt Hall Court

Excise Office

South Sea House

Crosby Square

Merchant Taylors Hall

St Christopher's

Royal Exchange

Cornhill

St Michael's Church

Leadenhall Market

Leadenhall St

East India House

African House

Billeter Square

Crooked Friars

Mark Lane

St Margaret Pattens

St Dunstans in the East

Navy Office

Monument

Tower

Old Swan

London Bridge

Customs House

H A M E S

Plate LVII

A PLAN OF THE CITIES
OF LONDON AND WEST-
MINSTER, ETC., ABOUT
THE YEAR 1725 DE-
LINEATING DEFOE'S
'CIRCUIT' AND 'LINE OF
MEASUREMENT'
THEREOF

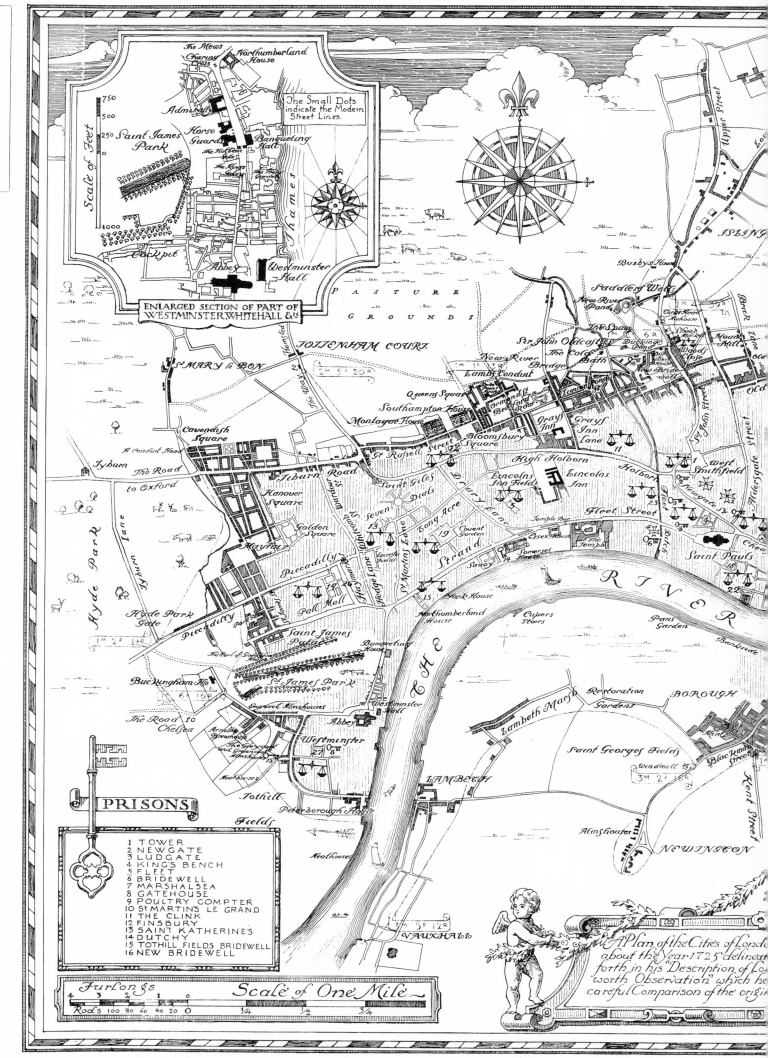

The Small Dots
indicate the Modern
Street Lines.

ENLARGED SECTION OF PART OF
WESTMINSTER WHITEHALL &c

PRISONS

1 TOWER
2 NEWGATE
3 LUDGATE
4 KING'S BENCH
5 FLEET
6 BRIDEWELL
7 MARSHALSEA
8 GATEHOUSE
9 POULTRY COMPTER
10 St MARTIN'S LE GRAND
11 THE CLINK
12 FINSBURY
13 SAINT KATHERINE'S
14 DUTCHY
15 TOTHILL FIELDS BRIDEWELL
16 NEW BRIDEWELL

Furlongs   Scale of One Mile

Rods 100 80 60 40 20 0   1/4   1/2   3/4

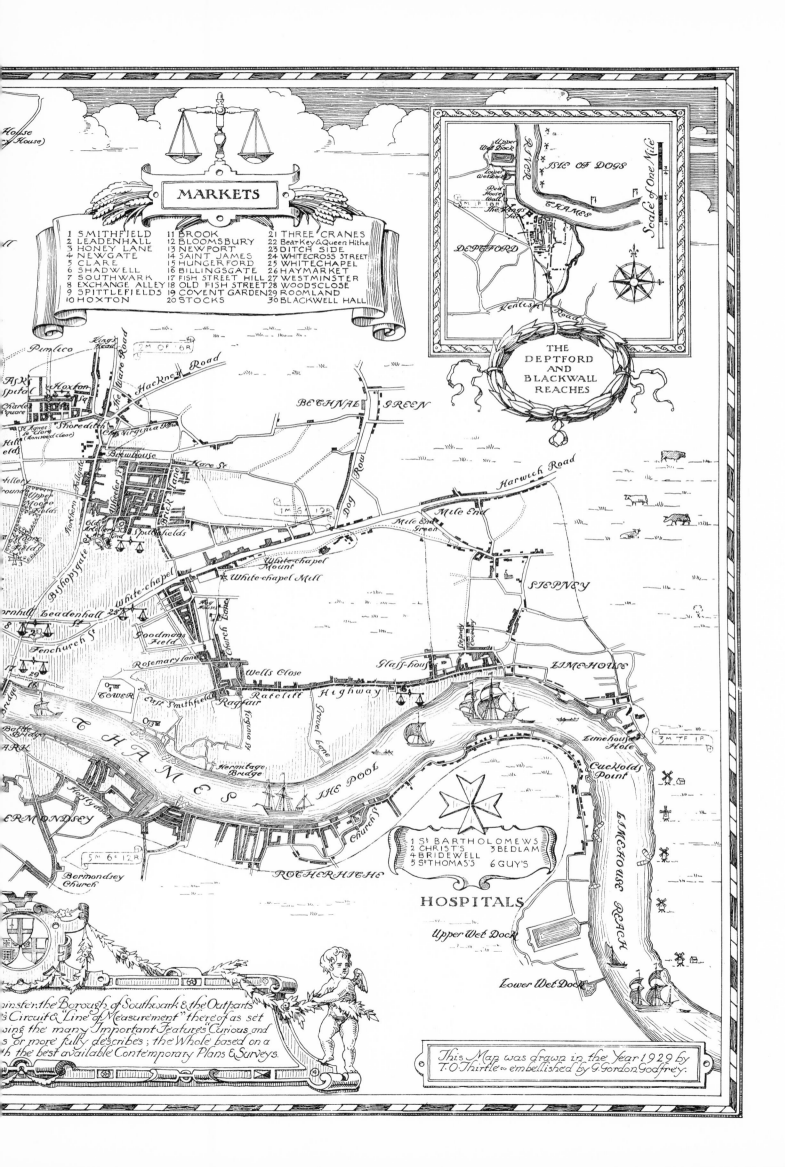

PLATE LVIII

PLAN OF THE PARISH
OF ST. GEORGE'S,
HANOVER SQUARE,
IN THE YEAR
1725

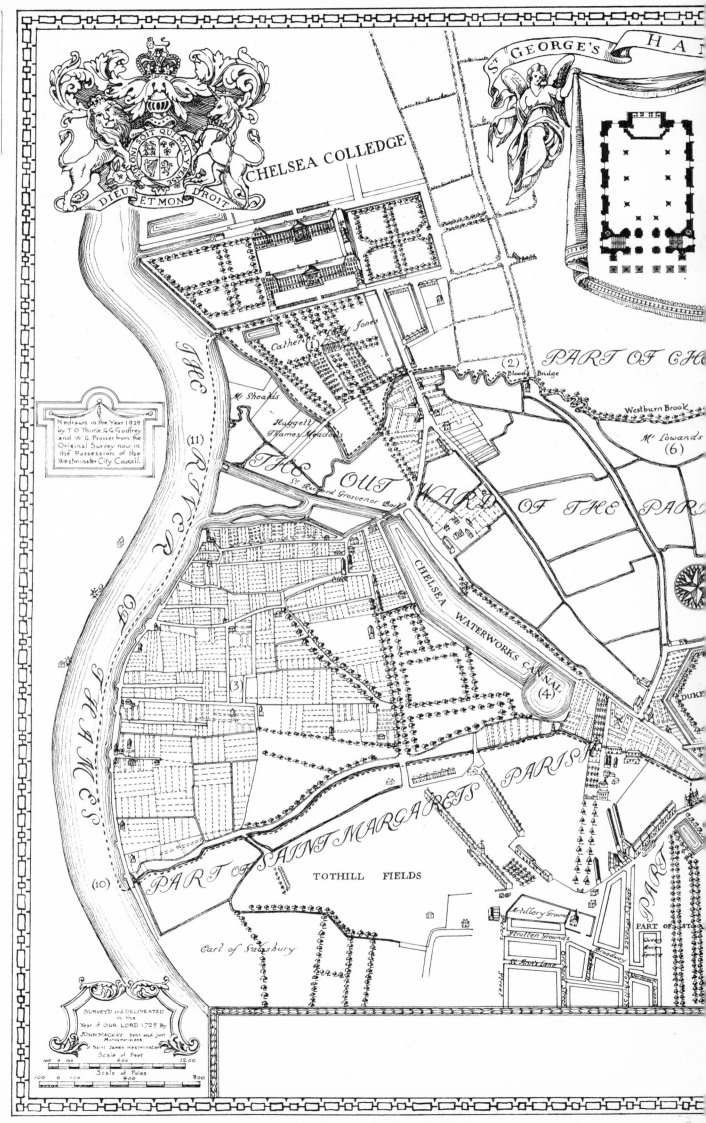

CHELSEA COLLEDGE

St GEORGE'S HA...

Redrawn in the Year 1929 by T. O. Thistle, G. G. Godfrey and W. G. Prosser from the Original Survey now in the Possession of the Westminster City Council.

THE RIVER OF THAMES

THE OUT WARD OF THE PAR...

PART OF CH...

Bloody Bridge

Westburn Brook

Mr Lowands's

Catherine Jones

Mr Sheard's

Huggett Thames Meadows

Sr Richard Grosvenor Baron

CHELSEA WATERWORKS CANAL

DUKE

PARISH

PART OF SAINT MARGARETS

TOTHILL FIELDS

Earl of Salisbury

Artillery Ground

Strutten Grounds

St Ann's Lane

PART OF ST...

SURVEY'D and DELINEATED in the YEAR of OUR LORD 1725 By JOHN MACKAY Gent and just MATHEMATICIANS at Saint James Westminster

Scale of Feet
100 0 100   600   1200

Scale of Poles
100 0 100   400   800

PLAN OF THE PARISH OF ST. GEORGE'S, HANOVER SQUARE, DATED 1725

PLATE LVIII

ER SQUARE

PART OF ST MARGARETS PARISH

PART OF HIS MAJESTY'S
NEW GARDEN

To the Right Honourable
GEORGE Earl of CARPENTER
The Right Honourable
WILLIAM STUART, ESQ
FIRST CHURCHWARDENS
of the
PARISH of ST GEORGE HANOVER SQUARE
To the Reverend
Mr TREBECK Rector
AND the Rest of the Noblemen and Gentn
of the
VESTRY
This Plan being an Actual Survey of the Parish is humbly Presented by Your most Obedient humble Servant John Mackey

A PARISH

KNIGHTS BRIDGE
(9)

Sr Thomas Cross

OF SAINT GEORGE HANOVER SQUARE

THE RING

MARTINS PARISH

CONSTITUTION HILL

PART OF HYDE PARK

Chelsea Waterworks

(Tyburn Gallows)

PART OF KENSINGTON PARISH

PART OF PADINGTON PARISH

PART OF ST MARY LE BONE PARISH

(8)

Park Lane

Hyde Park Street

Audeley Street   Grosvenor Sq   Street

(7)

GROSVENOR STREET WARD

Charles St   Duke Street

Wellbeck St

Nimble St

Chandois St

Earl of Oxford

Harley St

New Bond Street

Cavendish S

Ogle Street

Ice Houses

(5)

Great

CONDUIT STREET WARD

George   Street   Holles St

Cork Street

St James Street

Earl of Burlington   Saville Row

Sackville St

Duchess of Marlborough

PART OF ST JAMES PARISH

A Scale of 165 Feet in an Inch

A Scale of 10 Poles in an Inch

PLATE LVIII

PLAN OF THE PARISH OF ST. GEORGE'S, HANOVER SQUARE, DATED 1725

The following particulars are taken from the original survey :

"Ascension day being May the 14th 1725, The first Procession of the Parish of St. George Hanover Square began in Swallow Street at a S E Angle of Conduit Street Ward, where the Parish Mark S^{H}G was painted on Bostocks Brewhouse Abutting on St. James's Parish, from thence along Swallow Street to the N E Angle of the Parish in Oxford Street, from thence along the Oxford and Worcester Road to the S E Leg of Tyburn where S^{H}G was mark'd, then back thro' Hyde Park Gate near the N E Angle thereof, then along by the Wall Side within Cross Westburn Brook to Portman Seymours Wall where S^{H}G was Mark'd at the N W Angle of the Parish, then along on the N side of ye Ponds where four Parish Marks are Design'd on the Heads of four of the said Ponds, then along by Ditto Brook to the King's Bridge where S^{H}G was Mark'd, then still on by Ditto Brook to Hyde Park Wall where S^{H}G was Mark'd, then Cross'd the said Wall into Exeter Road in Knights Bridge where S^{H}G was Mark'd on the Bridge, where the Processioners were met by the Right Honourable George Lord Carpentet, The Right Honourable William Stuart Esqr. First Church Wardens, Sr. Thomas Clargys Bart. and the Reverend Mr. Trebeck Rector of the said Parish, then all Enter'd Knights Bridge Chapel where Prayers was Read by the said Rector, then went thro' the Widow Dennis's Brewhouse and along by Ditto Brook to Bloody Bridge where S^{H}G was Mark'd, then along by Ditto Brook to Stone Bridge in Chelsea Road where S^{H}G was Mark'd, then along by Ditto Brook to Lady Catherine Jones's Visto where S^{H}G was Mark'd on the Bridge thereof, then Cross'd into Thames Meadow along by the Brook to the S E Angle of Ditto Lady's Kitchen Garden to the S W Angle of the Parish and Ditto Meadow where a Post with S^{H}G is Designed, then along by the Thames Side to the King's Scholars Pond and S E Angle of the Parish where S^{H}G was Mark'd on the Sluice thereof, then along by Brook to the Willow Walk where S^{H}G was Mark'd on the Pales against the Bridge, then along by Ditto Brook pass Mr. Greens thro' the Gardens along the said Brook and thro' Tart Hall Washhouse into James Street where S^{H}G was Mark'd on St. James's Park Wall, then into St. James's Park where the First Church Wardens saw S^{H}G Mark'd on one of the Wings of Buckingham House, then along by the Wall on the outside of St. James's Park to the N W Angle of Ditto Duke's Wall where S^{H}G was Mark'd, then along by the said Wall to St. James's Park Gate at Hyde Park Corner where S^{H}G was Mark'd, then along by the said Wall to Arlington Street End, then down Arlington Street Bennet Street and part of St. James's Street to Park Place, then up Park Place to Esqr. Drakes Door where S^{H}G was Mark'd, then thro' his House to the End of his Garden where S^{H}G was Mark'd, then up to St. James's Street and along Piccadilly to near Burlington Wall where S^{H}G was Mark'd, then up old Bond Street and down part of Vigo Lane where S^{H}G was Mark'd near Burlington Garden Wall, then along New Bond Street where S^{H}G was Mark'd near the Coin over against the Duke of Grafton's, then along to near Clifford Street End where S^{H}G was Mark'd, then up Conduit Street to Trinity Chapel where S^{H}G was Mark'd on Burlington Garden Wall within the Yard thereof, then up Conduit Street to the first turning on the Right where S^{H}G was Mark'd in a line with Bostocks Brewhouse where the Procession Ended. The length of the said Boundary being Eight Miles and a half and contains 993 Acres 3 Roods 09 Pole more or less, and the Number of Houses are Rated 1200. The Land Tax about £3600 and the Poors Rate about £1400 pr. Annum. The Parish is Divided into three Wards. Grosvenor Street Ward, Includes the West Side of New Bond Street, Oxford Street to Tyburn Lane now Park Lane, and Brick Street, then along by the End of Clarges Street and back of Devonshire Garden to the End of Dover Street and to Lady Falcons Bridge House, Conduit Street Ward Includes the E Side of New Bond Street, the South Side of Oxford Road to Swallow Street and all Conduit Street. The Out Ward Contains all the Rest of the Parish.''

It will be observed that this plan has an east and west orientation, as the compass on it indicates. In order to mark approximately the relation between the topography of this part of London in 1725 with that of the London of 1929, some of the spots identified with existing landmarks are here shown by figures in circles.

(1) Ranelagh, (2) Sloane Square, (3) Bailwick of Neat (Neat houses or cattle sheds, with market gardens, pastures, and ditches), (4) Victoria Station, (5) Lancaster House (London Museum), (6) Site of Lowndes Square, (7) Stanhope Gate, (8) Grosvenor Gate, (9) Albert Gate, (10) Vauxhall Bridge, (11) Chelsea Bridge.

A New PLAN
of LON
WESTM
and SOU

DOMINE DIRIGE NOS.

Part of Eslington

St Pancras the wells

Battle Bridg

Pinder of Wakefeld

Sadler's wells

New River Pond

Black well
St John Old Castle

St Mary's

PASTURE

GROUNDS

The way to Hamsted

Road to Hamsted

Road to Hgate

Conduit

Wards Clo

The Coach Way

These Enclosures where

St Mary le Bon

Marybon &
Tottenh Court

Tottenham Court

Montague House

South Hampton

Marybone Park

Water House

Salt Peter House

Holborn

Lincolns Inn Fields

Tiburn Roade

A Conduit Head
L. Mayors Banquet
ing House

Road to Oxford

The Rectors House

Hanover Square

Pest House Ground

Pasture

Ground

Somerset House

HIDE

PARK

Road to Exeter

St JAMES'S

Road to Kensington

St James Palace

St JAMES'S

PARK

Buckingham House

Road to Chelsey

The Decoy

RIVER OF THAMES

Scotland Yard

White Hall
White Hall Stairs
Privy Stairs

Baris Garden

Westminster Stairs
Parliament House
Parliament Stairs

Stangate Stairs

Abby

Tuthill
Fields

Horse Ferry

Peterborough house

Lambeth House

Lambeth